OUR EUROPEAN FUTURE

The Foundation for European Progressive Studies (FEPS) is the think tank of the progressive political family at EU level. Our mission is to develop innovative research, policy advice, training and debates to inspire and inform progressive politics and policies across Europe. We operate as hub for thinking to facilitate the emergence of progressive answers to the challenges that Europe faces today.

FEPS works in close partnership with its members and partners, forging connections and boosting coherence among stakeholders from the world of politics, academia and civil society at local, regional, national, European and global levels.

Today FEPS benefits from a solid network of 68 member organisations. Among these, 43 are full members, 20 have observer status and 5 are ex-officio members. In addition to this network of organisations that are active in the promotion of progressive values, FEPS also has an extensive network of partners, including renowned universities, scholars, policymakers and activists.

Our ambition is to undertake intellectual reflection for the benefit of the progressive movement, and to promote the founding principles of the EU – freedom, equality, solidarity, democracy, respect of human rights, fundamental freedoms and human dignity, and respect of the rule of law.

Our European Future

CHARTING A PROGRESSIVE
COURSE IN THE WORLD

Edited by
Maria João Rodrigues

With the collaboration of
François Balate

Copyright © 2021 by Foundation for European Progressive Studies

Published by London Publishing Partnership
www.londonpublishingpartnership.co.uk

Published in association with the
Foundation for European Progressive Studies
www.feps-europe.eu
European Political Foundation – N° 4 BE 896.230.213

Published with the financial support of the
European Parliament. The views expressed in this
report are solely those of the authors and do not
necessarily reflect the views of the European Parliament.

All rights reserved

ISBN: 978-1-913019-32-7 (pbk)
ISBN: 978-1-913019-33-4 (ePDF)
ISBN: 978-1-913019-34-1 (ePUB)

A catalogue record for this book is available
from the British Library

Typeset in Adobe Garamond Pro by
T&T Productions Ltd, London
www.tandtproductions.com

Contents

Introduction   ix
By Maria João Rodrigues

PART I   1
Rebuilding the European Economic and Social Model for Ecological, Digital and Post-Covid Challenges

Synthesis of the debate   3
By Jean-François Lebrun

Aspirations: Europe in the 2020s – setting the course for all future Europeans   21
By Halliki Kreinin and Lukas Hochscheidt

A European Health Union   25
By Vytenis Andriukaitis

The care crisis and a feminist society   30
By Emma Dowling

The ecological transformation: the main driving factors and the social implications   35
By Saïd El Khadraoui

Social policies and the ecological transformation   40
By Georg Fischer

The digital transformation: the main driving factors and social implications   46
By Justin Nogarede

Nordic inspiration for the European socioeconomic model   52
By Britta Thomsen

Reinventing the state to deploy smart green growth and well-being, while disarming populism   57
By Carlota Perez

A European Social Union 63
By László Andor

PART II 69
EU External Action with Strategic Autonomy and Multilateral Engagement

Synthesis of the debate 71
By Giovanni Grevi

Aspirations: for an EU External Action with strategic autonomy and multilateral engagement 84
By Barbara Roggeveen

Scenarios for global governance and the EU open strategic autonomy: a window of opportunity for a 'Spinellian moment' 86
By Mario Telò

A digital and green European foreign policy that speaks to EU citizens and the world 94
By Guillaume Klossa

The EU and global economic governance 99
By Paolo Guerrieri

Defending the momentum, delivering on progress: the future of European defence 104
By Vassilis Ntousas

The European External Action regarding migration 109
By Hedwig Giusto

The European External Action and the EU constitutional system 114
By Diego Lopez Garrido

PART III 119
Economic Governance for an Empowered European Union

Synthesis of the debate 121
By Robin Huguenot-Noël

Aspirations: empowering progressive ideas in the EU's economic governance by matching 'policy with politics' 136
By Alvaro Oleart

European economic governance: key issues to assess its
recent past and its desirable evolution 139
By Vivien Schmidt

A European economic policy mix to support the
European project in the long term 145
By Michael Landesmann

Next Generation EU public finances 152
By David Rinaldi

A European budgetary capacity to support the
European project in the long term 161
By Peter Bofinger

What can we learn from federal experiences around
the world? 167
By Tanja Boerzel

A republican framework for EU economic governance 172
By Stefan Collignon

PART IV 177
The EU and the Next Democratic Transformation

Synthesis of the debate 179
By François Balate

Aspirations: : the EU's next democratic transformation 194
By Lora Lyubenova

Key changes to be introduced in the European political
system 197
By Olivier Costa

The new prospects for the European electoral and party
systems 203
By Ania Skrzypek

The digital revolution and our democratic lives:
meeting the challenges 209
By Gerda Falkner

What are the potential and the limits of the Lisbon Treaty? 215
By Mercedes Bresso

After the pandemic: a republic of Europe – what would
it mean? 221
By Ulrike Guerot

New horizons for a political union 227
  By Jo Leinen
Conclusion: a European legend 231
  By Maria João Rodrigues
Acknowledgements 234
Glossary 235
About the editor and authors 237

Introduction

By Maria João Rodrigues

A civilization's future depends on the internal forces it has to recreate itself. We are referring here to human civilization, but the same can be said about the rich set of components that are part of it, including the European one.

Right now, humankind is struggling against global existential challenges: pandemics, irreversible climate change, scarce resources in the face of ongoing demographic expansion, and deepening inequalities between countries and between people. There are different ways to respond to today's challenges: paralysis, competition, cooperation or coordination for upward convergence.

The European Union can play a key role in influencing which road is taken, but it must start with itself. It must assert itself as a full-fledged political entity, with economic, social and cultural dimensions, and it must take internal and external actions that are decided democratically by its citizens.

That is why a Conference on the Future of Europe is so necessary at this particular historical juncture. This book comes out of a larger intellectual and societal movement in Europe that is willing to make a contribution to a conference that should meet its historical responsibility.

A VISION FOR OUR EUROPEAN FUTURE

Our vision of how to live on this planet will doubtless be deeply transformed by our current collective experience of the Covid-19 pandemic and by the looming climate disaster. Now is therefore the right time to develop a common vision together.

The first step in this process is to change the relationship between humankind and nature. We are part of nature, and we therefore need to respect it by looking after its resources and biodiversity. This aspiration comes at a time of technological developments that will enable new ways of producing, consuming, moving around and living. Now is the time to create and disseminate a new generation of products and services that are not only low carbon and zero waste, but also smarter, because they are built on artificial intelligence. Our houses, schools, shops, hospitals, meeting places, cities and our way of life can all be completely transformed.

New economic activities and jobs will emerge while others will decline. An immense transformation of the structure of employment is already underway, and it has been accelerated by the various Covid-related lockdowns. Although there are jobs for which the main tasks can be replaced by automation and artificial intelligence, there are also new jobs dealing with climate action, environmental repair, human relationships and creativity of all sorts, and these roles can be multiplied. We need to support this transformation through massive lifelong learning programmes, as well as by using social protection to cover the various social risks.

All of this requires us to build a welfare system fit for the twenty-first century, based on the assumption that we will all end up combining a range of different activities – paid work, family care, community service, education and personal creativity – throughout a life cycle. And, of course, we also need to find new ways of financing this welfare system, by tapping into new sources of added value and by updating our tax structures.

These new aspirations will be claimed by many citizens, from all generations and from all countries, and this will inevitably create a push for deep policy shifts.

In the meantime, the current gap between global challenges and global governance is becoming more and more evident, and it requires an ambitious renewal of the current multilateral system.

This renewal is needed initially to cope with the current Covid-19 pandemic and the resulting social and economic crises that are unfolding. Indeed, we need to have large-scale vaccination for universal access, and we need more powerful financial tools to counter the recession and to turn stimulus packages into large transformations of our economies in line with the green and digital transitions that are underway and with the need to tackle increasing social inequalities.

Our response to the Covid crisis should not delay our urgent action on climate change, however, otherwise the damage caused to the environment will become largely irreversible, with implications across the board.

Additionally, our digital transition is in a critical phase, where the diffusion of artificial intelligence to all sectors risks being controlled by a small set of big digital platforms. But there is an alternative: we can agree on a common set of global rules to ensure that we have different choices, and to ensure that we improve fundamental standards regarding the respect of privacy, decent labour conditions and access to public services. These global rules would also bring in new tax revenue to finance public goods.

It is crucial that we have a strong multilateral framework to underpin the green and digital transitions, so that we can better implement the sustainable development goals and reduce social inequality within and between countries.

Nevertheless, we need to identify which actors the multilateral system can be renewed with, and how we can therefore improve global governance. The way the global multipolar order is currently evolving means there is a real danger of fragmentation between different areas of influence, and there is the additional problem of increasing strategic competition between the United States and China. The recent election of Joe Biden in the United States is very good news, and it creates a fresh basis for updating the transatlantic alliance. But the world has changed. There are other influential players now, so we need to build a larger coalition of actors – governments, parliamentarians, civil society organizations and citizens themselves – to push for these objectives using a model of variable geometry.

The EU should take an active and leading role in building the coalition of forces necessary to renew the multilateral system. At the same time, it should develop its bilateral relations with countries and regional organizations so that we can cooperate and move in the same direction. The EU's 'external action' must cover other relevant dimensions: from defence and cybersecurity to energy, science and technology, education, culture and human rights. Promoting the sustainable development goals in all of the EU's relationships should also be a priority.

Alongside this, the EU needs to build on the recent historical leap forward that it made when it finally agreed on the launch of a common budget financed by the joint issuance of bonds to drive a post-Covid recovery linked to green and digital transformations. This is a unique opportunity that we cannot afford to miss. It requires all member states to implement national recovery plans to transform their energy and transport infrastructures and to promote clusters of low-carbon and smart activities while creating new jobs. This needs to be combined with the development of new public services and new social funding for health, education and care.

These things should be at the centre of a new concept of prosperity that is driven by well-being. A welfare state for the twenty-first century should support the necessary transitions to new jobs, new skills and new social needs, and it should be based on an advanced concept of European citizenship that includes not only economic and political rights but also social, digital and environmental rights.

This advanced concept of European citizenship, as proclaimed by the European Social Pillar, also needs to be underpinned by a stronger European budget, joint debt issuance, tax convergence and European taxation. This will be at the core of stronger European sovereignty – which is needed to cope with the current challenges we face – while strengthening internal regional and social cohesion.

Stronger European sovereignty must in turn be founded on strengthened democracy at the local, national and European levels, and it should better combine representative and participatory mechanisms. The current Europe-wide situation caused by the Covid crisis is opening up new avenues of hybrid democratic activity that offer interesting potential for exploration.

TAKING A HISTORICAL PERSPECTIVE

Taking a historical perspective, we are certainly now entering a new phase of the European project – a project that all started more than 70 years ago with the aim of uniting Europeans to shape their future together. The general approach of combining a large open market with social cohesion and deeper democracy has persisted, but the central problem to be addressed has changed over time.

In the beginning, that central problem was peace. This was secured with the bold and groundbreaking agreement that emerged from the ashes of World War II to build a common market along with the early stages of a social fund and a supranational power. This power was represented by a European Commission, which was accountable to a Council and to a European Parliament, as enshrined in the Treaty of Rome in 1957. A more ambitious approach – the single market agenda – was then introduced during the Jacques Delors period. This agenda was underpinned by the Single European Act, in 1986, which enabled more decisions to be taken by qualified majority voting. It also enabled a stronger Community budget, which in turn enabled stronger common programmes and greater regional and social cohesion.

A second phase of the European project came with the fall of the Berlin Wall and the need to conduct enlargement along with the deepening of European integration. This need was translated into a common currency and the creation of a political union, with legal identity and European citizenship, enshrined in the Maastricht Treaty of 1992.

A third phase came with large-scale globalization. This called for comprehensive action and a development strategy that included social policies: the Lisbon strategy. It also required reform of the European political system – enshrined in the Lisbon Treaty of 2007 – in order to strengthen European external action and deepen European democracy, notably the role of the European Parliament. This was done by extending co-decision to many new common policies.

A fourth phase of the European project was triggered by the global financial crisis of 2008, which then created a eurozone crisis exposing the flaws of the project's economic and monetary union. In order to reduce dangerous financial, economic, social and political divergences between and within member states, an initial solution was drawn up with the creation of a European Stability Mechanism and with stronger action to be taken by the European Central Bank. However, a European budgetary capacity financed by the joint issuance of bonds would only come to be be accepted when a larger-scale economic slump, triggered by the Covid-19 pandemic, threatened all member states. A European Pillar of Social Rights also had to be defined and implemented in order to create a safety net to protect against further divergences and growing anti-European populism.

Alongside this, several disturbances to peace in countries neighbouring the EU have translated into a large wave of inward migration. This has required renewed organization of European borders, as well as developments in EU neighbourhood policies for Eastern Europe, the Middle East and Africa. All of this, together with the unprecedented decision of one member state to leave the EU – the Brexit saga – has led to a new reflection about the possible ways to organize the European space according to different circles of integration and coordination.

While all these problems overlap, we might argue that the central problem marking this current new phase of the European project is the deep structural transformation that is taking place on the ecological, digital and demographic fronts. This transformation requires more strategic state intervention, larger partnerships, renewed social and regional cohesion, stronger global action, and deeper democracy and citizenship at all levels. The technocratic mode of conducting European integration has now become obsolete.

As an intellectual, a policymaker and an elected politician who has been able to work inside the various European institutions on a wide range of policies – and as someone who has circulated around Europe and beyond dealing with many different actors – I have had the opportunity to be deeply involved in these most recent phases of the European project.

This started in the 1990s when I served as a minister in the Portuguese government at the time when the European employment strategy was adopted to counterbalance the Stability and Growth Pact and when the membership of the eurozone was being prepared.

In 2000 I was in charge of designing the Lisbon strategy – the EU's first comprehensive development strategy – and I then worked to translate it into the EU budget and into the national policies with what is now called the European semester.

I was also a member of the team in charge of rescuing the Constitutional Treaty and of negotiating the Lisbon Treaty while a full set of strategic partnerships was being developed between the EU and other global players, including the United States, China, India, Russia, Brazil and Mexico.

In addition, I have worked with many other policymakers and experts, exploring a wide range of new instruments to address the dramatic eurozone crisis.

When I was elected as a member of the European Parliament, I worked to build a large parliamentary majority to adopt a European Pillar of Social Rights and overcome the resistance of certain national governments that were arguing there was no need for such a pillar to underpin European integration.

More recently, due to my work on the international front on proposals to renew multilateralism, I found myself in New York for the 2019 UN Climate Action Summit, where I was able to witness the confrontation between Donald Trump and António Guterres, whom I know well as a Portuguese minister and European sherpa for several years. This was the moment when, after the 2019 European elections, a Conference on the Future of Europe was announced.

Discussion about the future of Europe was already underway during Jean-Claude Juncker's term, which came to an end in 2019, and at that time I could identify four possible scenarios. I believe those scenarios remain relevant.

POSSIBLE SCENARIOS FOR EUROPE

Scenario A: status quo/inertia

The too little too late scenario would continue in the post-2019 EU legislature. In this scenario, the newly announced geopolitical EU would be first absorbed by post-Brexit complications and then weakened by them. The EU's strategic partnerships and trade agreements with other major global actors would be used neither to support the upward convergence of environmental and social standards nor to strengthen the multilateral system. European foreign policy would find it difficult to assert itself, even in cases of major international conflict, due to the unanimity voting rule. The development of a European defence capacity would remain hesitant and with ambiguities regarding engagement with NATO. The EU's new partnership with Africa would disappoint, clearly being less firm than China's engagement with the continent.

In a world with two competing world orders led by the United States and China, the EU would slide towards a secondary position in both political and technological terms, despite the size of its market remaining relevant and interesting. The EU would fail to become a relevant geopolitical actor through a lack of vision and ambition, and also through a lack of internal cohesion.

Internal deliberation within the bloc about its multiannual financial framework (MFF) would result in an insufficient budget, leaving it unable to support all of its member states and citizens in their transition to a successful low-carbon, smart and inclusive economy. This transition would be slow and unbalanced across the continent, with some regions advancing but many lagging behind. The new European Green Deal would remain an undelivered promise, or might even become a source of new social problems in certain European regions.

Meanwhile, the digital revolution, driven by American and Chinese standards, would extend precarious work and undermine the financial basis of existing social protection schemes. The general deficit in strategic public and private investment would remain evident due to a conservative banking and financial system, conservative budgetary rules, and the political inability to complete a banking union and create budgetary capacity within the eurozone.

The creation of jobs would therefore remain sluggish, and the systemic difficulties of sustaining and renewing European welfare systems would increase social anxiety, particularly among the younger generations, as the baby boom generation hits retirement age. Migration inflows would increase, but they would do so in the face of internal resistance to manage and integrate them as a dynamic factor for European societies.

Underpinning all this inertia we find not only political hesitation but also passive and active resistance to real European solutions in order to protect vested interests, to promote national preferences, whatever the collective costs, or simply to assert the viewpoint of authoritarian and conservative governments.

This would be a very disappointing scenario of external and internal decline. But it is possible to identify another plausible scenario that looks even worse.

Scenario B: nationalistic fragmentation

The shift we have seen in some places to inward-looking and nationalistic attitudes might spread across the world in the face of a range of insecurities: climate disturbances, conflicts over natural resources, technological change and job losses, migration inflows and security threats. The European political landscape might also move in this direction, building on the weak links of Hungary, Poland, Italy, France and Germany.

A United Kingdom led by Boris Johnson would strengthen this trend from the outside by developing a special partnership, undermining European solidarity on a permanent basis. Similar pressures would come from a Russia led by Vladimir Putin and a China led by Xi Jinping. The digital revolution driven by the American–Chinese war over spheres of influence would turn Europe into an increasingly attractive land for this guerrilla action.

In such a scenario, the European Green Deal would fail through a lack of basic political and financial conditions – starting with the incapacity to agree on a stronger multiannual EU budget, not to mention the minimum financial instruments to make the eurozone sustainable in the longer term.

Deepening regional and social differences, despite some countries adopting nationalistic social protection schemes, would increase Euroscepticism and criticism everywhere, leading to decreasing democratic participation at all levels. The inability to define a European policy to manage migration and to set up a new partnership with Africa would both multiply the tragedies of rejected migrants and refugees and create cultural hostility to any kind of foreign presence.

The survival of the EU would be at stake, when it comes not only to the political union but also to the European single market with a common *acquis* of economic, social and political standards.

Scenario C: a liberal–green European revival

This scenario would see a coalition of forces relaunch the European project with the triple ambition of responding to climate change, increasing EU trade agreements and building up a European defence capacity, despite American resistance.

The four freedoms of the European single market would be defended, despite attempts by a Conservative-led United Kingdom to undermine them, notably by using the digital revolution and through the redesign of global supply chains. Nevertheless, it would also be key in this scenario to attempt to ensure a win–win relationship with the post-Brexit United Kingdom.

Internal regional and social inequalities would increase due to a lack of active European industrial, regional, social and taxation policies, but migration inflows would be better managed and would contribute to limiting demographic decline. They would, though, deepen social inequalities.

The attention paid to the rule of law and to political rights at the European level would limit the scope for nationalistic and authoritarian surges in EU member states, but European citizenship would remain poor when it comes to social rights, education opportunities and real economic chances. The EU project would be modernized but would remain quite technocratic and elitist.

Scenario D: European citizenship at the core of a new European project

This scenario would see a paradigm shift.

A stronger sense of European citizenship would lead to the construction of new tools of European sovereignty, which would allow us to respond to common challenges while reducing internal differences. We would see a stronger European budget for research, innovation and industrial policy, for energy, digital and mobility infrastructures, and for defence capabilities. And we would also see a stronger budget for reducing internal differences in access to new technological solutions, to education and to social protection. This would require new sources of taxation to be launched and coordinated at the European level to ensure more tax convergence.

This European sovereignty would also be translated into a more active role on the international scene when it comes to developing strategic partnerships, building coalitions and strengthening the multilateral system to bring about more effective responses to the global challenges we face: climate change, sustainable development, the digital revolution, social inequalities, the promotion of democracy and human rights and ensuring peace and security. A crucial test would be Europe's capacity to cooperate with Africa in the interests of a visible leap forward on sustainable development, education, gender equality, peace and democratic governance.

The external influence of Europe would increase, not just as a large market but also as a geopolitical entity that acts in every dimension: economic, financial, social, political and cultural. This external influence would be higher if Europe could lead by example when it comes to responding to climate change with social fairness, by driving the digital revolution for better working and living conditions, by increasing gender equality, updating social rights and strengthening an inclusive welfare system, by developing scientific and cultural creativity and deepening democracy at all levels.

In conclusion, whatever happens, the critical factor will be progressive European leadership to turn European citizenship into a new political force that is able to overturn the inertia of the past.

Nevertheless, one fundamental question remains: what might be capable of bringing about such a scenario? A climate disaster? A cyberattack? New financial turmoil? The failure of particular social rights? Or maybe it could be driven by greater awareness and ambition of European citizens themselves, as is happening with climate change?

History always brings surprises: we know that the trigger has been the Covid crisis. Nevertheless, these four basic, contrasting scenarios remain relevant. This book aims to give some more precise content to this scenario D. It will start from the vision I proposed in the first part of this introduction, with other authors further elaborating on that vision, and mobilize yet more authors and actors to participate in a long-term undertaking: shaping a progressive path for the next phase of the European project.

A BOOK FROM A EUROPEAN INTELLECTUAL AND SOCIETAL MOVEMENT

The direction the EU will actually take will be the result of very complex interactions between contradictory factors: decisions that will be taken by top decision makers and by the interplay between the EU institutions; and orientations that will be defined by major organized political and social forces such as the European political families, social partners and organized civil society, but also much larger movements of public opinion inspired by new concerns, new preferences and new ideas.

This book is intended to contribute to these complex interactions by presenting some state-of-the-art progressive thinking about the European project. I am proud that we have been able to bring together the thoughts of such a remarkable range of renowned authors. The book's contributors are the leading voices in an intellectual movement for the renewal of the European project. We started working together as an expert group organized by the Foundation for European Progressive Studies – a political foundation located in Brussels that works closely with the EU institutions.

Through a well-organized sequence of online meetings, we have explored key thematic areas, guided by questions formulated both by EU policymakers and by EU citizens. The aim of this book is not to come up with a consistent blueprint of solutions, but rather to inspire people through new ideas and new views, some of which might differ from each other. The book's content is intended to feed into a much-needed larger public debate, and to advance far-reaching proposals that build on the most recent developments of scientific research in its thematic areas.

The four main thematic areas we explore are defined by what we can call the central equation of the next phase of the European project. This equation can be presented in the following terms: if we want to renew the European economic and social model to address the ongoing ecological and digital transformations, and if we want to improve global governance to address the current global challenges, we must ask how our economic and financial instruments should be developed and how we can deepen European democracy in such a way as to be able to take the necessary far-reaching decisions.

The book's four parts cover each of these four main thematic areas with:

- an overview, prepared by a qualified rapporteur, of our meetings and the discussions we had at them;

- an impulse statement from a young person who represents the youngest generation of researchers on European issues; and
- an organized sequence of expert statements by renowned authors who are central experts in their particular field.

These latter statements build on each author's principal research, and some web links are suggested in order to mobilize this wider work. We hope that this will turn this book into a richer hypertext.

Part I, 'Rebuilding the European economic and social model to respond to the ecological, digital and post-Covid challenges', starts with a vision of how these transformations, which are being combined and accelerated by the Covid crisis, will impact on the longer-term perspective. The state needs to reinvent itself to shape these transformations and provide clear guidance relating to them at all levels, from local to European. Major flaws in the current European architecture need to be overcome by building a European Health Union and, even more ambitiously, a European Social Union. This need should underpin both the European Green Deal for the ecological transition and the European way of driving the digital transition, with its impact on job destruction and creation, on the regulation of working conditions, and on living conditions in general. All these issues deserve special attention because they are, and will continue to be, at the heart of European citizens' concerns.

The EU is at the forefront of international progress on ecological transformation, even if this progress is clearly below what is needed to reverse climate change. On the digital front, however, Europe is seriously lagging behind America and China in the move to the new phase of digitization. This phase is being driven by the Internet of Things, big data, cloud computing and artificial intelligence, which will transform all sectors of activity. Lastly, a special focus on demographic trends and the care sector shows that the rebalancing of our societies towards real gender equality still has a long way to go.

Part II, 'EU external action with strategic autonomy and multilateral engagement', starts with a general overview of the main scenarios for global governance in a multipolar world that is at risk of bifurcation between the world order driven by America and another driven by

China. What role should the EU play in order to overcome this risk, relaunch international cooperation and renew the multilateral system?

An EU with stronger strategic autonomy is needed, but this should be understood not as an alternative to renewed engagement with multilateralism but as complementary to it. Moreover, this relationship should be not just complementary but fully intertwined because, on the one hand, a stronger EU is crucial for renewing the multilateral system and, on the other, European bilateral relationships with other global players should operate within the multilateral framework. This approach is developed in several key areas of Europe's external action: notably, climate change, the digital revolution, trade agreements, the international financial system, defence and security, and migration. Conclusions are drawn about some of the key changes that need to be introduced to the EU's constitutional architecture in order to underpin some of these policy developments in the longer term.

Part III, 'An economic governance for an empowered EU', starts with a critical assessment of European economic governance through its recent history of self-inflicted austerity. It then assesses the desirable evolution of this governance on several key fronts: the need for a European industrial policy combined with a new approach to competition policy; greater macroeconomic dialogue; and a European semester to coordinate national policies with the sustainable development goals in order to reduce social and regional inequalities. However, there also needs to be a new economic policy mix that can rely on more active national budgetary policy that supports higher levels of investment, including social investment. This means updating the Stability and Growth Pact, acknowledging that the previous one was crafted in a very different context, with different underlying trends, and based on biased ordoliberal preferences.

We will also need instruments that strengthen European budgetary capacity, including a European Treasury, to be at the centre of the next phase of the European project. This will nevertheless require major progress to reduce tax evasion and tax avoidance, as well as to promote tax convergence and fairer burden-sharing, redirecting taxation towards new untapped sources: pollution, financial speculation and corporate extra profits, notably in the digital arena. In the longer term, more fundamental issues must also be addressed: the *sui generis* character of the European architecture as a fiscal union and the need to overcome its current intrinsic contradictions. Developing a republican approach to the governance of public goods at different levels might become an interesting road to explore.

Part IV, 'The EU and the next democratic transformation', explores some of the key changes that will be introduced to the European political system for the new phase of the European project. A central concern when it comes to representative democracy is the development of tools that will allow European citizens to increase their role when selecting their representatives for the legislative and executive powers. The *Spitzenkandidat* procedure that enables the president of the European Commission to be elected by taking into account European electoral outcomes and the way they are expressed in a European Parliament majority is certainly a central feature that needs to be developed. The democratic legitimacy of a European Commission president could also be strengthened through a debate about the political priorities of the European Commission as well as its composition. All of these ideas would increase the weight of the European Parliament in its general balance with the Council, as a second chamber, and ultimately with the European Council. The parliamentarization of the European political system, in line with the tradition of most member states, would help deepen democratic ownership by European citizens. Nevertheless, for this political process to be properly operationalized, the role of fully formed European political parties should be developed by (i) organizing internal primaries to select candidates, (ii) being more visible during the European electoral campaigns, (iii) proposing transnational lists, (iv) negotiating possible majorities inside the European Parliament and in the European Council, and (v) preparing programmes for governing the EU.

Another dimension of democracy that needs to be deepened is the participatory dimension – at all levels, and in conjunction with the development of a more substantial concept of European citizenship. This concept can no longer be reduced to economic or political rights. While they are undoubtedly important, these rights must be coupled with new ones, such as social, educational, digital and ecological rights. Digital tools can also enable the much larger-scale involvement of citizens, and different forms of participation too.

Citizens will need to be protected from the risks of manipulation, but they should be able to use the available tools to maxize their use of professional, plural and transparent media and journalistic services.

Finally, any discussion about the future of Europe should not be restrained by taboos. On the one hand, this means that we need to identify precisely how we can improve the European polity within the framework of the current Lisbon Treaty – and there are indeed many unexploited possibilities. On the other hand, though, if the necessary actions show us that some changes should be introduced in this Treaty, this should also be discussed rationally. In the end, both approaches to dealing with our problems should be on the table. According to the Lisbon Treaty, if a crucial decision is blocked, it can be unblocked either by using the *passerelle* clause and starting to make decisions by qualified majority voting, or ultimately by resorting to enhanced cooperation. But alongside this, citizens can call for concrete and timely decisions, particularly if they start to perceive themselves as fully fledged European citizens with both rights and and responsibilities. The republican approach of citizens being willing to better govern their own public goods, at all levels, can act as a good compass.

This book is the outcome of an amazing experience of collective debate and creativity. Its creation has involved not only its authors but also hundreds – in fact thousands – of other Europeans. We hope many others draw inspiration from our collective efforts for a timely delivery.

Readers have a choice over how to navigate the book: you can read the contributions in the order in which they are presented, you can choose your own sequence, you can read the whole book or you can pick and choose. You are also invited to explore the suggested web links as points of entry into a much larger hypertext – the one we Europeans are about to write.

Let me start with myself: Maria Joao Rodrigues, President of the Foundation for European Progressive Studies.

PART I
Rebuilding the European Economic and Social Model for Ecological, Digital and Post-Covid Challenges

PART

Synthesis of the debate*

By Jean-François Lebrun

'If you don't take change by the hand, it will take you by the throat.' This quote from Winston Churchill, the same man who said in 1940 that he had 'nothing to offer but blood, toil, tears and sweat', could be taken as our introduction.

At least three major drivers of change – climate, digitization and the ageing of Europe's population – can already be seen to be upon us. For decades there have been warnings about the impact these changes will have on our working and living environments, and it is now eminently clear that these transformations cannot be avoided. Global warming is beginning to make its effects felt; digitization, in which we are not one of the key players, has already become part of our lives; and the ageing of our populations is already well underway.

We must now manage their impacts, and particularly their effects on employment, working conditions and living conditions. These transformations will change our society profoundly. We must start to think about the socioeconomic model we want for tomorrow. It is possible that the instruments available to us will lead us to a more inclusive society – one that is able to turn the challenges we face into opportunities.

But are we able to act, today, to prepare ourselves for the changes that are to come? There is no shortage of available examples to illustrate the extent to which most human beings tend to resist change. Usually,

---

*   Disclaimer. This chapter and the ones that open parts II, III and IV of the book are summaries of meetings of the FEPS Expert Group on the Future of Europe (which was established in November 2020 – see the composition in the acknowledgements). These chapters aim to reflect the discussions and the main ideas that were debated. The names of the participants who made the various arguments are not identified as these meetings were held under Chatham House rules.

we only change when our backs are against the wall – when our survival is at stake. All change has implications. But change brings gains as well as losses. We are generally very averse to risk even though Homo sapiens are capable of adapting. However, this capacity to adapt and to be resilient is not distributed equally. In this respect, socioeconomic conditions play an important role – something that the Covid-19 crisis has clearly shown us every day for the past year.

In addition to this risk aversion, there is a second element that holds us back: complexity. Our societies are becoming increasingly complex. This complexity takes many forms: multicultural populations, a diversity of sociocultural systems (think of social protection models), a breakdown of the wage model, growing heterogeneity, interdependence and interdisciplinarity.

And at the European level, and within the framework of the existing treaties, the number of member states makes decision making complex. But time is against us. The longer we wait, the less we adapt and the greater the social challenges will be, the more difficult they will be to correct, encouraging the emergence of simplistic, populist, 'short-termist' and individualistic responses. However, the consequences will play out in a globalized economic environment over the long term and will require structural adaptations of our economies and our lifestyles.

As the current transformations also bring opportunities, it is essential that the policies that are implemented allow us to enhance these opportunties. We need a vision and we need fresh perspectives. This vision must enable us to envisage a more orderly world in which the need for security is decreased, thereby allowing us to express our other need: freedom.

WHAT ARE THE MAIN DRIVING FACTORS AND SOCIAL IMPLICATIONS OF THESE TRANSFORMATIONS?

The green transformation

The green transformation is closely linked to global warming, but it also includes other impacts on nature. It involves energy, various sources of pollution, waste and loss of diversity. Environmental change will profoundly alter our consumption and production habits. A more virtuous dynamic towards our planet has become indispensable. It is all the more necessary as it is not yet too late to try to limit the current warming.

Some sectors will be more affected than others by the necessary green transition. The biggest winners will be the electricity production and construction sectors. By contrast, a contraction is expected in sectors linked to fossil fuels. Furthermore, some sectors – such as steel, cement and chemicals – will have to undergo transformation as part of the transition to a low-carbon economy. Agriculture will be faced with some positive changes, notably in relation to consumer demand and environmental requirements, but also some negative ones, such as crop displacement, yields that are more variable and greater price volatility. The EU will remain dependent on a range of agricultural imports. It will need to ensure that it supports adaptation to climate change in other parts of the world.

A new relationship with nature will also bring many opportunities, including (but not limited to) the use of renewable energy and improved energy efficiency, the development of biomimicry and green chemistry, and the management and recycling of our waste (a major source of raw materials for tomorrow). The implementation of policies that support these new developments will have positive repercussions both for our planet – which is, after all, the only place where we can live, and will remain so for a long time – and for our health and well-being.

Patterns of both production and consumption will be affected by the green transition. Short circuits, the circular economy, zero waste and renting instead of buying are just a few of the many examples of new modes of consumption. Often stimulated by collaborative platforms, these new modes could become increasingly important.

This transformation will therefore have an impact on employment, both in quantitative and in qualitative terms. In the future, there will certainly be jobs that can be described as green, but above all there will be a 'greening' of a large number of jobs. Our ability to provide workers with new skills will be decisive in reducing the negative effects and promoting the positive ones. One does not spontaneously become an installer of thermal panels or a specialist in thermal insulation.

In the social sphere, care must be taken to minimize the effects of the green transition. In this respect, the fight against energy insecurity and for affordable, high-quality food for all will be elements that should not be neglected. Indeed, it is the most vulnerable who will be confronted with the greatest consequences of the green transition. It is important to pay attention to the effects of the green transition on social inequalities.

It will be necessary to ensure that the burden of the green transition is shared fairly between individuals, groups, sectors and regions. Some regions are better prepared than others. Social protection and solidarity mechanisms between regions will have to be put in place to respond to the impacts of this transformation.

Sustainability must be a guiding principle for all our future policies. But the focus should be on an overall strategy for sustainability and welfare improvement rather than on separate policies in individual areas.

It will be useful to continue the work of moving beyond using growth in gross domestic product (GDP) as the major indicator of a country's success. People's well-being and cohesion, as well as their ecological footprint, will have to be included in policy evaluations.

The digital transformation

The digital transformation may be more complex than the green one, as it will spread across all sectors. It is a multistage process that started more than forty years ago, with the key stages including the development of the first personal computers, the dawn of the internet (first with Web 1.0, where information went from the professional to the individual, and then with Web 2.0, which was characterized by social networks and the production of information by the individual), the development of smartphones, industrial robots and now artificial intelligence (AI), and the era of blockchain and Big Data. Data is becoming a commodity. Networking has become the norm.

We are in the Fourth Industrial Revolution. The Third Industrial Revolution relied on electronics and information technology to automate production. The Fourth Industrial Revolution – the digital revolution – is characterized by a fusion of the physical, digital and biological spheres.

This revolution is developing at an exponential rather than linear rate, and it will radically change the way we produce, consume, work and approach life in society. All sectors will be affected in one way or another. For example, digitization will affect mobility (autonomous cars), retail (via e-commerce), health (AI-assisted remote medical consultations), housing (introduction of home automation), and our interactions with public services (via electronic counters) and with things (via the Internet of Things).

This will affect a huge number of jobs. While there will be 'digital jobs', there will also be a 'digitization' of (almost) all jobs. As with the green transformation, we are witnessing and will continue to witness creation–destruction cycles of activities linked in particular to automation.

Furthermore, by allowing teleworking (or 'remote working', the adoption of which has been accelerated by Covid-19), digitization can create increased competition between highly skilled workers at the global level. Digitization is also a breeding ground for the development of platforms that, without supervision, encourage the development of precarious jobs.

The digital divide must be tackled. Everyone must have access, tools and sufficient knowledge to be able to benefit from digitization. Once again, it will be necessary to ensure cohesion within the EU, as not all regions are equally well equipped to deal with digitization and the need for qualified human capital that it brings with it. Nor are all companies equipped to take part in the Fourth Industrial Revolution.

But digitization is also a challenge for the whole of the EU. Large companies, mostly American ones, now dominate the international scene and are more and more central to our daily activities. Taxing the profits of large foreign digital platforms is necessary, but it is not enough, because we are excluded from production. The EU is dependent; it is a digital colony. The development of AI, given its future importance, cannot be left to America and China, our great global competitors. We must have a central role in tomorrow's technology, and we need to support European companies in the field, both large and small. An 'industrial' policy in this area is needed: a long-term strategy requiring cooperation, public and private funding, appropriate infrastructure, research and, above all, a sufficient quantity and quality of human capital.

The Internet of Things (part of Web 3.0, which focuses on the interaction between humans and their environment) is one of the major areas of work for the future. The EU should not be left on the sidelines. A joint research effort is needed in this area, with research addressing all aspects of it, whether they are technical, economic, social or legal. Once again, we must defend the freedom of every EU citizen.

The strengthening of freedom is not only an external matter: it is also an internal concern. Indeed, digital transformation can strongly influence the balance between freedom and security, as in the case of social profiling, for instance. In this respect, the General Data Protection Regulation (GDPR) is a great success of EU action (as is the Registration, Evaluation, Authorization and Restriction of Chemicals (REACH) regulation for the green transition). It is through being a strong technological player that the EU can preserve its sovereignty and be a factor in democratic resilience. It is imperative that we can control technological developments – a necessary condition for trust in technology.

The demographic transformation

The demographic transformation is driven by falling birth rates and rising life expectancy. It is characterized by an ageing of the European population, which will only begin to stabilize towards the 2050s. This ageing brings with it a number of challenges, particularly in terms of health, dependency management and the financing of our pension systems. Here, too, this change will have many effects on employment and in the social sphere.

Longer life expectancy does not go hand in hand with better health. Medical progress will certainly be made, particularly in connection with genetics (such as with the possibilities offered by messenger ribonucleic acid (RNA)), but for the time being we remain mortals who see our capacities erode with time. Immortality – or, in its modern version, transhumanism, the augmented man – remains a quest: a quest that will certainly require a robust debate on the future of mankind.

Ageing also has both positive and negative effects on employment. On the negative side, there is a decrease in the labour force and an increase in the demand for social care, healthcare and public infrastructure. But on the other side, there are the opportunities offered by the 'silver economy'. The elderly are a market. They have specific needs for services and products (e.g. exoskeletons and home robotics).

With regard to ageing, many projects will have to be implemented rapidly to enable the elderly to remain independent for as long as possible in a place of their choosing (at home or in an institution). Two factors influence the level of dependency of our citizens: socioeconomic conditions (the kinds of low-paid, precarious and difficult jobs that are often associated with a low level of education are ultimately vectors of dependency) and age (more particularly, old age, whatever the socioeconomic conditions). A review of our personal and household support (PHS) services seems necessary if we are to have the means to cope with a double shift: more dependent people and fewer family carers. These services combine both direct care activities centred on people (the elderly, the disabled, young children, etc.) and indirect care activities centred on objects (houses, linen, meals, etc.). While they are essential for allowing dependent people to remain at home, they are also essential for promoting a better balance between family and working life.

While social services are essential for disadvantaged people (particularly in terms of their level of dependency and income), complementary service providers must be able to intervene for other groups. This is a significant source of employment, but it requires a review of the ecosystem of these services in order to avoid growth in undeclared jobs or in jobs that do not comply with normal working conditions. Are they local jobs? Currently, yes and no. Yes, because we need to act at the level of the dependent person's home. No, because the often low attractiveness of these jobs encourages the immigration of foreign care providers.

An increased need for security and stability will coexist with a desire for autonomy and freedom. Older people also have time and experience to share. Voluntary work and intergenerational cooperation open up many ways of strengthening social cohesion. Old age should not become an antechamber to death but an important phase of life.

Of course, in order to benefit from this new phase of life and for society to be able to take advantage of it, it is essential that older people have sufficient income. The question of the level of pensions and their financing must be central. Individual responsibility and collective solidarity will have to be combined so that we can draw on demographic transformation to create prospects for better well-being.

When we talk about demographic developments, we must address the question of net migration. At least two phenomena influence the evolution of this balance.

The supply side is determined by the socioeconomic conditions in the migrants' countries of origin, but also by the political and, in the future, climatic conditions. The population of Africa is expected to double in the next thirty-five years (from 1.34 billion now to 2.7 billion in 2055). If just one per cent of this additional population decided to cross the Mediterranean, that would see migratory pressure to the tune of 13 million people.

Demand is determined by our needs, particularly in terms of labour. With rises in the standard of living of Europeans, many jobs that are considered to be arduous and poorly paid are not readily taken up by the local population. In other cases, the ageing of the population could trigger migratory demands to meet the labour needs of the European production system.

Migration policy is of vital importance, as are policies that support the economic and social development of countries around us. The practice of burying one's head in the sand in this area is a major risk for our political systems.

Combining these three transformations

Each of these transformations is in itself a challenge in terms of both positive and negative impacts. In combination, they make the situation even more complex, but it is perhaps also thanks to this combination that favourable outcomes are possible.

Our future policies must combine these three transformations. We must be able to take advantage of each of them to reduce the negative effects of the other two and, conversely, to maximize the positive effects.

For instance, autonomous low-emission cars can help with the mobility of the elderly; a properly insulated house with the latest automation can help the elderly to remain in their homes; and artificial intelligence that supports medicine, combined with improvements in our diet and in air quality, will increase healthy life expectancy.

Homes should be used for the benefit of communities. Decentralized energy production is a possibly interesting example of this. The home can also become a central element of future policies. The development of teleworking is one aspect; energy use reduction, through better thermal insulation for example, is another; the introduction of 3D printers is a third; and the provision of services in the home (especially in relation to dependency) yet another. As a corollary, the fight against homelessness must be considered essential.

The digital transition must also be green because it is energy intensive.

But a lack of global vision risks accentuating the negative effects of these transformations. Maintaining the digital divide therefore risks excluding a growing number of European citizens. A mismatch of skills between greening and digitization will have an impact on employability, and ultimately on pensions too.

HOW SHOULD SOCIAL POLICIES BE UPDATED?

The impacts on employment

Perhaps the important thing is not the quantitative forecasting of the jobs of tomorrow or the day after, but rather the provision of instruments that are able to address future needs. In particular, it is a question of encouraging internal and external adaptation to companies' future skills requirements (take, for example, the transition from mechanics to electronics, and even to IT, in the automotive industry).

Skills will have to be adapted to our new modes of production and our new lives. Our education and training system must respond to future needs, otherwise we are heading for increasing polarization of our society – polarization between those who have gainful employment and those who do not. Skills will be at the centre of managing the effects of the current transformations.

We need education systems that are able to provide both soft skills (relating to communication, creativity, teamwork, entrepreneurial spirit, and so on) and technical qualifications that are increasingly specialized and evolve over time. We also need efficient employment services that are able to support jobseekers and workers who are undergoing retraining. And the ability to manage human capital internally within companies (skills assessment/recognition of acquired experience/career mobility/career paths) is also essential. On this last point, it might be useful to bring out the EU Quality Framework for Anticipation of Change and Restructuring (COM(2013) 882) and turn it into a guide for human resources management.

Education, all the way from early childhood to lifelong learning, is a central collective investment (early childhood is important, because the development of cooperative synapses is not to be neglected). Living in a digital society without knowing its language (e.g. the ability to create and understand applications) is no longer acceptable. The need for innovation and technology to cope with both the green and digital transformations requires our education systems to attract and train a significant number of STEM (science, technology, engineering and mathematics) graduates. It is worth stressing that this acronym does not only refer to 'male jobs'.

Moreover, in a world where change is becoming the norm, lifelong learning must become the rule for all and not just the prerogative of the few (usually those who are already the best trained). Our school systems will also have to ensure that early school leaving and school failure are limited. Young people without training will find it increasingly difficult to find jobs, because even if the polarization of the labour market continues (high-skilled jobs versus low-skilled jobs), there is a serious risk that 'intermediate' workers will find themselves partly performing tasks that require fewer technical skills, thereby putting pressure on low-skilled entrants.

Lifelong learning, or continuous training, must become a reality for all European citizens. Even greater investment is needed for those with reduced employability. The fight against long-term unemployment should become a priority – or rather, a reality. This fight is costly, but the consequences of long-term unemployment are even more so.

Interdisciplinarity will become the rule, not the exception. Tomorrow's society will no longer be able to work in silos as it has in the past. In the future, the interdependence between climate/environment and economy/society will become more visible with every passing day. The quality of human capital will be a key factor in increasing innovation and productivity.

The impacts on working and living conditions

Creating jobs and having the right skills is desirable, but it is not enough. Those new jobs have to be quality jobs. Pay-as-you-go work based on zero-hours contracts paid at the minimum wage, without the acquisition of social rights and in an unsafe environment, cannot be the basis for the jobs of tomorrow. The world of work is already changing. The wage model of the industrial age is crumbling. New forms of employment are emerging, and others are developing (such as teleworking, 'platform work' and self-employment). Many restructurings, especially in small and medium-sized enterprises, are not accompanied by enough effort to reintegrate workers. Part of the population is afraid of these developments, and often rightly so. But once again, solutions exist, at least on paper.

The quality of employment depends on both the regulatory work of public authorities and that of their social partners. Public authorities should be able to set minimum working conditions, ensure equal treatment of contractual and casual employees, and enforce labour legislation. The issue of platform work is crucial. Platform workers should be guaranteed the same rights as those in more traditional forms of employment, including social protection and access to collective bargaining.

Moreover, public authorities must support the dynamics of social dialogue so that their social partners can negotiate complementary and/or specific agreements. Social negotiations must be possible at all levels: European, national, cross-industry and sectoral, and lastly at company level. All sectors and activities must be covered by binding collective agreements. With due regard for the representativeness of the signatories, the procedures for extending agreements (*erga omnes*) must be supported by public authorities. The joint work of social partners must be allowed to extend to the effective management and implementation of instruments for the reintegration of workers (as is already the case in some member states).

Social dialogue must remain a central part of the social sphere. Industrial democracy, based on freedom of association and the effective recognition of the right to collective bargaining, must be widely supported by the EU throughout the world, for it is this that will enable workers both here and, above all, elsewhere to benefit from the economic progress that is linked to globalization. Trade union freedom is an important marker of political democracy.

Social protection must be in line with labour market developments (see in this respect the Council recommendation on access to social protection, adopted in 2019). Social protection must provide a safety net that is free of holes (and where non-use of rights must be reduced), and it must be able to respond to the care and service needs of the population. In the face of increased flexibility and an economy in transition, the question of income protection that would guarantee a basic income must be studied without preconceptions.

It is important to note the welcome arrival of the European Pillar of Social Rights (EPSR) in 2017. This is not so much about new rights as it is about requirements relating to social policies to be implemented, mainly by member states. The future action plan should enable member states to offer Europeans the implementation of the principles contained in the pillar. This action plan could constitute the beginnings of social governance in the same way as economic governance (the Annual Growth Survey, the National Reform Programmes, Stability and Convergence Programmes and Country Specific Recommendations).

The social, employment and education policies that are covered by the EPSR should promote professional transitions and cover all forms of employment. Implementation of the twenty principles set out in the EPSR would constitute a guarantee of a well-functioning labour market and of efficient social protection/coverage while respecting the principle of subsidiarity. It is primarily up to member states to implement actions that protect their citizens. European policies in these areas support national policies and should stimulate and initiate virtuous processes.

WHAT SHOULD EUROPEAN PRIORITIES BE IN SHAPING THESE TRANSFORMATIONS?

The future as a journey

We know the elements that could contribute to a long-term vision, but how can we put them together to make an understandable and credible package?

Let us forget about using the term 'model', which often refers to a static definition, and instead use a dynamic approach: perspectives, opportunities, even dreams – in short, a vision. But while a vision is essential, it is not the quantitative targets that should prevail but the path we intend to take to achieve them.

The path is first and foremost a basic value that we must not forget: we walk together. And while some of us might be able to go on a scouting trip, we must not leave anyone by the wayside. By following this path, we can maintain the support of the population and the flexibility necessary for a long-lasting journey in a complex and uncertain world.

Having a path means that you need a direction – a map, GPS, a compass. Uncertainty and complexity should not prevent us from developing indicators. In fact, they are essential because we need to know we are making progress. We need to know that our efforts are serving a purpose and that we are moving forward. Our political instruments must be easier to read and simpler to comprehend. Citizens must be able to understand and evaluate the policies proposed to them.

This readability and simplicity does not prevent the 'back office' from being complex. The integration of negative as well as positive externalities is not easy, but it is essential. The taxation of negative externalities must be effective and efficient, as must the subsidizing of activities with positive externalities. Prices must be transparent and easy to read, and they must fully play their essential role in the allocation of resources.

'Leaving no one behind' means that cohesion, convergence and equity should be central concerns. Solidarity and equal opportunities must permeate our political actions. An ordered world in which freedom prevails comes at a price that we must be willing to pay. Accepting the price of solidarity requires public services to be efficient.

Cooperation and subsidiarity backed by a demand for coherence must also be our guide. Cooperation between the various socioeconomic actors but also between the levels of power must be developed. In this respect, our practices of social dialogue must be given all the necessary support, in terms of both means and facilitation, to play their role and in terms of the possibility of completing, or even exceeding, the regulatory framework. This framework must allow equal treatment of all forms of employment. Subsidiarity must remain the rule, but it must be accepted in both directions: more local if necessary, or more European if that is needed. We must not be afraid of either, but we must demand that people work in a coherent way. In this respect, debate must regain its rightful place. Everyone must be able to express themselves, but democracy must prevail and therefore enable decisions to be made. Yes to consensus, no to unanimity.

Solidarity, freedom and investment

A protective framework within which freedom can be expressed must be provided.

The expression of freedom is also the expression of solidarity. Solidarity guarantees support in times of difficulty and allows everyone to be free. Freedom and solidarity are inseparable. As Nelson Mandela said: 'For to be free is not merely to cast off one's chains, but to live in a way that respects and enhances the freedom of others.'

Solidarity is useful to society – to each and every one of us – because it makes society more balanced and more stable. It is therefore not only beneficial to the weak and the poor.

Solidarity enables our societies to be resilient. It enables individuals and communities to cope with, adapt to and recover from crises. The primary elements of resilience are prevention, education and training. The new demands that will be brought about by changes and new production processes, combined with an ageing society, will create jobs. We will therefore need to have the ability to meet these labour needs in both quantity and quality. Our education systems will have to be very agile and responsive, which can be a challenge. Supervised training can be an important element of support.

Resilience in our societies, but also at the individual level, cannot therefore be achieved without an ability to invest. Investment must be at the centre of our concerns, including social investment in its broadest sense. Investment and structural deficit are two notions that must be kept separate. Investment means money. Money remains the backbone of war – even a peaceful war that moves us in the direction of more equity, resilience and freedom.

The 'European model' of social protection will be put under great pressure in the coming years, particularly through the costs of ageing and the support that will need to be offered to people affected by job losses, to enable their reintegration. Faced with such tensions, a reimagining of the social contract that exists between the state, its citizens, workers and companies must be put on the table. In this respect, we need to rethink the relationship between the state and its citizens. Businesses will have a crucial role to play in meeting environmental objectives. This is all even more true in a globalized world where profit shifting by multinationals, tax evasion and tax competition undermine the financial viability of our society and the ability of governments to prepare for the future by investing in innovation or in education and retraining people.

It is important for public budgets to be able to support the three main functions of public action: allocation, redistribution and stabilization. These three functions must be carried out at all levels of government.

In addition to the taxation of negative externalities (a reduction in the social cost), which must become fundamental (that is, by definition, erodible), we must return to progressive taxation of income – all income – in a fair and stable manner. One that allows for collective investment.

Being taxed should become a positive social marker. But to achieve this objective, public services must become strong examples of effectiveness and efficiency. There is a need for public spending to be meaningful and to generate investment. This requirement must be complemented by a second, too: that there is coherence and complementarity between the spending carried out at various levels of power. We must move forward together, including in the budgetary field.

Among the investments that public authorities can support are subsidies that raise social welfare (also called Pigouvian subsidies). Giving meaning to social welfare – in other words to the community – must become a hard and fast rule. It is well known that the identification and, especially, the quantification of positive externalities are complex but solvable problems.

Innovation and industrial policy (including that relating to services) are elements that must be eligible for Pigouvian subsidies if social welfare is to be increased. If competition remains a central element of the social market economy, it would certainly need to be understood in its international dimension as well, as in the case of the aerospace sector (see the examples of Airbus and Galileo).

Defence policy (which is aptly named) must not be forgotten. This policy, which also includes space, is a crucial factor in maintaining our independence, preserving peace and strengthening our freedom. But it is not only that. It is also a major source of technological innovation, and it is an area in which other countries are seeing steady development. We must strive to do the same because, as the saying goes, if you want something done well, do it yourself.

The development of abilities and capacities is essential at the individual level, but the same is true at the territorial level too. We are not all in the same boat. Some regions will be harder hit by climate change than others, and some regions are better prepared to cope with the effects of both climate change and digitization than others. It is therefore crucial that solidarity is exercised at the interregional level. The EU has a history of being able to develop such instruments.

The instruments of European solidarity in the social field have been developed over time. This solidarity now takes several forms. Firstly, the EU has a redistribution mechanism aimed at strengthening the structural capacities of its member states to manage adaptations: the European Social Fund. Secondly, it has a redistribution mechanism between the winners and losers from certain policies: the European Globalisation Adjustment Fund. And thirdly, and more recently, it has created a stabilization mechanism following a major shock: the Support to Mitigate Unemployment Risks in an Emergency. This new instrument was launched by the EU in the context of Covid-19 and it is a very interesting example of reinsurance. In this case, it is financial assistance in the form of loans from the EU to enable member states to cope with a sudden increase in public spending to preserve employment (short-time work). Other reinsurance mechanisms could be created to strengthen the possibility of solidarity at the EU level. One example is a European unemployment benefit scheme.

Without sufficient provision of such instruments – and, therefore, without mobility of capital, and more precisely of public capital – it will be the people who move. This is a choice that we will have to accept and that does not offer many collective solutions.

ALL THESE ELEMENTS ARE KNOWN, SO WHAT STOPS THEM BEING COMPONENTS OF A SHARED VISION?

Having a vision is one thing. Having a shared vision is quite another. Faced with the transformations that are currently underway, we must be able to move beyond the question of rights that were acquired in the past. We must convince ourselves that the vision being offered will generate more winners than losers, and that for the losers, solidarity will be real and effective.

The winners must help the losers. Only then can changes be accepted. This preamble is important to enable the necessary adaptation to change. The second factor in the success of a process of change is a shared assessment of the current and future situations (a shared assessment implies a dialogue). It is within the framework of these conditions that the cooperation of all actors will make it possible to offer everyone a new perspective.

The EU has already demonstrated in the past that it is able to transcend its differences and offer a clear vision (notably when the internal market was established). All European citizens must be able to be proud of being European and of living in a geographical area in which solidarity and freedom are everyday realities. It is in this framework that European citizenship will play its full role and that Europe will have a future. This future, built on the twin values of freedom and solidarity, will become a beacon for other parts of the world.

Let us not forget that these transformations are taking place in an environment that already poses a number of significant challenges, such as those posed by globalization and European integration. In the past, we could not know what was happening on the other side of the seas, or over the mountains and deserts, and we could live in autarchy. It is the exchange of goods as well as of ideas and knowledge that has allowed the world in which we live to emerge. Interdependence is a reality. Globalization, like the three transformations that are currently underway, offers opportunities if we work out how to deal with its negative impacts. We will be able to do this if we preserve and develop our values of freedom and solidarity.

Let us end as we began, by quoting Winston Churchill: 'There is nothing wrong with change, if it is in the right direction.'

Aspirations: Europe in the 2020s – setting the course for all future Europeans

By Halliki Kreinin and Lukas Hochscheidt

We will look back at the 2020s as the decade in which we either did right by or failed *all* future Europeans. If we are lucky enough to be alive, it is likely that we will have to revisit this period and account for our actions, much like the Europeans of the 1930s and 1940s. What did we do to change the course we were on? Did we fight for what was moral, even if it sounded inconvenient? Or did we give in to inertia, accepting what was 'normal', but harmful?

THE FUTURE OF EUROPE: PERPETUAL CRISES?

The 2020s will set the course for the rest of European – and world – history. Per capita, Europeans currently emit quadruple the carbon emissions that are allowed under the Paris Agreement. Will we stay below 1.5–2 °C of warming in the coming years and avoid the 'Hothouse Earth' scenario? Or will we shoot over that limit and, because of the Earth's inbuilt feedback loops, assign humanity to perpetually rising temperatures, the collapse of agricultural systems (starting in or around 2035), famines, climate genocide and, ultimately, the collapse of civilization? Will we change societal institutions and laws to allow for everyone to meet their needs with *sufficiency*? Or will we allow rising inequality and obscene material consumption for a select few at the expense of establishing a firm basis for a good life for all?

The multiple crises that Europe faces – environmental, societal, economic – require us to rethink how we provide for societal well-being while staying within the planet's 'carrying capacity'. These interrelated crises demand that we find solutions using a systems approach. Instead of 'going back to what we had' after the Covid-19 crisis, let us move forward to something better. Let us revisit our ideas about what is 'normal' and what is 'important'. Let us try to get off the hamster wheel of more.

FROM VISION TO ACTION

If this vision is to become a reality, the European social and economic model will need to change fundamentally. Only by adapting our social contract to become an eco-social contract that encompasses the ecological and digital transformations that face us will we be able to set up social structures that provide sustainable welfare for all future generations. The twin challenges of the climate crisis and the digital revolution are not therefore merely about innovation and disruptive technologies: we have to address each as a social issue, and we need to give ourselves the means to succeed in this challenge.

First, we have to rethink industrial policy. Instead of linking investment decisions to traditional conceptions of economic growth, we have to redirect investment flows towards industries that promote sustainable welfare and allow for climate-neutral production and decent jobs. Public investment should only benefit those who are committed to respecting climate targets and creating good work in new sectors, including the digital world of work. We need to be honest about which industries cannot continue in their present states, instead of promoting dangerous discourses about climate delay on behalf of industries that are harmful to the environment and harmful to workers kept in unsustainable jobs.

Second, we have to provide workers and their families with the safety they need to thrive in a more dynamic working environment. Industry transitions require workers to change their jobs, and even the sectors they work in, more frequently. In order for workers to be willing to commit to these changes and be capable of doing so, they need security of both employment and income, in the form of better (and universal) social services, robust unemployment benefits, reskilling programmes and, eventually, a universal job guarantee.

Reductions in working time can be a useful tool for sharing work more equally and for reducing structural unemployment. Of course, this must not come at the expense of workers already pushed to the limit. Instead, we need to create minimum- and maximum-income corridors for a more just and sustainable wage distribution. For this New Social Deal to succeed, strong codetermination and collective bargaining mechanisms have to be put into place to allow workers' voices to be heard all over Europe.

Third, to reduce social and environmental risks across Europe, we need to build a much more welfare-oriented and crisis-averse tax policy. A comprehensive social–ecological tax framework must be EU-wide if it is to avoid becoming a race to the bottom (we are looking at you Ireland); it must include decreased labour taxation and increased taxes on emissions, materials use and energy use (starting with a kerosene tax). Our tax system must include much more progressive taxes on capital, wealth and inheritance in order to reduce inequality and raise welfare without increasing emissions. Tax avoidance by multinational companies must be fought against strongly, notably when it comes to digital services firms who have done business in Europe without paying their fair share of taxes. Through lowering inequality and promoting welfare, a comprehensive social–ecological tax system would also help us to stay within the earth's carrying capacity, as inequality is a driver of the environmental crisis.

STRONGER EUROPEAN DEMOCRACY FOR A BETTER FUTURE

For the EU to be capable of delivering the needed social–ecological and digital transformations, the institutions of our union have to change fundamentally. The European Parliament must have the final say on *all* the issues pertaining to the transformations – as a true democratic legislator. Europeans should be able to decide on the future course for Europe by majority voting in the European Parliament rather than by relying on unambitious compromises resulting from unanimous Council decisions. This would make the parliament the home of a genuine European democracy.

Democratic legitimacy and listening to 'the voice of the many' are prerequisites if we are to build a society that is more equal, slower, happier, more focused on well-being, and not exploitative of the environment, or of resources and labour elsewhere. This cannot be the mission of any single member state on its own, only the EU working together.

A European Health Union

By Vytenis Andriukaitis

The Covid-19 pandemic has shaken Europe. This is, first of all, a health crisis. Just in the EU/EEU alone, more than 610,000 deaths have been caused by Covid-19, with hundreds of thousands more excess deaths having been caused by disruption to health systems and with long-term mental health problems brought on by broken societal life that will be felt for years to come. It is also an economic and, finally, a social crisis, and it is one that challenges the entire European project.

Until recently, development goals such as saving lives, promoting good health and increasing longevity were off the radar of European policy. For decades, health-related matters were considered by the EU to be almost exclusively the business of member states or of quasi-markets. Until Covid-19 came along, health remained a minor topic in European Treaties, in the European Semester and when it came to the EU's budget. The 'EU does not take action' prevails unless it is more effective than action taken at national, regional or local level – this is how in usual everyday practice the subsidiarity principle and the role of the EU in health is interpreted.

The experience of the pandemic has shed light on the weaknesses of the existing mechanisms for collaboration among member states and with the European institutions. Covid-19 has inspired a rethink of the role that health plays in European politics. To many Europeans – including patients, healthcare practitioners and progressive societal leaders – it is clear that health is a big issue, and we have to seize this window of opportunity to ensure strong public action is taken to transform cooperation at the member state and EU levels.

Each previous health crisis (e.g. bovine spongiform encephalopathy (BSE), Ebola) has added a health policy layer and created new EU institutions (the European Medicines Agency and the European Centre for

Disease Prevention and Control, for example). In the face of this crisis, then, does Europe need to look at taking forward new EU competencies in the field of health, as well as in the other areas of EU policy that impact on health?

After the outbreak of SARS-CoV-2 in spring 2020, the Progressive Alliance of Socialists and Democrats came up with a set of proposals that would establish a European Health Union (EHU). Since September 2020, the EU Commission has supported the initiative by designing the first building blocks of an EHU. These relate to a stronger capacity to respond to cross-border health threats and better crisis preparedness. They will in time be followed by two major EHU initiatives: a Pharmaceutical Strategy for Europe and Europe's Beating Cancer Plan.

So what is a European Health Union, exactly? Are those proposed first building blocks of the EHU cohesive enough to serve as a strong basis for it? Does the creation of an EHU mean that the differences in average life expectancy at birth that exist between old and new member states, of up to 7–9 years, will reduce in the future? Will an EHU bring innovations closer to every hospital bed in Europe, and will it irrigate 'medical deserts' across the member states?

In all European nations health is one of the most important pillars of well-being. Can you think of a better way for the EU to reach out to its citizens than through health solidarity? Unfortunately, the Commission's most recent initiatives are unlikely to provide encouragement when it comes to the health-related expectations of Europeans. The current Commission proposal to build an EHU without treaty changes gives no chance of a strong EHU being built.

A genuine European Health Union would first and foremost have to build on the EU Pillar of Social Rights, on the EU and member state commitments to the Sustainable Development Goals, on the European Green Deal, on the Recovery and Resilience Facility, and on the Digital Agenda for Europe. It is now time to combine these and add to them the concept of a Health and Well-being Deal.

I propose some suggested features that the future EHU might have below.

- The role of health policy in the European Treaties should be reconsidered and strengthened. The objectives that should be

kept in mind are more proactive and preventive health measures, more solidarity when it comes to public health activities in Europe, and more cooperation in building resilient health 'care and cure' systems.
- There should be a sufficient capacity to safeguard EU solidarity when there are shortages of medical supplies simultaneously in different member states. The EU should be empowered in some areas to ensure centralized distribution of emergency medicines, 'orphan drugs' or medicines for rare cancer treatments, and supplies based on medical needs.
- A cross-border healthcare directive is not enough. We also need the EU to share some responsibility in 'care and cure' in the areas of rare cancers and rare diseases while preserving subsidiarity as a core principle. We need the European health insurance fund to cover rare diseases and to ensure that the pledge that 'no one is left behind' is a reality in Europe. No European country is capable, on its own, of guaranteeing universal health coverage for all of the 30 million EU patients who are suffering from rare cancers or rare diseases, but the EU can do it.

Let us be clear: the challenge is not one of making EU institutions responsible for all health matters but of finding the right form of integration and cooperation between the EU and its member states so that they can act more effectively both in 'normal' times and in times of pandemic.

One can imagine a range of different scenarios for the development of an EHU. If we follow the existing constraints and legal limits enshrined in the European Treaties, two scenarios can be envisaged:

- Scenario A would utilize existing legal, financial and managerial instruments, improve functioning institutions, and improve the implementation of already-agreed policies.
- Scenario B would see the fine-tuning of existing instruments of health policy in parallel with the development of secondary legislation and the establishment of new institutions that are capable of creating added value for European health.

By opting for either of these scenarios, Europeans would be restricting the benefits they might obtain from deeper cooperation on health.

The aim of the EU and all of its main objectives are enforced by Article 3 of the Treaties of the European Union (TEU). Health is not currently included in Article 3; it appears only as a 'shared competence' between the EU and the member states in Article 4 of the Treaty on the Functioning of the European Union (TFEU) in a very limited form: as 'common safety concerns in public health matters, for the aspects defined in this Treaty'. According to Article 6 of the TFEU, the EU shall have competence to carry out actions to support, coordinate or supplement the actions of member states in the protection and improvement of human health. Article 168 of the TFEU – which is quite renowned by the health community – is a development of the legal norms enforced by Articles 4 and 6 of the TFEU. Some powers are given to the EU over ensuring the safety of sanitary–phytosanitary drugs and medical devices.

Following the logic of the TEU, the TFEU is prioritizing the articles that are devoted to the development of an internal market over the articles that deal with other activities of the EU. Development of health care is considered to be important to the EU insofar as it better serves the functioning of the internal market. But Europe is not just the market per se. Europe needs to speak explicitly about good health being an aim of the EU, and about an EHU being a tool that could ensure the good health and longevity of Europeans. The need to speak about good health being an aim of the EU requires us to look at a third scenario.

- Scenario C sees the status of health policy in the European Treaties being strengthened, with provisions made for an EHU to be incorporated into the TEU and amending the TFEU, giving the EU some responsibilty over health policy in very concrete areas while preserving the principle of subsidiarity at the core.

The best choice for Europeans would be to adopt the most ambitious scenario: scenario C. This would provide citizens with the opportunity to reap all the benefits that would stem from deeper cooperation over health. Europe lives according to its treaties, so the demands of its citizens that cooperation in health matters is taken seriously should be enshrined in the TEU. Europeans need to see a 'healthier' face of Article 3 of the TEU.

Let us replace part 3 of Article 3, which currently starts with 'The Union shall establish an internal market', with one sentence: 'The EU shall promote universal health coverage by establishing a health union.'

And then let us amend point (k) of paragraph 2 of Article 4 of the TFEU about shared competence between the EU and its member states in the area of health, specifying it in order to (subsequently) further clarify Article 168 of the TFEU.

The Covid-19 crisis taught us to build solidarity. The response to future cross-border health threats could be strengthened through a health solidarity clause that amends Article 222 of the TFEU – a clause that will work in a similar way to the EU civil protection clause.

Maybe some of us would prefer development to be slow, but without being ambitious there is a risk that we will miss a window of opportunity for evolving the EHU beyond the internal market, and beyond a narrow paradigm that does not fit the realities of the twenty-first century.

The citizen-led Conference on the Future of Europe should be very ambitious about taking over Europe.

The former European Commission president Jacques Delors described the EU's lack of solidarity over its response to the pandemic as a mortal danger to the bloc. But a lack of solidarity in health is also a mortal danger. Let us be inspired by this insight, and let us be brave, building a strong and genuine EHU.

The care crisis and a feminist society

By Emma Dowling

Feminist scholars and activists have long been pointing to a growing care crisis. Since the 1970s there has been a rise in female labour market participation without there being a fundamental transformation of the sexual division of labour. A dual-earner household model has replaced that of a male breadwinner, yet this has gone hand in hand with wage stagnation (Guschanski and Onaran 2020). Households require more waged work to be done to make ends meet, and that has a knock-on effect on the time available for the unpaid work of cooking, cleaning and caring for children and other kin. The situation is exacerbated by the rise in the need for care due to demographic changes such as ageing, meaning more people need care.

At the same time, welfare retrenchment and privatization are putting pressure on public services. The idea of cost saving – whether to prop up profits or to operate under conditions of austerity – leads to a depletion of reserve capacities. This exacerbates vulnerability to unexpected events like the Covid-19 pandemic. All the while, dividends to shareholders continue to increase (Coffey 2020). The interest of private investors in the care sector is rising, and the personal and household services sector is the second-fastest growing sector in Europe (Decker and Lebrun 2018). Care platforms are already part of the precarious gig economy. Yet, leaving care to the market drives a wedge between those who can afford expensive services and those who cannot. It also assumes people who need care usually have the capacity and the time to navigate providers and pricing options, which is simply not the case. An effective care infrastructure cannot be built on personal responsibility alone. By definition, care involves needing the help of others. When it comes to care, it is more efficient for societies to pool risk and resources over the life course.

WHO CARES?

Women still do most of the unpaid work of care and social reproduction, and they usually carry the overall responsibility for care in households (Gimenez-Nadal and Molina 2020). In paid care work, women are also in the majority, which means that the low earnings and the low quality of jobs in the care sector affect women more (see International Labour Organisation 2018). Economic disadvantages for women include those inadequate employment conditions and the loss of earnings due to caring responsibilities (Folbre 2017). A lack of affordable childcare is often a reason why mothers are not engaged in paid employment or work part time. Across the EU, more women than men find it difficult to combine paid work with caring responsibilities (Manoudi *et al.* 2018). Women with caring responsibilities more often tend to be employed informally or are in self-employment, and they are therefore less able to pay into social security or are deterred from taking jobs that demand irregular hours (as per the aforementioned 2018 International Labour Organisation study). Furthermore, class, ethnicity and migration background are significant factors when it comes to filling care gaps. Wealthier households can afford to pay for marketized services, while those who cannot have to fit the work in themselves or go without. In fact, a high proportion of migrant workers and ethnic minorities work in long-term care and household services, often for very low pay and in precarious conditions. Cross-border care work is prevalent where there are discrepancies between working conditions and salaries across the EU, an issue that affects Eastern European citizens in particular (see Eurofound 2020).

The coronavirus crisis has highlighted the fact that something is seriously amiss in how we care for one another. It brought into view the lack of resources and equipment that are available to health and social care workers, as well as the understaffing, long hours and low pay that are prevalent in the care sector. The situation in care homes for the elderly has been especially troubling. During lockdowns, households had to turn their homes into offices, nurseries and schools, and more people became informal carers as a result of the pandemic, with uneven care burdens mostly falling on women.

At the same time, the unpaid and underpaid work of maintaining lives has received more attention. Many people went out on their doorsteps to 'clap for our carers' every week. This ignited a debate over whether and how such symbolic appreciation could evolve into a real valuing of healthcare workers, and of *all* care givers and receivers. One thing is clear: profound change is needed.

TOWARDS A FEMINIST SOCIETY

A feminist politics is attentive to the structural conditions for care deficits and injustices. Hence, we can ask: what might a feminist society look like? First of all, there would be an end to gendered and intersectional inequalities. Gender, ethnicity, migration background, sexuality, age and disability would no longer determine access to resources, nor would they be the basis for the valuation or devaluation of labour power. A feminist society would truly value the work of care and social reproduction.

Labour market vulnerabilities that stem from discrepancies in working conditions and wages across different countries would not exist. Existing wages and working conditions in the care sector would be improved. There would be more jobs and better ones – ones that included training and qualification. Trade unions would be recognized and there would be coverage of collective agreements across the entire sector.

There could be a common European strategy for social protection and social security (see European Women's Lobby 2020). This would require a shift away from thinking of the welfare state as a residual protection in the last resort to a vision of society in which access to high-quality public services across education, health and social care, and transport are guaranteed for everyone.

More time, money and societal capacities would be allocated to care and social reproduction. More public funding would be made available through progressive taxation, including measures such as corporation tax increases and the introduction of a financial transaction tax. Care would be decoupled from the profit expectations of private providers, and it would be shielded from the volatilities of financial markets, not drawn deeper into them. The realms of care would therefore not be available to high-risk forms of financial investment, including private equity and debt-based forms of financial engineering, where expectations of high returns on capital are upheld at the expense of quality of employment and quality of care. There would be stringent regulations against tax havens.

In a feminist society, care and social reproduction would be reorganized. Remunicipalization movements in Europe are already seeking to bring services back into the public hands of local authorities (Kishimoto and Petitjean 2017). Key here has been the elimination of the profit motive and the rollback of corporate control. There is scope for bottom-up innovation to devise models of democratic and participatory ownership, access and decision making. Worker-managed organizations affiliated to trade unions that collaborate with local authorities and put the expertise of care workers as well as the needs of care receivers centre stage could also be part of this model.

A feminist vision is far from being limited to a focus on professional care work. Caring for each other remains a crucial aspect of social life and an important element of what gives our lives meaning and purpose, and people of all genders require time to do so in their everyday lives. This necessitates a shorter working week and an active envisioning of collective caring arrangements beyond the confines of the nuclear family and the division of labour that rests on.

Finally, in a feminist society, care and social reproduction would not be placed at the service of economic growth. Instead, these activities would be orientated towards individual and collective well-being.

REFERENCES

Coffey, C. 2020. *Time to Care: Underpaid and Unpaid Care Work and the Global Inequality Crisis*. London: Oxfam International.

Decker, A., and Lebrun, J. 2018. *PHS Industry Monitor – Statistical Overview of the Personal and Household Services Sector in the EU*. Brussels: European Federation for Services to Individuals.

Eurofound. 2020. Long-term care workforce: employment and working conditions. Report, Publications Office of the European Union, Luxemburg, p. 1.

European Women's Lobby. 2020. Purple pact: a feminist approach to the economy. Report, European Women's Lobby, Brussels, p. 15.

Folbre, N. 2017. The care penalty and gender inequality. In *The Oxford Handbook of Women and the Economy*, edited by S. Averett, L. Argys and S. Hoffmann, pp. 749–766. Oxford University Press.

Gimenez-Nadal, J., and Molina, J. 2020. The gender gap in time allocation in Europe. IZA Discussion Paper, no. 13,461. Institute of Labor Economics, Bonn.

Guschanski, A., and Onaran, Ö. 2021. The decline in the wage share: falling bargaining power of labour or technological progress? Industry-level evidence from the OECD. Socio-Economic Review, mwaa031.

International Labour Organisation. 2018. *Care Work and Care Jobs for the Future of Decent Work*, pp. xxxv, xxxxv. Geneva: International Labour Office.

Kishimoto, S., and Petitjean, O. 2017. *Reclaiming Public Services: How Cities and Citizens Are Turning Back Privatisation*. Amsterdam: Transnational Institute.

Manoudi, A., Weber, T., Scott, D., and Hawley Woodall, J. 2018. An analysis of personal household services to support work–life balance for working parents and carers. Report, European Commission Directorate Employment Social Affairs and Inclusion, Brussels, p. 14.

The ecological transformation: the main driving factors and the social implications

By Saïd El Khadraoui

The planet will somehow survive another few billion years, but our current lifestyle and socioeconomic model are truly becoming an existential threat to life on earth. Science tells us that soon, in a matter of decades, climate tipping points will be exceeded if we do not take immediate action, and the intensity and severity of extreme weather events and rising sea levels will have an unprecedented impact on our food systems, our infrastructure, and much more, with repercussions being felt throughout the economy. But this transformation will also have wider ramifications and will raise social and political tensions with unknown ripple effects. The longer we wait to act, the more severe the consequences will be and the more difficult, and costly, they will be to remediate.

Global warming is not the only threat. Our inability to live in harmony with nature includes other pressing and interconnected issues, such as different forms of pollution, the alarming rate of biodiversity and natural habitat loss, the unsustainability of resource use, and so on.

In and of themselves, global warming and the gradual degradation of our environment generate a wide range of social challenges. The most vulnerable suffer first and most because of the places where they live (in the areas of our cities most exposed to floods, leaving them at risk of losing everything), or because their houses are badly insulated, or because they cannot afford air conditioning during extreme heatwaves, or because good healthcare and healthy food may well become increasingly expensive. By contrast, it is the richest segments of the population that are contributing most to higher emissions due to their consumption patterns: they tend to occupy larger living spaces, have higher energy use and meat consumption, and travel further by car and plane.

Let us not forget that, even if the world succeeds in implementing ambitious climate policies quickly, the disruptive forces of nature will continue to get stronger for some time anyway, because any positive effects of climate mitigation efforts will come with a delay. So regardless of what happens, our climate adaptation policies, our spatial planning and our housing and health policies will have to absorb these additional social risks so that we can adapt to the new reality: a hotter planet with more disruptive weather patterns.

For progressives, failing to take action is therefore not an option. Taking ambitious actions, on the other hand, is also likely to have social implications, because the cost of environmental policies may affect vulnerable groups more than others. Pricing the negative externalities of products and services – a key measure that is necessary to achieve behavioural change – or phasing out unsustainable practices may disproportionately affect lower-income households, because they spend relatively more on energy, for example, or because the necessary investments are unaffordable. At the same time, subsidies to promote innovative and sustainable technologies such as electric cars and solar panels are often taken up first by wealthy and middle-class citizens, creating wealth transfers away from those in need.

It does not have to be like that, but the examples I have mentioned show that the social dimension needs to be structurally embedded in the design of climate policymaking from day one.

This is not easy, because addressing the intersections between social and environmental policies is also about balancing short-term costs against long-term benefits, or about losing something in one area and gaining something elsewhere. Indeed, developing a socio-economic model that is compatible with planetary boundaries is a complex, systemic endeavour, and it requires a fundamental transformation of our economy across a range of sectors. To make this a successful journey, fairness should be at the heart of it. People will oppose change if it creates or aggravates inequalities, or if they feel there is no place for them in future.

I would like to mention a few critical success factors.

First, we need a clear vision of the future we want: we need to describe the way forward and set targets as orientation points in order to help all actors in society understand where we are heading. The European Green Deal narrative offers this, with climate neutrality as a key objective to be achieved by 2050 and with a revised 2030 target to make clear that we need to kick-start things straight away. But this framework for the future should be complemented with stronger ideas on how inequalities will be addressed and a new definition of what it means for an economy to be successful. This definition needs to capture a wider set of economic, social and environmental objectives and indicators than GDP does. The way public institutions – bodies such as Eurostat – and 'influencers' speak about what is important for policymakers can have a huge impact on the direction of travel.

Second, the transition will not happen without the endorsement of and buy-in from citizens. Coalition building will be crucial. Top-down government interventions at different policy levels have to be combined with bottom-up initiatives from multiple stakeholders. The role of cities, local communities and new types of organizations can therefore no longer be underestimated. A successful ecological transformation has to be a societal project – one that empowers people to be part of the journey. Building on the Future of Europe Conference, a new type of governance that can capture this complexity needs to be designed, and novel tools will need to be developed to engage with citizens beyond the very technical 'public consultations' and non-committal 'citizen dialogues' that have no real feedback loops. Moreover, policies need to showcase the fact that climate action can change people's lives for the better, and they need to bring fairness and green policies together and close to home. For instance, by accelerating visible and targeted investment in the massive renovation and upgrading of social housing, we can achieve multiple benefits such as addressing energy poverty and creating local jobs. By developing more green areas and transforming mobility infrastructure in cities and villages, we can increase people's quality of life, reduce local air pollution and decrease the number of traffic accidents. Also, where the intention is to shift consumer behaviour – away from driving polluting vehicles, for example – sustainable alternatives must be accessible. This is about redefining public services in a decarbonized world.

Third, we know that half of the cumulative emissions reduction that is needed will have to come from technology that is not yet commercially viable. We therefore need to find technological solutions and innovations and scale them up through smart industrial policies, and we also need to identify strategic sectors and make sure they can be developed, thereby creating new jobs in various new sectors across Europe. Lifelong learning, reskilling and upskilling people – regardless of their current job positions – will have to be at the core of our economic policies. But the transition towards a clean economy will not be a walk in the park. Sectors will be disrupted, and they will need to adapt or risk disappearing. Others will emerge. That is what creative destruction is all about. Similarly, some regions will face bigger transformations than others. That is why it is important to manage this transition well, anticipating future challenges well in advance and developing new strategies that involve all local stakeholders. The current set-up for designing and implementing the national recovery and resilience plans, and their interaction with the European Semester, can be inspiring, but it should be transformed into something more structural and comprehensive, with robust tracking and assessment tools. At national or regional level, 'just transition' bodies – in which social partners, knowledge institutions and local and regional authorities come together – could be tasked with a more operational role and with designing tailor-made transition plans. Moreover, the European dimension, linking the different national plans, should be reinforced, because the transformation of our socioeconomic model also has cross-border and geopolitical implications. The EU emits only eight per cent of global emissions but it consumes much more by importing carbon-intensive products from elsewhere. Raising the bar for our own production facilities might risk replacing further EU production and causing potential job losses in Europe. That is why the Carbon Border Adjustment Mechanism, which is going to introduce a carbon price for imported goods, is a crucial tool to push third-party countries to develop similar instruments and create a global level playing field while decarbonizing the world economy.

Next, we need to have the financial means to accelerate investment in sustainable infrastructure and methods of production. This requires further reflection on how the temporary Next Generation EU can be transformed into a more long-term transition investment instrument – one that is structurally integrated into future EU budgets. It also requires developing banks that can be used more strategically, inspired by the ongoing transformation of the European Investment Bank into a 'climate bank'. Furthermore, the financial system as a whole should be redesigned so that capital flows are reoriented towards achieving our long-term societal objectives. Ongoing efforts as part of the EU's sustainable finance agenda to foster transparency and facilitate pricing of environmental externalities should be complemented with social considerations. Central banks, and particularly the European Central Bank (ECB), can become crucial levers by integrating the necessary ecological and social transformations into their banking supervision, their financial stability analysis and their market operations.

Finally, we need to be ready to face unintended consequences and surprises. There are many unknowns about the future. Agility will be crucial, and that is why it is good that the European climate law provides the mechanisms for evaluating progress every five years, checking where we are and adjusting as necessary. In addition, everywhere in Europe, some communities and individuals will be affected more than others. In order to achieve a fair transition and better anticipate problems, we need to better understand the dynamics and the impacts on people and the distributional effects of policies, technologies and market developments. That is why more research is needed to assess the vulnerability of sectors, regions and specific communities and understand better how to manage a socially just transition. At the EU level, the European Environment Agency could further integrate socioeconomic issues and be transformed into a 'transition agency', with a clear mandate and additional resources. It could become a policy hub that brings together the available knowledge and provides policymakers with evidence-based policy options.

To conclude, the climate crisis is clearly a threat, but it can also be turned into an opportunity to address a wide range of issues and create a socioeconomic model that is truly progressive and fair. Before we can do that, though, we need to put the conditions in place to make it happen.

Social policies and the ecological transformation

By Georg Fischer

THE RELATIONSHIP BETWEEN SOCIAL POLICIES AND ECOLOGICAL TRANSFORMATIONS IS A TWO-WAY PROCESS

Social and employment policies are historically both a response to major economic transformations and have also often shaped them in some way. In view of the massive changes they will bring, the development of greening and social policies should be a two-way process: social considerations should be built in when designing green measures and investment programmes.

The impacts of climate change are not at all neutral when it comes to the distribution of well-being. Those who will feel the greatest impact of climate change in their daily lives are generally those who contribute least to the production of high levels of carbon dioxide. Lower-income populations are more affected by global warming than wealthier groups, and the latter also have the means to avoid or mitigate some of the extreme effects of climate change, such as heatwaves, floods and, in particular, air pollution. A successful ecological transition will directly improve the well-being of many lower-income households, workers and their families.

Note, too, that policies to address climate change are not necessarily neutral in terms of their impact on workers or on income distribution.

The overall impact of the ecological transformation on employment is generally considered to be relatively small, because there is substantial potential for job creation with the greening of our economies (urban renovation, modernization of transport, the provision of new services). It is probably unnecessary to add that well-designed greening strategies have substantial potential to create jobs. Three points deserve our attention.

First, job losses might be highly concentrated in certain regions and sectors, so strong transitional support for the affected communities will be needed. Second, not all new 'green' jobs will be well remunerated or provide decent working conditions, while some of the disappearing 'brown' jobs might have been better in these areas. There is a challenge, therefore, to ensure that green jobs are also quality jobs. Third, most jobs will need to be adapted to a zero-carbon production mode and job holders will need to update their skills accordingly.

How will adjusting housing, energy and transport costs impact on incomes? It is a fact that richer groups consume a lot more energy and produce more CO_2 than poorer groups, and they might therefore be expected to shoulder a substantial part of the costs of transformation. But rises in heating, energy and transport costs will, if unchecked, be a considerably higher burden, proportionally, on disadvantaged and low-income households, who are least able to adjust their housing or their means of transport.

Looking at Europe as an entity, the starting point for the green transition across the bloc differs widely, partially because of the economic and social divergence that emerged from the Great Recession and that is likely to be exacerbated by the Covid-19 pandemic. If Europe is to succeed with its ecological transformation, it can only do so jointly, so the divergence between its constituent parts poses a major challenge to achieving a socially fair transition. Social policies that support the ecological transition have both a member state dimension and an EU-level one.

SOCIAL POLICIES AND ECOLOGICAL TRANSITION

A change in perspective on social policies is already underway. For Europe, the adoption of the European Pillar of Social Rights reflects such a change, as does Joe Biden's recovery plan in the United States. Unlike in recent decades – when the idea of social policy being a productive factor was that of a fairly limited group of policymakers and economists – many people now expect modern social policy to positively affect long-term development via higher employment and productivity and economic growth in crisis situations, via the demand side, not least because this will reduce income inequality. In such a way, modern social polices contribute to a more sustainable and less carbon-intensive development path. Modern social policies require a broad spectrum of income support, labour market policies, adaptable labour relations and work schedules, interventions across the life course (from early childhood education and care), lifelong education, paid leave, adequate and adjustable retirement, and long-term care.

Here I list a few examples of what this entails.

- Ex post interventions when job losses occur will always be needed, but the rule should be anticipation and early action, ideally as part of a broader package of green development, and particularly in sectors and regions that depend heavily on carbon-intensive modes of production. The 'retain, retrain and re-deploy' principle should replace 'open unemployment' as far as possible, and it should apply to all workers independent of their legal status, gender or age.
- The development of skills relating to green transitions needs to be accessible to all workers, as skill adjustment will be necessary across the board and not just in certain 'old industry' regions. Training programmes need to be designed to actively encourage those that usually receive the least training: the unemployed, the low skilled, atypical workers and, in particular, disadvantaged youngsters. A specific task is to boost STEM participation among women as much as possible.
- Green jobs can be good jobs, but they are not automatically so. History tells us how to transform jobs into quality jobs: collective bargaining, worker participation, and job training being a right for workers and an obligation of employers. And given the employment structure by sex in the sectors in question, mobilizing women workers to campaign for better working conditions and remuneration will be essential. Public policy has a wide range of tools at its disposal here, including mandating employers to provide care and training infrastructure, and implementing social and green requirements in public procurement.

- Income support is important for mitigating the negative distributional impacts of the green transition, particularly as low-income groups have already suffered through the Great Recession and the Covid-19 crisis. While measures to compensate low-income households for rising energy costs can be an element of green policies, the focus of social policies should be on adequate income support and access to essential services more broadly. We know that income support for the unemployed and for those on low incomes is insufficient in many member states. We also understand the central importance of supporting children in the process of fighting social misery, so children – and especially those in disadvantaged communities – deserve special attention. Although they are outside of the remit of this chapter, tax policies are an essential component of a socially fair transition. They must ensure adequate contributions come from wealthy/high-income populations.

THE ROLE OF THE EU

Some regions and countries that are facing the biggest ecological and social transformations are those that are least well prepared to address them, in terms of both their capacity to cope and their fiscal space. As it is in the interests of the EU that everybody succeeds (otherwise greening might fail for all), it has a role to play in encouraging modern social policies to be adopted across the bloc. The European Pillar on Social Rights focuses on these challenges, and recent initiatives, in particular the Action Plan to implement this Pillar, address several of them: for example, the Council Recommendation on Access to Social Protection; the Work–Life Balance Directive; the Minimum Wage and Collective Bargaining Directive; and, more recently, the proposal for a 'child guarantee', with proposed targets on child poverty, the poverty gap and adult education, with the latter underpinned by an indicator of outreach of training to the low skilled and the unemployed. Another new (Sustainable Development Goal) indicator – the income share of the bottom forty per cent – will indicate whether economic development has actually reached this population group. These EU initiatives provide guidance and mandates for action while rightly emphasizing that the EU cannot replace action by national, regional or social partners. Implementation might prove that stronger social mandates are needed to ensure that the green transition is fair, and these could form part of a 'social rule book'.

The question of the EU's role also has a different dimension. The EU rightly emphasizes national responsibility, but it also asks member states to provide quality social policies when coping with climate change, on a comparable level across the whole bloc. In reality, technical and funding capacities differ widely between regions and also over time (during deep recessions, even some fairly rich countries can face massive difficulties). EU assistance in the frame of the different policy coordination processes and the EU funds has great potential to support a socially fair transition if the EU insists that member states use these funds in such a manner. The EU's response to the Covid-19 pandemic clearly went one step further: its Support to mitigate Unemployment Risks in an Emergency (SURE) scheme supported national job retention programmes for workers in regions and countries that were facing the greatest challenges. In the words of the Spanish finance minister Nadia Calviño, SURE has been used as an 'EU backstop for people' (Calviño 2021) in addition to all the measures that offer a backstop for financial markets. Could the EU develop this €100 billion 'embryo' (again in the words of Calviño) to help national unemployment benefit systems to provide income support, job subsidies and training when workers lose jobs (Vandenbroucke *et al.* 2020)?

A precursor to SURE was the 'youth guarantee' (which has recently been reinforced), which combines guidance on policy and commonly agreed standards and a measurable target with funding where need is greater. Support for children is the third area in which an EU-level funding instrument is frequently discussed. Such an instrument would complement the Child Guarantee proposed by the present Commission. The late Tony Atkinson proposed an EU child benefit scheme to reduce child poverty and foster equal opportunity across and within member states (Atkinson 2015, Proposal 12). Such schemes require not only agreement among member states and with the EU on standards and objectives, but they also need funding. This leads to the question of additional resources being needed, raised through new forms of EU-level taxation.

In summary, the ecological transformation will require labour and social policies to anticipate labour market changes in order to help workers in carbon-intensive industries and to ensure that green jobs are indeed quality jobs. This requires public capacity and resources to act early and to strengthen labour market institutions such as collective bargaining. Workers and their families, low-income households and disadvantaged communities all need access to adequate income support and essential services while they are undergoing this transformation. They will then be able to fully benefit from fighting climate change, which is certainly in their interest. As success depends on progress everywhere across the Union, there is a case for EU-wide support systems that combine guidance on standards and good practices with funding where and when it is most needed, not to replace the efforts of member states but to enable them to provide modern social policies that support and complement the ecological transformation.

REFERENCES

Atkinson, A. B. 2015. *Inequality: What Can Be Done?* Cambridge, MA: Harvard University Press.

Calviño, N. 2021. Recovery plans: Spanish and EU perspectives. FEPS Talks, no. 74.

European Commission. 2019/2020. Employment and social development reviews. Report, European Commission, Brussels.

Fischer, G. 2017. Social Europe: the Pillar of Social Rights. In *Structural Reforms for Growth and Cohesion: Lessons and Challenges for CEESE Countries and a Modern Europe*, edited by E. Nowotny et al., pp. 32–42. Cheltenham: Edward Elgar.

OECD. 2021. The inequalities–environment nexus: towards a people centred green transition. Report, OECD.

Vandenbroucke, F., Andor, L., Beetsma, R., Burgoon, B., Fischer, G., Kuhn, T., Luigjes, C., and Nicoli, F. 2020. The European Commission's SURE initiative and euro area unemployment reinsurance. Article, VOX/CEPR, London.

The digital transformation: the main driving factors and social implications
By Justin Nogarede

The digital transition ranks highly on the EU policy agenda, and policymakers are looking to accelerate, manage and control it. But which technologies are we speaking of, exactly, and when did the transition start? With the first computer in 1946? The rise of the personal computer in the 1970s? The development of the internet protocols in the early 1980s? The World Wide Web in the early 1990s? Or perhaps with the popularization of the smartphone? It is impossible to answer decisively.

More broadly, one can ask if it is even useful to look at the digital transformation in isolation. Rapid technological innovation has been a constant feature of Western societies since the Industrial Revolution, and although digital technologies feature prominently today, they are by no means the only significant class of technologies. They interact with developments in biotechnology, for instance, which may become very impactful in their own right.

Nevertheless, most will agree that today's mass digitization and data collection, the near omnipresent reach of the internet and smartphones, and digital platforms' intermediation of social activity does present a combined phenomenon about which something useful can be said in the aggregate. This chapter will limit itself to identifying the key driving force of the digital transition, as it has been unfolding in post-war Europe, and some of its main social effects.

THE POLITICAL, SOCIAL AND ECONOMIC CONTEXT MATTERS

When discussing technology, the late US historian Melvin Kranzberg still said it best when he said that 'technology is neither good or bad, nor is it neutral'. What he meant by this is that technology often has 'environmental, social and human consequences that go far beyond the immediate purposes of the technical devices and practices themselves, and the same technology can have quite different results when introduced into different contexts or under different circumstances'.

This is a really important point, and one that is often overlooked when the digital transition is discussed. In the 1990s, many people lazily assumed that the decentralized design of the internet would lead to an unrestricted increase in human freedom and democracy, and these claims were repeated two decades later during the Arab Spring. But things have unfolded differently. The Arab Spring was largely crushed, because it was not just activist organizers who could use social media: state apparatuses could use digital technologies too, to mobilize counterforces and more effectively monitor and repress protestors. In addition, the internet is not a monolithic entity: it consists of an ensemble of technologies that give different results depending on the political, social and economic conditions in which they are deployed. The internet in China looks rather different from the one in the EU. In summary, technologies do not inherently produce specific social outcomes.

Therefore, instead of looking at the superficial design values of digital technologies, or the public claims made about them, it is worth analysing the actors involved and the context in which they operate. In the words of Benjamin Peters, 'the history of a computer network is first a history of the organizations that tried to build it – and only secondarily a reminder of our collective failed romance with their design values'.

If we leave aside deterministic accounts and instead focus on the institutions that are currently pushing the digital transition – and on their ideologies and interests – then one characteristic looms large: a major driver of the digital transformation are the dynamics of capitalism itself.

This becomes clear when we look at the history of the internet. In the immediate postwar decades, with the wartime managed economy still fresh in people's memories, the state played a much more prominent and active role in economic life and technological development. And indeed, the internet was created through a combination of decades-long public investment, non-commercial academic collaboration and military involvement (in the context of the Cold War). However, under the influence of exuberant belief in market forces and an increasing dislike of state intervention, this radically changed in the 1990s. In that decade, the United States decided to privatize the entire infrastructure of the internet without setting any rules or public oversight mechanisms. The EU largely followed suit, with laissez faire regulation, a lack of public investment and a general deference to Silicon Valley investors and entrepreneurs, who, it was hoped, could bring back the strong economic growth rates of the 1950s and 1960s.

SILICON VALLEY MINDSET

Since the 1990s, the imagination, values and mode of infrastructure development that have come out of Silicon Valley have driven the digital transition forward in the West. The success of US firms has been enabled by the widespread availability of cheap capital looking for a productive outlet, as investors have sustained large platforms such as Amazon, Uber and WeWork through billions of dollars of losses, sometimes for more than a decade. As a result, different business models and non-profit alternatives have largely been snuffed out. The influence of Silicon Valley firms has had some peculiar characteristics: what has been called the 'Californian ideology' combines a strong belief in the benign power of digital technology and the start-up entrepreneur with a distaste for state intervention and democratic regulation.

This set of political and social conditions has led to a specific type of technology development: one that emphasises quick scaling in the hope of reaping (monopoly) profits, the mass surveillance of citizens for commercial motives, and the pushing of technological fixes to all sorts of complex social problems. To some extent, this explains the constant hyping of digital technologies: from social media and blockchains to autonomous driving and artificial intelligence. The optimistic predictions never seem to come true, but that does not seem to matter much. Public authorities – not least the European

Commission – are susceptible to this type of marketing, as can be clearly seen if we look (for example) at the Commission's White Paper on AI from February 2020: 'AI will change our lives by improving healthcare, increasing the efficiency of farming, … increasing the security of Europeans, and in many other ways that we can only begin to imagine.'

It is unfortunate that both the public imagination and the actual development and control of digital infrastructure are dominated to such a large extent by private actors that view the future primarily through the lens of profit. Digital technologies have come to occupy a crucial place in modern life: citizens use digital technologies to find information, to communicate with one another, to work and to find work, and to seek entertainment. However, the infrastructure only appeals to people as consumers or entrepreneurs – it ignores public values such as democracy, transparency, sustainability and solidarity. This is a mismatch. At the moment, this paradigm is slowly being challenged, as the failures of public infrastructure that is run according to purely commercial logic become clear. In particular, the Covid-19 crisis has underlined the importance of digital infrastructure and the need for more active public involvement in its design and management. That said, the mismatch is very far away from being adequately addressed.

RISING INEQUALITY AND THE CRUMBLING OF INSTITUTIONS

While it is impossible to review all the effects of the digital transition as it developed in Europe, two broad trends stand out. First, digital technologies have tended to map onto and exacerbate existing inequalities; and second, they have undermined existing institutions, from democracy and journalism to social security and a range of human rights. Let us look at each of these trends in turn.

As is usually the case with technological change, inequality has risen. This cannot be seen in isolation from the existing trends of globalization, the financialization of economies and the weakening of labour, but digital technologies are likely to have facilitated and accelerated those trends and contributed to a multiplier effect on the return on capital. This is often attributed to the fact that data can be copied pretty much freely, effortlessly and instantaneously. This allows the most successful firms to sell software to a global market, with very low marginal costs. At an individual level, it means that individual entertainers can suddenly reach a global audience and demand corresponding fees.

These deepening inequalities, however, are not just an intrinsic quality of data: they are, just as much, a consequence of political and economic priorities. When analysing EU policy initiatives, the preponderance of laws to expand and strengthen intellectual property rights and global capital movement is striking. Policy initiatives to strengthen knowledge commons, public ownership or public interest technology have been much less forthcoming. As a result, the digital transition seems to have so far especially benefitted large organizations: from the global surveillance apparatus uncovered by Edward Snowden in 2013 to telecoms and big tech firms such as Apple, Google, Microsoft, Amazon and Facebook.

Turning to our second broad trend, the digital transition has been accompanied by declining trust in the institutional pillars of post-war democracies. Historically speaking, new forms of communication have facilitated new modes of politics, and authorities have taken a close interest in them. For instance, mass communication media like radio are linked to the rise of mass parties and also, unfortunately, fascism. They are heavily regulated, and rightly so. This has not been the case for social media, although the amount of hate speech they carry and misinformation they spread, and the way they have degraded journalism and fractured the public sphere pose a real problem. On the other side, one can ask whether, in an environment of instant and constant communication, limiting citizens' influence to a vote once every four years or so still suffices.

In the same vein, there is an increasingly large disconnect between Western welfare state institutions and the practical realities of the world of work. Digital platforms have accelerated trends towards the unbundling of jobs into ever-more-specific tiny tasks and towards an increase in precarious and flexible work. At the moment, many workers carry out their tasks via digital platforms and effectively operate outside legal protections on minimum wages, social security and human dignity. Beyond the workplace, citizens find that their fundamental rights to data protection, a private life and equal treatment effectively do not exist online, and consumers and small businesses experience the same thing when they try to enforce their economic rights on the internet.

These developments are undermining the legitimacy of public authorities just as they need to take a more active role in the design and management of digital infrastructure. In the wake of the Industrial Revolution, Western states set up new institutions: from those that handle public education, healthcare and social protection to public libraries, trade unions and the general vote. This history should inspire public authorities when they are pondering how to invest in and govern data, crucial digital platforms and network infrastructures.

REFERENCES

Kranzberg, M. 1986. Technology and history: Kranzberg's laws. *Technology and Culture* 27, 545–546.

Peters, B. 2021. A network is not a network. In *Your Computer Is on Fire*, edited by T. Mullaney, B. Peters, M. Hicks and K. Philip. Cambridge, MA: MIT Press.

European Commission. 2020. White Paper on Artificial Intelligence. A European approach to excellence and trust. COM 65, European Commission.

Nogarede, J. 2021. Governing online gatekeepers: taking power seriously, Report, 15 January, FEPS.

Harrop, A., Murray, K., and Nogarede, J. 2020. Public Services Futures: Welfare States in the Digital Age. FEPS/The Fabian Society.

Nogarede, J. 2020. EU digital policy: time for a holistic approach. Report, 10 November, Friedrich Ebert Stiftung.

Nordic inspiration for the European socioeconomic model

By Britta Thomsen

The digital transformation and the fight against climate change have for many years been high priorities on the political agendas of the Nordic countries.

In the case of Denmark, the current Social Democratic government is determined to use public investment to promote the green agenda and climate action in order to revitalize the economy after the Covid-19 crisis. The government has chosen a different path for its economic policy rather than taking the austerity approach that we saw after recent financial crises.

The government has a good foundation for its green policy. After the oil crisis of 1973, a public debate about the future energy mix was initiated by politicians and NGOs because Denmark was, at that time, 100 per cent dependent on oil. The debate resulted in a strong, popular anti-nuclear movement, and a decision was subsequently taken in the Danish parliament in 1985 to eliminate nuclear energy from future energy planning.

When the Social Democrats took over the government, under PM Poul Nyrup Rasmussen (1993–2001), the Ministry of the Environment and Energy was allocated very large resources. The minister in charge, Svend Auken, had not only a green agenda but also high ambitions to become a leading voice in both global and European climate negotiations. At the same time, Auken succeeded in gaining support among Denmark's trade unions because his expensive environmental and energy projects created many new green jobs for specialized workers during a time when shipyards and steel mills were being shut down, not least in many provincial cities. Auken secured the setting up of wind turbine factories, and the ministry also campaigned, together with NGOs, to change the behaviour of the population by convincing people to reduce their energy consumption and, at the same time, save money. This initiative made many citizens feel that they were actively participating in the country's energy-saving policy.

Gaining the support of trade unions by linking green development with job creation was an important lesson for future politicians to learn, and it was because of this that Denmark has never seen an attempt to create movements like France's *gilets jaunes*.

Denmark has, since the 1990s, been an active driving force in the EU's environmental and renewable energy policy. When the EU approved its first binding target for CO_2 reduction and renewable energy in 2008, Denmark insisted that the target for energy efficiency should also be binding. At that time, the Commission and the Parliament were not prepared to agree, but during Denmark's presidency in 2012 the EU approved the first ever directive on a binding target for energy efficiency, and since then binding targets for energy efficiency have been part of European green policy.

Denmark's present Social Democratic minority government, under the leadership of Mette Frederiksen, along with its supporting parties won the election in 2019 by promising to fight climate change and improve welfare. After the election, the parties agreed to make Denmark one of the world's leading countries in the green transition, with an aim to reduce the country's CO_2 emissions by 70 per cent (compared with 1990 levels) by 2030.

This will be achieved via national strategies in all areas of energy use: from buildings to transportation and other industries. Since the agreement was signed, concrete initiatives have been taken. For instance, a new green tax reform has been undertaken that should lead to uniform taxation on CO_2. Renovation of social housing is underway. A new law has been approved that only permits private landlords to increase rents after they have renovated their property if the renovation has been undertaken based on green principles. A green road transport plan has been announced, with a target of having a million electric cars. Just one and a half years after the election an action plan has been adopted, and with the initiatives already in place a target of 46–50 per cent reduction by 2025 will be reached. To achieve the aimed-for 70 per cent reduction, the government is aware that investment in research and innovation is necessary to develop new CO_2-saving technologies.

In accordance with the so-called Danish model (which entails the involvement of all social partners in negotiations), 'Climate Partnerships' have been established in thirteen different sectors of the economy, with stakeholders drawn from enterprises, trade unions, employers' associations and others. Each sector has to present a strategy and a catalogue of solutions for their specific area.

The concept of Climate Partnerships will be presented to the EU by MEPs from different Danish parties and by Denmark's Minister of Energy as a way of improving CO_2 reduction in all member states.

A survey undertaken by the Danish think tank Cevea has shown that people with a lower level of education prefer investing in welfare even if doing so implies a relaxation of the climate effort, while people with higher education prefer increased climate effort at the expense of public welfare. The government is aware that the green transition should be socially fair and must be combined with investment in welfare and jobs.

DIGITALIZATION

When the first step was taken in the digitalization of the Danish public sector in 2004, the intention was not to create jobs. On the contrary, the centre-right government of Anders Fogh Rasmussen wanted to reduce the number of public employees and it wanted the public sector to become more efficient by using technology both in its communication with citizens and in the interactions between institutions. The public sector went through a long and challenging period of transformation into new forms of organization and management based on digitalization. After that it was the citizens' turn. Since 2015, citizens have only been able to communicate with the public sector through digital means. However, 20 per cent of the population – primarily older citizens – were initially exempt from the law, as they did not know how to operate computers. After just two years, though, that proportion decreased to 10 per cent because of the effort made to teach people new ICT skills. But it is important that people have the same rights even if they are offline.

Danish citizens have a high degree of trust in the state, so a fear of surveillance has not been an issue in relation to digital personal data. Although gaps in personal data security have come to light, people see the benefits of digitalization as being greater than the associated problems.

With online service available around the clock, many citizens are happy not to stand in lines and instead interact with the public sector from home, whether it relates to tax issues, their children's schools or the results of a health test.

During the Covid-19 pandemic, experts, politicians and citizens have become more aware of the many advantages of digital development and of how data can provide knowledge that helps to control the disease. New digital challenges and opportunities have been presented by teleworking and home schooling, and we will certainly see new ways of organizing work after the pandemic is over.

In Denmark, digitalization has not meant fewer public employees, as it was thought it would in the beginning, but the new digital tools have meant that the content of work has changed in many professions.

In the future we should demand that all citizens have the necessary access and sufficient skills to take part in the digital transformation. We also need to focus much more on data security and to discuss the role of artificial intelligence in the public sector. We should demand transparency about how algorithms are composed in relation to gender, age, etc. Technology should be for all, and it needs to be trustworthy!

THE SOCIAL DIMENSION IN THE EU AND THE NORDIC COUNTRIES

The Nordic member states are not always happy with the EU's social dimension, not because they are afraid that new legislation will lower the level of the Nordic welfare state but rather because they fear that initiatives like minimum wages will weaken the role of national trade unions, which are considered the best protector of workers' rights. Some parts of EU legislation in the social area are incompatible with Danish social policy. The Nordic welfare state is based on universal principles: everyone pays for everyone, which means high taxation. The European Commission recently presented a proposal that poor children should have a free meal at school, but that would be against the philosophy of social welfare in the Nordic countries, which is based on rights and not on charity. A free meal will, in that context, stigmatize the poor. In the Nordic system, the principle is that there is access for everyone or for no one. Every student receives a scholarship, every retired person receives a basic pension independently of other pensions, every student has the right to free education at all levels, and every citizen has the right to free healthcare.

RECOMMENDATIONS

The role of progressives in relation to the future of Europe should be to ensure that the European Green Deal and the digital transition are socially fair and that they do not create further inequalities or conflicts between young and old or between people in the provinces and those in big cities.

The gender dimension seems to have been forgotten both in the EU and in member state strategies for the recovery fund. In all European member states, labour markets are to varying degrees gender segregated, and both the energy sector and the digital sector are male dominated. New skills will be needed for many of the new jobs that will be created, and it must be ensured that women also get access to new qualifications and a fair share of those new jobs.

Reinventing the state to deploy smart green growth and well-being, while disarming populism

By Carlota Perez

THE CURRENT HISTORICAL MOMENT

Although it is always risky to make historical parallels and try to identify recurring phenomena, there is strong evidence to suggest that technological revolutions have, in the past, led the market economy to experience periods of 'creative destruction', bubbles, recessions and golden ages, and that the latter have resulted from a shift in economic thinking and from the action of a proactive state.

Following that historical pattern, a paradigm shift in economic policy and thinking is now overdue: it should have happened after the financial crisis of 2008. Until the 2020 pandemic hit, governments had remained trapped in austerity, reluctant to interfere in the free market and therefore letting finance, rather than production, define the direction of the economy, from one bubble to the next. The inequality that inevitably resulted was eventually brought to light and governments could no longer ignore it, and nor could they allow the pandemic to wreak havoc on their economies. The parallel with World War II and with the proactive states that led reconstruction efforts after it was captured in the slogan 'build back better' and by the call of the World Economic Forum to 'reset'.

The historical shift in the late 1940s saw the unleashing of the mass production revolution. The time has now come for the state to provide the context for an information society golden age.

WHY HAS POPULISM FLOURISHED?

It is not by chance that populism has gathered strength, that political parties are dividing, and that new movements have emerged. This has happened during every technological revolution – in the 1840s, 1890s and 1930s – after major financial collapse.

Populism is an alarm bell. The system is not performing for the majority. In fact, it has gone backwards. 'Make America great again' implies that life was better before. 'Take back control of our borders' implies that we have lost something that we previously had (and that others are now benefitting). The rejection of immigrants comes from a fear of losing one's space to 'invaders'. Many people fear for their future and feel that their children will be worse off than them. Resentment grows and populist leaders ride the resulting wave.

In the 1930s Hitler and Stalin promised a better future via ethnic nationalism and communism, respectively. Yet it was social democracy that actually delivered a better society, through the policies of the New Deal and the welfare state.

WHY IT IS TIME FOR SOCIAL DEMOCRACY

Social democracy is about a positive-sum game between business and society, and that is what is currently needed. Now is the time to boldly occupy the centre ground with a creative entrepreneurial state working with a dynamic private sector and an actively participating society, all moving in the same direction. It is when that happens that capitalism regains legitimacy – when the wealth of the few truly benefits the many.

Success is possible because, once a technological revolution is underway and its logic is well understood (as is the case with information and communications technology (ICT) today), it is possible to tilt the playing field in a direction that will lead to the optimal social and economic outcome. This requires a set of systemic policies that will favour business innovation and investment in a synergistic direction that results in improved social conditions while also being profitable. There is no technological determinism: the same mass production revolution was shaped very differently by Hitler, Stalin and the Keynesian democracies. Something equivalent can happen with ICT.

The social democratic policies that favoured suburban homeownership (and also funded innovation for the Cold War) were responsible for the post-war boom, for '*les trente glorieuses*', when good profits were accompanied by good wages and diminishing inequality. Similar times can come again, but the state must shape the information revolution to bring them about. Social and environmental sustainability represents an obvious course to set.

THE CONDITIONS FOR, AND RISKS OF, MOVING IN A GREEN DIRECTION

The age of ICT has brought two waves of pain to significant portions of the population of the advanced world. The first wave resulted from the globalization of production in search of low-cost labour. The second wave saw technological unemployment and deskilling. This has been underway since the 1980s and could well intensify in the coming years, with advances in artificial intelligence and robotics. The rise of populism owes a lot to the destruction of livelihoods and hope that resulted.

Covid-19 has brought a third wave of job losses. Governments must not let the green transformation bring with it yet another wave of skill and job destruction. Facing up to the challenges of climate change and planetary limits on resources is an urgent task, and it is also our best hope of a healthy economic recovery that sees the creation of both jobs and wealth. There are green policies that create jobs and others that destroy them. Which route we choose will make an important social difference.

HOW CAN BOTH ENVIRONMENTAL AND SOCIAL SUSTAINABILITY BE ACHIEVED?

There are four elements that we need to think about if we are to achieve growth and maintain it, or even enhance it, while changing its nature towards social and environmental sustainability. A new sustainable growth model needs to be smart (meaning digital), green, fair and global.

Smart growth implies using ICT to help dematerialize growth, fulfilling needs with services rather than products – as has already largely happened with music, films and books – thereby reducing energy and materials use. It includes using artificial intelligence and robotics to increase productivity in certain sectors of the economy while creating a huge number of jobs in the new green sectors. This will require policies that encourage such a direction in innovation while also using ICT to modernize the public sector so that it is as effective and as easy to use as some of the private sector platforms.

Green growth does not simply mean a shift to renewable energy; it also requires a radical reduction in waste, the development of biomaterials and biofuels, a 'circular economy', sustainable homes and mobility, the redesign of cities, durable goods that are truly durable in a rental and maintenance model, and so on. All of these changes would require policy action to promote smart green production methods as well as greener lifestyles. These are particularly important as the greatest source of new jobs.

Fair growth is not just a question of using redistribution to overcome inequality after the fact, but rather it is one of creating the right conditions for reducing differences in opportunity and promoting a fairer proportion of rewards in the wealth creation process. A universal basic income could be part of such 'predistribution'. Greater equality involves money, certainly, but also skills and education. While a home was the most important asset in securing life in mass production times, education has become the most crucial in our new knowledge society. Government support – equivalent to that which promotes home ownership – should now take aim at education.

Global growth is not solely for humanitarian goals. While Asia has become the factory of the world when it comes to the mass production of consumer goods, Europe could make itself a centre for specialized, custom-made, sustainable equipment and engineering, and it could provide education to support a broad development effort in a sort of Marshall Plan for the lagging countries. As well as the resulting trade relationship being mutually beneficial, the process would stem the immigration tide, which is a brain drain for developing countries and a political problem for developed ones. And finally, given the globalized economy and the new nature of cross-border finance, an orderly future is likely to necessitate supranational institutions with more power than the UN and with complete transparency.

WHAT CAN BE DONE TO SHAPE GROWTH IN THESE DIRECTIONS?

It is clear that achieving such a complex set of interrelated aims would require designing appropriate policy tools. We are fortunate, then, that the threat of the pandemic has seen the tide turn in favour of a greater role for the state.

In addition to clearly focused regulation, some of the most powerful tools we have at our disposal are Pigovian taxes and subsidies that punish undesirable behaviours (as was the case with cigarette smoking) and support positive ones (as has been done with renewables). Doing this would change the relative cost structure in the same direction for everyone, thereby tilting the playing field to stimulate innovation and investment in the same – socially desired – direction.

It is vitally important to understand that many of our current policies and institutions are obsolete. They were geared towards helping the spread of the previous mass-production revolution, and they did so successfully. But shaping the direction taken by the information revolution will require considerable institutional and policy innovation, using ICT to do so in an agile and effective way. That will mean adopting a post-war-style reconstruction mentality and a truly social democratic way of approaching the problems.

Crucially, this implies choosing the route for the greening of the economy that will generate the most employment in its early phases. This will both repair the pain inflicted by globalization, the technology revolution and Covid-19, and it will enlist the majority of citizens in support of the transformation. The goal would be to set up a win–win game between business and society, between advanced, emerging and developing countries, and between humanity and the planet.

It is, to be sure, a full redesign of the state in its organization and its tools. Such a consensus can only be reached by repopulating the centre ground and designing policies that will balance the various interests involved to harness the technological revolution towards a sustainable global golden age with optimal social conditions.

REFERENCES

Mazzucato, M. 2021. *Mission Economy: A Moonshot Guide to Changing Capitalism*. London: Allen Lane/Penguin.

Palma, J. G. 2020. Behind the seven veils of inequality. *Development and Change* 50(5), 1133–1213.

Perez, C. 2021. Using the history of technological revolutions to understand the present and shape the future. *The Progressive Post*, 17 February.

Perez, C., and Murray Leach, T. 2018. Smart & green: a new 'European way of life' as the path for growth, jobs and wellbeing. In *Re:Thinking Europe: Positions on Shaping an Idea*, pp. 208–223. Austrian Council for Research and Technology Development. Vienna: Holzhausen.

A European Social Union

By László Andor

In recent years the vision of a Social Union has been developed and promoted by leading social scientists including Frank Vandenbroucke, Maurizio Ferrera, Anton Hemerijck and Colin Crouch. The Conference on the Future of Europe should bring this concept centre stage, not least to ensure that the recovery following the Covid-19 pandemic is inspired by a renewed commitment to the European social model.

FROM THE EPSR TO A SOCIAL UNION

The latest conceptualization of the social dimension of the EU took place when the European Pillar of Social Rights (EPSR) was discussed and eventually signed in 2017. Though the creation of the EPSR was predominantly an ideological process, it has achieved a major step forwards by incorporating the questions of the welfare state into the concept of the European social agenda. The three-chapter approach of the EPSR – and in particular its third chapter – can be compared to the original construct of the late 1980s and the subsequent legislative cycles that practically identified social policy with coordination in the area of employment, and with legislation in the area of working conditions in particular. In spring 2021 the European Commission came forward with an action plan to implement the EPSR, and the Portuguese presidency of the Council staged a major conference in Porto about strengthening the social dimension of the EU.

The idea to build up 'social Europe' was championed by Commission President Jacques Delors (1985–1995), who not only was rhetorically strong on the social dimension but also elevated social dialogue to the EU level, reformed cohesion policy to be able to counterbalance the single market and launched a cycle of social legislation to prevent a race to the bottom. Indeed, he acted in the spirit of Karl Polanyi, who stressed in his seminal work, *The Great Transformation* (1944), that moves to extend markets need to be accompanied by moves in social policy.

Table 1. The pillars of a Social Union.

An EU safety net for the national safety nets; guarantees	Social investment strategies driving cohesion policy	Keeping economic and social policies connected
... to prevent divergence	... to facilitate convergence	... to avoid marginalization

However, the concept of a Social Union represents a qualitative leap from the EU construct in which social policy is an appendix to the main body of economic integration and governance. As Vandenbroucke very importantly underlines, 'a European Social Union is not a European Welfare State: it is a union of national welfare states, with different historical legacies and institutions'. However, since the functioning of the EU, and of its economic governance in particular, has massive consequences when it comes to national industrial relations and welfare systems, there is a need for an EU safety net for the safety nets of the member states. What follows is a short explanation of the various components of the envisaged Social Union.

A PARADIGM SHIFT TO SOCIAL INVESTMENT

Placing the social investment welfare state centre-stage represents a paradigm shift, or even a conversion, in the field of European social policy. The totemic issues of earlier social policy debates, such as the posting of workers, are no longer the focus. Recent debates have, for example, highlighted proposals for a 'child guarantee', following up on 2013 EU recommendations for investing in children, together with legislation relating to paid parental leave.

Within national budgets, broadly defined welfare expenditures amount to around 40 per cent of total expenditure. From this category, narrowly defined social protection budgets receive about a third of the total. The EU budget will never be able to rival or centralize these budgetary components, but the social compartment of the EU budget can, and does, provide vital contributions to social assistance (through the Fund for European Aid to the Most Deprived (FEAD)) and social investment (through the European Social Fund (ESF) and the Youth Employment Initiative (YEI)) programmes within member states, which also function as incentives for reforming employment and social policies and designing more effective programmes on the ground. Research by Maurizio Ferrera has established that a larger EU budget aimed at promoting economic and social investment – for helping people in severe poverty and for providing financial help to member states experiencing a rise in unemployment – has majority support not only in EU countries with larger populations (Spain, France, Italy, Germany, Poland) but also in smaller ones.

SETTING DECENT WAGES

Wages and wage setting represent an area in which the EU has no direct competences, but in various ways these issues have gradually come under EU influence. The EU response to the eurozone debt crisis brought pressure to move towards a decentralization of wage-setting mechanisms. This came on top of a longer-term trend of a declining wage share in a number of countries. In order to counter such negative trends, a campaign was launched by trade unions for a European Wage Alliance in 2018.

How to facilitate upward wage convergence is the central question. The idea of guaranteeing a wage floor in each country, based on a coordinated approach towards minimum wages at the EU level, had gained traction by 2020, and an EU legislative initiative was the result. It not only ensures that minimum wage levels are set above the poverty threshold and represent decent pay for the work undertaken, but it also encourage collective bargaining within member states. A Europe-wide component to minimum-wage strategies (adjusted for local costs of living) would also help to prevent unfair competition from – and exploitation of workers within – the poorer countries of the union.

UNEMPLOYMENT INSURANCE

Existing monetary unions all have examples of automatic stabilizers. In fact, all monetary unions are also insurance unions, so they also self-evidently cover unemployment. A fair, rules-based and predictable transfer mechanism at the Economic and Monetary Union (EMU) level will also have to be acceptable to the 'surplus countries', in order to stabilize the single currency economically, socially and politically. Creating an EU-wide unemployment insurance (or reinsurance) scheme would also allow for a limited amount of harmonization, e.g. stamping out anomalies where the duration of unemployment support is limited to 90 days. Some consider the EU's Support to Mitigate Unemployment Risks in an Emergency (SURE) instrument (launched in 2020 to help workers through short-time work schemes during the recession caused by the Covid-19 pandemic) to be the basis for a common unemployment scheme.

A basic European unemployment insurance scheme, serving to partially pool the fiscal costs of cyclical unemployment, is the most important example of possible automatic stabilizers at EMU level. Such a tool would form a direct link between reducing imbalances in GDP growth and helping the innocent victims of recessions and financial crises. It would help to uphold aggregate demand during asymmetric cyclical downturns and it would provide a safety net for national welfare systems. Various models of unemployment insurance have been explored. Together with a genuine unemployment benefit scheme, reinsurance mechanisms have also been considered. If it was carefully designed, a reinsurance scheme could function well, and it could be politically feasible.

SOCIAL POLICY AND ECONOMIC GOVERNANCE

When it comes to strengthening the social dimension of economic governance, very important work has been done in the past decade on consolidating social policy coordination at the heart of economic governance, i.e. within the so-called European Semester. First, in 2010, it was ensured that employment and social policy would play a part in this new method of coordination, and subsequently the share and weight of social analysis and recommendations gradually increased. But the European Semester is only a starting point: for better social outcomes, it is also important to continue regulating finance and reforming globalization, and, most importantly, to revamp the monetary union.

The EMU was launched at Maastricht as a monetary union without a fiscal union, common financial sector regulation or a lender of last resort. The dangerous potential of this badly designed EMU was only partially exposed in the late 1990s, during the only period in EU history when the centre-left dominated European politics and also the European Council. The Lisbon Strategy was introduced during this period, and it confirmed a European commitment to a 'social Europe', but it aimed to deliver a remedy without revising the macroeconomic framework.

The recent financial crisis caused such great social damage primarily because of the inherent bias of the current model of monetary union towards internal devaluation during times of crisis. But the capacity of EU social policy to compensate for the mistakes of economic governance remain limited. It is therefore vital to ensure that economic policies at the EU level produce fewer problems. Since 2012, a number of reforming steps have been taken (there have been two pillars of Banking union, a permanent European Stability Mechanism has been introduced, even if it is outside the Community framework, etc.), but the reform process itself is incomplete. There is a long list of outstanding reform elements: from creating a deposit insurance sceheme and safe assets to amending the mandate of the European Central Bank (ECB).

Table 2. A paradigm shift on Social Europe.

	Delors–Lisbon	Social Union
Sociology	Pact with labour aristocracy (Val-Duchesse)	Inclusion of marginal/vulnerable groups
Policy focus	Definition of rights (1989, 2017)	Resources and policy coordination
Arrangement	Social Open Method of Coordination	Consistency with EMU reform

THE NECESSARY POLITICAL ALLIANCE

The concept of a Social Union springs from a social democratic vision. Christian democrats are also invited to align themselves with this vision, and this particularly applies to the true followers of Pope Francis, who has stood out among contemporary Catholic leaders with his campaign for inclusive egalitarianism. The inspiration of the Pontifex should help to put the reduction of material (income) inequality back at the heart of the social agenda.

For the European left, the institutions of the EU are central to its objectives and identity. They are not an add-on. The Covid-19 pandemic, with which Europe has been struggling since spring 2020, is an additional reason to push for more European solidarity and greater safety nets. This can be a new chapter in the history of the EU – a chapter that will not open unless social democrats argue more forcefully than they have in the past. At the same time, this new chapter has the potential to define the power of social democracy in Europe for generations to come.

REFERENCES

Andor, L. 2018. A timely call for a Social Union. *EU Visions*, 13 December.
Crouch, C. 2020. *Social Europe: A Manifesto*. Social Europe Publishing.
Vandenbroucke, F. Barnard, C., and De Baere, G. (eds). 2017. A European Social Union after the Crisis. Cambridge University Press.

PART II
EU External Action with Strategic Autonomy and Multilateral Engagement

Synthesis of the debate

By Giovanni Grevi

The debate undertaken by the FEPS Expert Group on the Future of Europe underscored the connection between Europe's External Action and the question of the future of Europe. If the EU is not equipped to cope with the geoeconomic, geopolitical and transnational challenges that it faces – and if it is not determined to do so – it will not be able to deliver on its citizens' priorities and expectations concerning their prosperity, welfare and security. That would, in turn, affect the legitimacy of the EU, bringing into question the purpose and rationale of the whole European project. There is also a connection between the future of multilateralism on the global stage and the future of the EU as a *sui generis*, deeply integrated multilateral institution. The preservation and reform of the multilateral order requires strong leadership from the EU, alongside its global partners, but the crisis of multilateralism challenges the principles at the core of Europe's rules-based integration.

The EU and its member states therefore have a choice: they can take a strategic and joined-up approach in order to advance their interests and values; or they can be on the receiving end of the decisions of others, vulnerable to the impact of multidimensional competition among major powers. Effective external action requires a vision of what the EU stands for and what it wishes to accomplish on the international stage, including both the means to attain these goals and a viable strategy to align ends and means. This is why the EU must become more strategic and more autonomous. Advancing Europe's open strategic autonomy is not about Europe turning its back on its partners, taking an isolationist path or reneging on its commitment to multilateral cooperation – it is about empowering Europeans to define their own objectives and enhancing their capacity to act, while avoiding one-sided dependencies. On that basis, the EU should always pursue cooperation with others where agendas converge.

WHAT SHOULD THE LONG-TERM EUROPEAN GLOBAL STRATEGY BE?

The EU operates in a challenging and unprecedented global context marked by a multipolar distribution of power, a dense web of multilateral frameworks, and a growing bifurcation of the international order due to the increasing rivalry between the United States and China. The United States remains the largest global power by most measures, but power is shifting. China – an authoritarian political system that is deeply integrated into international economic flows – is well on its way to becoming the world's largest economy (indeed, it already is in purchasing power parity terms). There is a clear risk that Sino-American competition becomes the dominating factor in the shaping of the international system – across politics, economics and security affairs – potentially leading to the splintering of globalization and to a new Cold War. The multilateral order has entered a difficult and uncertain transition. The Covid-19 pandemic has exposed both the limits and fragmentation of multilateral responses and the fact that multilateral cooperation is essential if we are to cope with transnational risks. As major powers take increasingly adversarial positions, there is a risk of international organizations becoming gridlocked, with no agreements being possible on new rules to extend global governance to critical areas of interdependence, such as digital connectivity. At the same time, however, there are examples of governance resilience and innovation, such as when it comes to dealing with climate change. Regional organizations may also prove to be an important driver of collective action, but the pace and the extent of their consolidation will likely differ between regions.

Participants at the meeting felt that the drift towards a new Cold War between the United States and China, which would further disrupt multilateral cooperation, would be detrimental to the interests of the EU. With a view to preventing that and containing bipolar confrontation, the EU should renew its investment in multilateralism through a stronger web of norms, rules, institutions and platforms for dialogue. The point was made that, for the EU, multilateralism is not just an instrument in its toolbox for external action: it is a goal in itself. It is a central element of its identity as an international actor and political project. This is about seeking to mitigate power politics and, where possible, elevate rules-based cooperation as the grammar of international affairs.

In a contested and turbulent strategic environment, there is no doubt that Europe needs to 'learn the language of power', as High Representative Josep Borrell has often stated. However, the EU should not accept the zero-sum logic of power politics. While strengthening its resilience, its ability to counter the coercive practices of others and its capacity as a security provider, the EU should speak its own distinctive language of power through trade, investment, rules and democratic values. The EU should put the promotion of global public goods, such as environmental sustainability and public health, at the centre of its external action and its multilateral approach. This agenda would both address pressing global challenges and help create the right conditions for dialogue among all major powers in areas of shared concern, with competition prevailing in other domains. This approach would also match the recent call by the Secretary General of the United Nations for a new global deal to cope with the impact of Covid-19 on social and economic systems worldwide. The pandemic has heightened inequalities, exposed governance deficits, and threatened the pursuit of the Sustainable Development Goals.

The importance attached by the Biden administration to renewing US leadership through multilateral engagement and cooperation with its partners and allies opens up a major opportunity for advancing the transatlantic partnership. Participants at the meeting noted that the EU and the United States share various concerns related to China's unfair trade practices, including the question of subsidies distorting the level playing field, and it was agreed that there is a need to better coordinate their approach. The European Commission intends to launch a new transatlantic green agenda in the summer of 2021. There is also a need to deepen transatlantic dialogue on digital matters, from the regulation of big tech to questions concerning the taxation of digital companies. It was noted that, across these and other issues, the EU should engage based on a clear understanding of its interests and positions, which do not always correspond to those of the United States. Doing so would form the basis for a strong partnership grounded in a common agenda, while empowering the EU to define and pursue its own priorities when need be. In other words, there is no contradiction between the pursuit of open strategic autonomy and fostering the transatlantic partnership. In relation to China, it was argued that the EU will need to balance elements of cooperation, when possible, and confrontation, when necessary. This is in line with the strategic outlook presented in 2019 by the Commission and by High Representative Borrell, where China was defined as a cooperation partner, an economic competitor and a systemic rival promoting alterative models of governance. There is a need to engage with China to address global challenges like climate change and pandemics and to deliver global public goods, but the EU should stand firm on values and tackle the challenge posed by those activities of China that promote forms of authoritarian governance on the international stage.

The debate at the meeting about the various central dimensions of EU external action pointed to the gap between the growing demand for, and the faltering supply of, international cooperation. This has led to a serious deficit in global governance. This deficit is in part driven, and certainly amplified, by the surge of competition between the world's great powers, which may result in a bifurcated or otherwise fragmented global order, particularly in the economic and digital domains. Starting from this realistic assessment, the EU should play a proactive role in shaping the green and digital transitions in Europe and beyond and in preserving an open, rules-based and fair global trade order.

To succeed, the EU will need to work at two levels. On the first level, it must strengthen its own power base by setting the agendas, developing the assets and adopting the rules that are needed to withstand competition and engage in effective cooperation. In other words, the EU needs both the resources and the regulatory frameworks necessary to manage interdependence in line with its interest and values. And on the second level, the EU will need to operate simultaneously through different partnerships, networks and multilateral institutions. The mix will depend on the issues at stake, its convergence with likeminded partners, and the importance of involving different actors to deliver solutions and global public goods.

HOW SHOULD THE EU TACKLE THE CLIMATE AND SUSTAINABILITY CHALLENGES?

It was stressed at the meeting that the multiple and interrelated implications of climate change – whether related to human development, resource scarcity, health, security or further loss of biodiversity – call for a comprehensive response backed up by adequate resources and relying on international cooperation. Working at the interface between internal and external policies, the implementation of the European Green Deal can provide a major contribution to both mitigating climate change and adapting to its impact, sustaining the energy transition in Europe and in various other regions. Technology will play an essential role to drive sustainable growth. This emphasizes the importance of both technological innovation and technology transfers, where they are needed to help EU partners cope with climate change and move towards a cleaner energy mix. That will require large investment, drawing on both public and private funding through innovative finance models, and adequate incentives, e.g. the establishment of a suitable price for carbon. The EU should also anticipate and address the far-reaching geo-economic implications of the energy transition. Over time these will create new opportunities for those countries that are able to harness renewable energy sources such as the wind and the sun, but they will negatively affect the income of countries that rely disproportionately on revenues flowing from the export of fossil fuels.

It was noted that, in many ways, EU policies and standards are already making a significant contribution to shaping climate governance in third countries and at the multilateral level. Through market regulation, the EU is mainstreaming environmental sustainability clauses and requirements in trade deals, and it could develop them further, with a stronger focus on implementation. The EU was the first player to develop an emission trading scheme, which has served as a useful experience for designing similar frameworks in other countries and for making progress towards an international carbon market. The EU is also innovating by adopting a taxonomy of sustainable economic activities and working on a 'green bond' standard to provide clarity to market operators and boost sustainable investment. The design of the envisaged EU carbon border adjustment mechanism – which is intended to avoid carbon leakage by pricing the carbon content of products imported from countries with looser environmental regulations – is another important and sensitive aspect of the EU's external green agenda. The question is how to develop a mechanism that both advances the EU's climate goals and preserves a level playing field, market wise, while addressing the concerns of those EU partners that perceive the measure to be protectionist, thereby preventing trade disruptions.

The launch or rollout of massive recovery plans in most major economies during the course of 2021 offers a key opportunity to unlock adequate investment to foster the energy transition and the green economy. Agreements on the EU's multiannual budget and on the Next Generation EU plan have been pivotal in setting the European Green Deal on a strong footing. It was noted that, at the multilateral level, the sequence of summits taking place in 2021 gives the EU and its member states multiple entry points to advance their environmental agenda, to strengthen global environmental governance and to ensure that the post-pandemic economic recovery contributes to attaining the Sustainable Development Goals. President Biden has announced that he will host a Leaders Summit on Climate in April; the UN Biodiversity Conference will take place in China in May; the G7 and G20 summits will follow in June and October, respectively; and November will see the UN Climate Change Conference (COP26) take place. At the same time, the EU needs to advance bilateral partnerships with key players, such as by building on the proposal of the European Commission to establish a comprehensive transatlantic green agenda in the coming months.

WHAT SHOULD THE EU'S APPROACH TO TRADE AND GLOBAL ECONOMIC GOVERNANCE BE?

Meeting participants stressed that the EU should continue to invest in an open and rules-based international trade order. That means working with partners to reform the World Trade Organization (WTO) and modernize its agenda to tackle contested issues such as trade-distorting subsidies. Working through the WTO does not preclude fostering plurilateral coalitions and expanding the EU's network of bilateral free trade agreements. These are important vectors of cooperation that can complement multilateral engagement and contribute to strengthening and diffusing social and environmental standards for fair and sustainable trade. A robust trade policy also needs to meet the priorities of EU citizens, who expect measures to cushion the impact of trade and globalization on inequality and welfare.

Strengthening the resilience of Europe's supply chains is another central challenge, and one that lies at the intersection of several EU policy agendas: trade, innovation, climate, health and security. Advancing Europe's energy transition and supporting Europe's leadership in green technologies, and its technological sovereignty more generally, will depend on reliable access to the critical raw materials used in strategic industrial sectors such as electronics and the renewable energy, automotive, aerospace and defence industries. The extraction of many of these raw materials is concentrated in just a few countries, which raises issues concerning the potential disruption of supplies and the manipulation of interdependence for geopolitical purposes. The EU will need to adopt a more focused approach to manage interdependence and reduce its vulnerability to external dependencies, e.g. by near-shoring and diversifying its supply chains and by building stockpiles of critical goods.

It was pointed out that, as well as taking a proactive stance on trade, the EU should be prepared for the emergence of a multipolar monetary regime on the global stage. In this context, enhancing the international role of the euro will not only bring more predictability for EU citizens and companies but also contribute to international financial stability and reduce the EU's vulnerability to the weaponization of financial power, such as through secondary sanctions. Strengthening the euro as a global currency requires, among other steps, completing the bloc's banking union and its capital markets union, issuing common euro-denominated safe assets (as envisaged under the Next Generation EU recovery plan) and establishing swap lines between the European Central Bank and other central banks. The meeting participants ultimately regarded the euro, the EU's trade power and Europe's capacity for technological innovation to be the main sources of EU influence on the global stage.

WHAT SHOULD THE EU'S AGENDA ON SHAPING THE DIGITAL REVOLUTION BE?

The ongoing technological revolution is affecting international affairs, politics and societies in profound ways.

First, it was stressed that the production and control of new technologies changes the international balance of power. Technological leadership can be leveraged as a source of both soft and hard power – to attract and to coerce others – while digital connectivity cuts across borders and breaks the traditional link between sovereignty and territory. This also generates new security threats in cyberspace and brings new priorities to the fore, such as the securitization of data.

Second, new technologies will have a major impact on the economic trajectories of different countries and regions, and Europe is currently lagging behind. All of today's top internet and digital companies are either American or Chinese, while the United States and China are also way ahead when it comes to the distribution of large start-ups (so-called unicorns) in key fields such as artificial intelligence, advanced robotics, cloud computing and geo-localization. This is particularly consequential for Europe because the dominant tech companies are also those that generate most productivity growth, thereby enhancing their competitiveness, sidelining potential challengers and leading to oligopolistic or monopolistic markets.

Third, it was argued that the spread of digital technologies also creates new challenges for democracy and human rights. This concerns, for example, the right to truthful information, which is essential for sound democratic politics and is affected by the behaviour of social media platforms that refuse to take responsibility for the content that they carry. Looking ahead, the intersection between big data, surveillance techniques and progress in behavioural science creates more potential for governments and other actors to control and manipulate people's behaviour and affect individual agency, which is another pillar of liberal democracy.

Europe's performance at the frontier of technological innovation will be of critical importance if it is to switch from a reactive mindset to a proactive one – moving from being on the receiving end of technologies generated elsewhere to shaping Europe's own digital future. With China intent on strengthening social surveillance and with the United States focused on gaining market share and reluctant to regulate big tech, it was argued that the EU needed to define and implement its vision for a digital economy and society – one directed to deliver public goods in Europe and on the global stage. Recent policy proposals such as the Digital Services Act and the Digital Markets Act go in the right direction, but a step change is needed. In particular, the EU needs to make sure that its recovery plan channels and pools adequate funding towards transnational projects for research and innovation.

Strengthening Europe's resilience and strategic autonomy in this domain requires securing digital values chains and expanding Europe's knowledge and skills base, including attracting talent from abroad. The launch of a digital euro would support the digitalization of the European economy while also enhancing its resilience. Completing the digital single market and creating European spaces for data sharing are other essential steps. However, these measures will not, on their own, be enough, since the EU's market would be too small anyway. Cooperation with like-minded countries, such as Japan, the Republic of Korea and Canada, is called for. This should be part of a broader partnership strategy that engages those countries that share EU norms and values in the digital domain. The EU should also establish a strategic dialogue on technology and innovation with the United States, not least to address the differences between their respective approaches. The EU and its like-minded partners should set up a 'Schengen for data', enabling free data flow under appropriate rules. They should also develop frameworks for global digital governance in line with UN objectives, take a shared approached to the highly competitive area of standard-setting, and use digital technologies to deliver global public goods such as earth observation to support environmental sustainability. The EU should also put the digital transition at the centre of its partnership with Africa, with a focus on sustainability and health issues.

HOW TO ADVANCE THE EU DEFENCE AGENDA

With the conflict in Ukraine and the destabilization of the EU's eastern and southern neighbours over the last decade, defence issues have climbed the bloc's priority list. The 2016 EU Global Strategy called upon Europeans to take more responsibility for their security, which required an appropriate level of ambition and strategic autonomy and the enhancement of cooperation over defence matters. Defence and security have been among the most dynamic areas of implementation of the EU Global Strategy, with a range of new arrangements framing and supporting cooperative efforts to develop military capabilities and stronger operational capacity. These arrangements include the so-called Permanent Structured Cooperation, the Coordinated Annual Review on Defence and the European Defence Fund. The ongoing Strategic Compass process aims to build on the shared analysis of the threats facing the EU that was completed in late 2020 and provide clear objectives for EU defence policy in the domains of crisis management, resilience, capability development and partnerships.

Strengthening the coherence of the recently established cooperative defence arrangements and reaffirming the commitment of member states to join forces over defence matters are necessary steps to enhance the so-far-limited output of the Common Security and Defence Policy (CSDP) of the EU, whether in terms of capabilities or operations. Progress is required to fill long-standing capability gaps, to equip EU member states to deal with new security challenges (such as those driven by new technologies), and to establish integrated multinational force packages for rapid deployment. The protection of the global commons – space, cyberspace and the oceans – is an increasingly important dimension of the defence agenda, and one that requires close cooperation between the European External Action Service and the Commission. In this context, the specific role of the military should be clearly defined within a much larger approach that draws on the full EU toolbox and regulatory power.

It was noted that the intergovernmental decision-making process that presides over the EU's security and defence policy and the related requirement for unanimous decisions affect the bloc's performance when it comes to security and defence. Additionally, responsibility for defence issues is quite fragmented across the EU institutional architecture. While the application of majority voting in this domain would undoubtedly accelerate decision making, it would require a change of Treaty provisions and it is highly unlikely that member states would agree to that. However, some proposals were made at the meeting that would not require Treaty change but would strengthen both the institutional dimension of EU defence policy and Europe's capacity to act.

For one, the member states should decide to set up a Defence Ministers Council instead of holding informal meetings of defence ministers as per current practice. This would raise the visibility of defence in the EU institutional framework as a policy area in its own right – one that is regularly addressed through high-level political discussions – and it would facilitate EU–NATO cooperation.

For another, the process for planning CSDP military operations should be reformed to enable decisions to be made more quickly in times of crisis. In particular, the Military Planning and Conduct Capability should be strengthened and tasked with carrying out advanced planning based on generic scenarios, with subsequent operational plans submitted to the Political and Security Committee to provide a basis for rapid decisions if the scenarios materialize. Related to this, it was argued that the command structure of CSDP military operations should be reinforced too, attributing their operational command to the head of the EU Military Staff.

WHAT PRIORITIES LIE AHEAD?

The EU needs to face up to the more uncertain and competitive strategic environment it finds itself in with a strong sense of purpose and a clear set of priorities to guide its external action. Meeting participants felt that the message at the heart of the EU's foreign policy and external action should point to the promotion and delivery of global public goods through rules-based cooperation. Three basic requirements were highlighted to empower the bloc to defend and advance its interests and its values in the world.

First, the EU needs to strengthen its own political cohesion, its institutional structures, its instruments and its capabilities as the bedrock for effective external action. In other words, Europe needs a stronger domestic power base if it is to pull its weight in the world. The Covid-19 pandemic has starkly demonstrated that promoting international cooperation is essential to addressing transnational health challenges, but it has also shown that the EU needs to enhance its capacity to produce and distribute medical equipment and vaccines if it wants to be effective at home and abroad. It was felt that the three principal sources of EU power are the single market, which underpins Europe's regulatory power and trade policy, technological innovation and the euro. Among the various measures outlined to strengthen EU external action, enhancing the international role of the euro was considered of particular importance to improve both the bloc's resilience and global financial stability.

Second, strengthening the domestic pillars of the EU's external influence also means improving the effectiveness of EU decision making by using all the options offered by the treaties. This includes, in particular, using the so-called *passerelle* clause to extend the application of qualified majority voting to some important areas of EU external action, as proposed by the Commission. In addition, it was argued that consideration should be given to reform of the EU's constitutional framework, where need be, such as extending EU competencies in the domains of health, social, climate and digital policies, and pooling of EU and national resources on the basis of the principle of subsidiarity.

Third, meeting citizens' concerns and expectations is a necessary condition for the legitimacy, credibility and effectiveness of EU foreign policy and external action. There is a need to fully integrate citizens' priorities into foreign policy making and to carefully assess the costs and benefits of relevant policies for the prosperity, welfare and security of Europeans. It was stressed that the upcoming Conference on the Future of Europe offers a significant opportunity to engage citizens in a thorough debate over the priorities of EU external action and on how to achieve them. This debate should address, among other issues, the close connection between internal and external policies, e.g. concerning trade, the environment, digital affairs, and security and defence. The choices made at home have an impact abroad, and the forces that are shaping Europe's strategic environment carry far-reaching implications for the prosperity, cohesion and security of the EU itself.

Aspirations: for an EU External Action with strategic autonomy and multilateral engagement

By Barbara Roggeveen

Earlier this year, High Representative Josep Borrell visited Moscow. It turned out to be a controversial trip. During a meeting with the Russian foreign minister Sergey Lavrov, Borrell's host referred to the EU as an 'unreliable partner', condemning EU sanctions against Russia over the annexation of Crimea and accusing the EU leadership of lying about Alexei Navalny's poisoning.

Instead of discussing the 'shoulds' and 'oughts' of Borrell's response to these provocative statements, I merely mention the Moscow trip in order to highlight two systemic weaknesses in the EU's external action: the first is the lack of consensus regarding the bloc's strategic ambitions; and the second is the EU's two-track approach, through which Europe tries to pursue both normative conditionality and pragmatic engagement in its interaction with 'rival' actors in the international sphere. This short analysis highlights a number of ways we might overcome these roadblocks in the EU's external action.

To conquer the first weakness identified above, the EU has to get to grips with the concept of strategic autonomy – a topic that is widely discussed in European policy circles. If the EU wants to become a global actor in the sphere of foreign policy, it needs to take ownership of its relationships with its main counterparts. This is easier said than done, since the EU derives its current leverage from trade and market access, rather than via a strong political or military position vis-à-vis its counterparts in the international sphere.

Additionally, where current debates surrounding strategic autonomy focus on the EU's external relations, introspective dialogue is lacking. Borrell's recent Moscow visit illustrates that the EU's strategic ambitions are an empty shell if Europe's internal dynamics do not allow for decisive action to be taken on behalf of the bloc as a whole. Therefore, if the EU wants to achieve a serious level of autonomous decision making, it first needs to reach a consensus among its member states. This will not be an easy exercise, as it would require member states to agree on the aims and instruments of strategic autonomy, as well as on the political preparedness to deploy them.

To overcome the second weakness, the EU needs to rethink its two-track approach towards 'rival' actors, such as China and the Russian Federation. Currently, the EU tries to combine pragmatic engagement with normative conditionality in its interactions with these so-called systemic rivals. This two-track approach can only succeed if the EU's normative demands align with the de facto political and economic leverage it holds over these actors – that is, if the EU is capable of enforcing the normative demands that it sets.

To turn the two-track approach into a successful model for multilateral engagement, the EU should veer away from aspirational assessments of its normative bargaining power and instead rely on a critical evaluation of its *actual* enforcement capacities. In other words, the EU should only make demands that it can truly back up. Borrell's visit to Moscow last February illustrates what happens when the EU's normative demands and its enforcement capacities do *not* line up: the bloc's credibility as an actor in the foreign policy domain is harmed.

To effectuate an external action that consists of strategic autonomy and productive multilateral engagement, the EU must address these two systemic weaknesses. Ultimately, the solution to these roadblocks is highly intertwined: the EU needs to reach internal consensus regarding its aims and instruments of strategic autonomy, and this consensus needs to be based on a critical evaluation of the EU's real, existing bargaining power in the foreign policy domain.

REFERENCES

Financial Times. 2021. Botched Moscow visit is a wake-up call for the EU. *Financial Times*, 11 February.
European Commission. 2019. EU–China – a strategic outlook. Report, European Commission and HR/VP contribution to the European Council, 12 March.

Scenarios for global governance and the EU open strategic autonomy: a window of opportunity for a 'Spinellian moment'

By Mario Telò

INTRODUCTION: IS 'OPEN STRATEGIC AUTONOMY' A PRIORITY FOR THE CONFERENCE?

Open strategic autonomy is an extremely relevant and ambitious concept relating to the EU's future: it has to do with our liberty and welfare within the complex and dangerous world we currently inhabit. However, it is quite a vague notion: the task of making it more concrete should be a priority both for EU institutions and for the Conference. Research may contribute by deepening its conditions and consequences – notably, what is and is not feasible in the global context of the twenty-first century. While for 70 years European unity was mainly concerned with internal conflict prevention and stability (after two world wars), the main issue at stake in the decades ahead will be the coherent link between the internal multilateralism and the capacity of shaping, an an autonomous actor, the globalization and the world order.

The EU represents only 5 per cent of the global population but is comparable with the United States and China in terms of GDP (15.4 per cent in 2019) and trade power (15 per cent), is still a monetary power (the euro is the world's second reserve currency), remains a major actor when it comes to aid to developing countries and humanitarian aid, and is still the world's number one in terms of creating arrangements and agreements with international partners, both near and far. How can it, through a deeper cooperation and integration process, not only survive but also better influence the multipolar, non-European world and its governance according to its own interests and values? It must, first of all, proactively promote multilateral convergences for common goods: peace by conflict prevention, public health, sustainable development, protection of the environment, and fair regulation of the globalized economy and trade.

If the EU misses this opportunity, a tragic backwards step is possible. We might find ourself retreating from the constructive years between the 2001 Laeken Declaration, the European Convention and the Lisbon Treaty, when ambitious objectives were strictly linked to new institutional modes of governance.

ALTERNATIVE SCENARIOS: ANALYTICAL FINDINGS

Will the current global multipolar context allow new actors like the EU to emerge? Research suggests that there are four alternative scenarios for the EU's potential role.

An asymmetrical multipolarity characterized by US military primacy

Since 1989–1991, the global context has evolved towards an unprecedented multipolarity, both asymmetric and bifurcating, combined with a multilayered, multilateral network of cooperation, which is to some extent very fragile but in some ways resilient and dynamic.

Why asymmetric? Contrary to the eurocentric order of the nineteenth century, the new multipolarity is asymmetric in terms of geographic extension, demography, economic power and the soft power of the main poles. The main asymmetry, though, is that relating to military capacities and defence budgets. The United States remains by far the biggest superpower. The rhetoric about China's strengthening military competitiveness must be submitted to deeper scrutiny, with data showing that China's defence budget (US$209 billion in 2020) is still only a quarter of that of the United States (even if it is increasing).

The consequences for European nuclear and non-nuclear security, notably in a context of global rearmament (SIPRI 2019), is that the

EU still needs to combine its own open strategic autonomy with a new transatlantic deal – for the coming 20 years at least (and with the benefit of NATO's Article 5 for its security). This does not mean 'NATO first' for ever, and reviving transatlantic cooperation will not be easy. What is new is that the global changes and experiences of the last few decades have made European leaders (Merkel, Macron, Borrell) aware that the EU can no longer solely rely on the United States for its security. The United States's declining role and the transatlantic rift over strategic interests and models for society are long-term achievements of scientific research, even if only extremists would neglect the relevance of shared values and the liberal model. The Eurobarometer surveys have shown how EU citizens no longer rely on the United States, as they did previously, and they are worried about the growing relevance of American domestic politics by provoking oscillations of the US will (and capacity) of leading global cooperation.

This mean that the EU cannot return to the obsolete role of being a junior partner in the alliance. After Trump's defeat, bringing the United States back into the multilateral game is in the EU's interest and in the general interest of all players. That said, a few months into Joe Biden's presidency, it is already evident that he will often be obliged to choose between internal consensus and leading global change in a multilateral way. The George W. Bush unipolar dream is gone, but the steps taken towards a revived US global hegemony risk taking the form of an uncertain compromise between national US interest and a defensive/exclusive concept of internationalism – far away from the 1944–1945 grand multilateral commitment, from Roosevelt and Kennedy, and even from the Obama approach.

A status quo multipolarity? The emergence of China as an unprecedented historical challenge

The second evidence is the dramatic global economic power shift within the process of consolidation of a multipolar world. Since 2007 the rest of the world has overtaken the West according to share of global GDP. China is already the world's largest economy in purchasing power parity terms, and it will also be largest in nominal terms within a decade. China is the number one import and export power: the largest trading partner for 100 countries, as well for the EU. Having an authoritarian regime (with a poor human rights record and an alternative understanding of fundamental principles) as the world's dominant economy – a highly internationalized, interdependent and technologically advanced country – is unprecedented in history, and it demands innovative thought.

Furthermore, while China is an authoritarian regime, it is a well-functioning one: never in history has such growth in benefits and welfare been provided to so many people in such a short time. In the USSR, for instance, maintaining superpower military status came at the cost of people's welfare. And finally, China, unlike the USSR, is much more integrated into the multilateral system – something that provides multiple opportunities for cooperation over common goods.

The strong trend towards a bifurcation

The multipolar global order is increasingly bifurcating between the United States and China: trade tariffs are being introduced, technological digital competition is rife, there are increasing splits in supply chains, mutual threats have been upgraded and political rhetoric is heightened. A second Cold War is not an abstract scenario but a matter of everyday decisions. In fact, it is openly considered as inevitable by relevant scholars on both sides. In the aftermath of the Anchorage US–China hard confrontation in March 2021 and the following series of reciprocal sanctions, a two-part question arises.

- Is a serious reduction in global production chains and complex interdependence possible, or is it too late to contain China's economy in an effective way? See, for example, Ericsson's support of Huawei's competitive presence in the West, in the hope that China will support Ericsson's business in China.
- How can we cope with the risk of endless multiplication of ineffective reciprocal sanctions, good only for bolstering Xi's regime?

The EU is interested in averting tow risks: either passively adjusting to a hard global bifurcation or sticking to the status quo may end up dramatically weakening the EU and multilateral organizations such as the World Trade Organization (WTO), the World Health Organization (WHO) and the UN, but also the G20, as well as their various binding agendas. The António Guterres UN reform agenda would be at risk; the revision of WHO governance would be frozen; and the commitment of the new WTO director general Ngozi Okonjo-Iweala for subsidies reform, investment facilitation, domestic services regulation and Appellate body revival would be harmed.

How, then, should we deal with China– the country that benefitted most from globalization and multipolarity? Trump tried to combine his defensive and inward-looking programme priority – 'America first' – with a tough outward stance: trade wars and political confrontation with the aim of bringing about an internal collapse of the People's Republic of China regime. It became quickly evident not only that his tactics would fail, but that economic containment is not a feasible option. Two alternative avenues are possible: either we strive for a realistic plural multilateralism that is a mirror of a consolidated multipolarity, making room for China and for other non-Western actors, their economies and also their different background cultures; or we search for innovative combinations of realism and transformation.

Of course, the EU must put human rights and the promotion of democracy at the top of its agenda: EU sanctions are justified on the basis of neutral investigation of human rights violations, and if there are retaliations against European Parliament members, researchers and research centres, China's actions must be firmly rejected. However, are sanctions – if they are singled out mainly as a means of external pressure – the best way to defend human rights and promote democracy? Is the revival of an anti-reformist and fundamentalist political culture ('if we don't obtain all we ask for, then we obtain nothing') a good way to assert European global influence, or is it the route to dangerous self-isolation?

An EU alternative: combining realism with dialogue and transformation towards a new multilateralism

UN Secretary General António Guterres has mentioned the 'Helsinki process' (also known as the Commission on Security and Cooperation in Europe (CSCE)) several times in relation to authoritarian regimes. When the CSCE was established in 1976 as the outcome of the famous Helsinki conference of 1975, the idea of its promoters – from Helmut Schmidt to Olof Palme, and many others – was to profoundly change the authoritarian Eastern European regimes through dialogue and functional cooperation in three areas: security, economy, and culture and human rights. The Brandt *Ost-Politik* inspired this innovative approach, in spite of the 'Archipelago Gulag'.

Combining a defence of our values with increasingly sophisticated negotiations over our interests – by using our market power, e.g. by including the level playing field and a chapter on 'sustainable development' in the EU–China Comprehensive Agreement on Investment (CAI) – is the EU way, and it is consistent with the aim of open strategic autonomy. This way is realistic and ambitious at the same time. It is realistic because it is a simple fact that, through the recent Regional Comprehensive Economic Partnership, all the Asia-Pacific states, including the region's most important democratic entities (Japan, Korea, Australia, New Zealand), have recently signed an agreement with China, and so too has the United States, with the 'Phase One Deal' (January 2020). But it is also ambitious because the EU seems to be aware that if realism is not combined with strong demands for China to respect human rights, the upgrading of treaty contents and revival of the WTO, the objective risk is a de facto shift to a conservative and status quo multipolarity, framed by weak and fragile multilateralism. At the same time, the EU's future as a multilateral entity is directly linked to reform of the multilateral network, and the future of multilateralism is, to a large extent, dependent on the EU as a key driver of multiple coalition building.

Contrary to some comments, strategic autonomy is the opposite of 'going it alone'. With good reason, the Franco-German Declaration of 20 November 2020 asserted the European alternative to a Cold War – that is, the perspective of a new 'alliance for multilateralism' – whereas the Cold War scenario would divide the current and potential multilateral coalitions for common goods and weaken multilateral regimes and organizations. The main role of the EU is that of bridge-building, and of forming coalitions at the global, regional and interregional levels, thereby leading the process of multilateralizing multipolarity and every bilateral agreement. Since 'the status quo is not an option', defending multilateralism is only possible if one is reforming it. That is why the EU is politically obliged to promote various political and functional coalitions

With good reason has Josep Borrell argued that the EU must use the language of power with authoritarian regimes. I would go further: we must use out *distinctive* language of power. Market power, trade power and the euro are the most effective levers of international influence available to the EU.

CONCLUSION: A 'SPINELLIAN MOMENT'?

In 2021 we celebrate the 80th anniversary of the 'Ventotene Manifesto'. This was the founding statement of the European construction, drafted by Altiero Spinelli and his colleagues during their fascist detention. Would it not be a largely consensual idea to propose to make 2021–22 a 'Spinellian moment' for the EU? Dedicating the Brussels parliament building to Spinelli was one way of recognizing the main driver of the EU democratization process. However, in a period where the EU needs both more democracy and an enhancement of its role in the world, the bloc's citizens would feel more enthusiasm for a Spinellian moment than for a 'Hamiltonian moment' (to quote Wolfgang Schäuble and *The Economist*). Hamilton's fight was aimed at building the United States; the EU cannot become a second United States, as it is not a state in the making. Spinelli represents not only the federalist idea and movement, but also a much larger array of forces and hopes for European unity, rooted in every member state and political culture – an internationally ambitious European project that is very timely in the current world. Underlining this solid inspiration would help to avoid two wrong turns: on the one hand, a merely instrumental approach to Europe's unity, whose demise was confirmed by Brexit; and, on the other, an emphasis on the building of a European sovereign state or a Eurocentric dream of a 'European civilization'. Taking Spinellian inspiration for open strategic autonomy may help upgrade the global EU's distinctive project of European modernity and be a driver of new multilateral cooperation. This project is more actual than ever. Through such a symbolic reference, the Conference of 2021 could make the EU's 'open strategic autonomy' more credible and more able of representing the will of millions of citizens for peace and an inspiring political and socioeconomic model in an uncertain world.

REFERENCES

Telò, M., and Viviers, D. 2021. *Europe, China, USA: Alternative Visions of a Changing World*. Brussels: Académie Royale.

Tocci, N. 2021. European strategic autonomy: what it is, why we need it, how to achieve it. Report, Istituto Affari Internazionali, March.

A digital and green European foreign policy that speaks to EU citizens and the world

By Guillaume Klossa

AN OPPORTUNITY

We currently have an opportunity to make sustainable development and digital technology the two central – and citizen-friendly – pillars of the EU's external action.

In addition to a rebalancing of power from West to East unlike anything that has been seen since the beginning of the nineteenth century, the world today faces two urgent challenges: it must address the rapidly deteriorating habitability of the planet, and it must deal with a fast-paced digital transformation that calls into question our ways of accessing information, our working lives, the way we organize our economic and social lives, the distribution of economic value, our security, our rights and our freedoms. More profoundly, these two challenges, which know no borders, raise both an ethical question, about the world we want for future generations, and political questions about the relationship between national and European sovereignty for the member states of the EU. More broadly, at the level of the planet, there is the question of a collective global will.

It is in the EU's interest to make these two challenges central pillars of its external action, with the objective of ensuring that these priorities are understood not only by diplomats but also by opinion leaders and citizens throughout the rest of the world. This should be easy for two reasons. Firstly, these priorities already form two pillars of the EU's internal action, led by the 'geopolitical European Commission' under Ursula von der Leyen, and of the European recovery plan negotiated in July 2020. And secondly, they are now the subject of broad consensus among EU member states – something that has not always been the case.

In this context, the Conference on the Future of Europe – which is already underway and which will continue into the first half of 2022 – is an opportunity to define a vision of the EU's future that has the digital and green dimensions at its centre. It is this vision that could then be carried into the world by the EU's external action service and by the diplomatic services of the member states. Doing this would allow us to have a European foreign policy that speaks to the citizens of the EU, which is not the case when the EU seems to be dealing exclusively with conflict resolution. It would be a broader response to the 'middle class foreign policy' advocated by the Biden administration.

A CONTRAST

In contrast to the EU, the United States and China have long-established policies on digital technology and recent ones on sustainable development.

A long time ago, President Bill Clinton's United States made the 'information superhighway', and the resulting new digital society, a political and geopolitical priority. As early as the mid 1990s, America understood the stakes of positioning itself as a power of the future and also of attracting the talent that this dimension, which today we describe as digital, required. From that moment on, America made the digital dimension central to its foreign policy message. From a concrete point of view, the country oriented its State Department's leadership programme towards digital issues, almost systematically organizing visits to Silicon Valley, with the aim of rooting America's digital leadership in people's minds. The country quickly identified the transnational nature of digital technology and data circulation, and consequently developed powerful extraterritorial legislation such as the Patriot Act and the Cloud Act. America is now pursuing an external strategy of active support for the economic and fiscal interests of its digital giants, which for the sake of simplicity we will call GAFAM (Google, Amazon, Facebook, Apple and Microsoft). The Trump and Biden administrations have identified these giants as decisive levers of American power in the twenty-first century.

Since the beginning of the 2010s, China has used digital technology to support its vision of the country's future but also to support its power. China made digital sovereignty a priority in 2012. It has set up ambitious talent-attraction programmes (such as '1000 Talents') and has massively supported the development of BATX (Baidu, Alibaba, Tencent, Xiaomi; to which must now be added Huawei), both domestically and abroad, with the idea of establishing China as the country with the best digital infrastructure in the world in order to serve a society of efficiency. The West rightly analyses this as a society of control and surveillance. These companies are also used as levers of Chinese power, particularly in the context of the Belt and Road Initiative.

Only recently – with the Paris Agreement of December 2015 about the fight against global warming (which was put on hold during the Trump administration) – have America and China begun to prioritize the international issue of sustainable development. This will undoubtedly become one of the few areas of Sino-American cooperation.

In contrast, Europeans made sustainable development a priority at a very early stage, enshrining it in the Lisbon Treaty and playing a major role in setting the UN's seventeen Sustainable Development Goals. After the disastrous failure of the Copenhagen Climate Change Conference in 2009, which followed the very ambitious Climate and Energy Package introduced during the French presidency of the EU Council in 2008, Europeans gave themselves the means to succeed at the Paris Climate Change Conference by anticipating and coordinating their actions and by creating coalitions, including with civil society. This conference will remain a founding moment of the European external sustainable development strategy. It is regrettable that the EU failed to pursue a soft power strategy in this area from 2008, by promoting its Climate and Energy Package. Such an approach would have enabled the EU to establish its leadership in world public opinion.

In the digital field, it must be noted that until recently there was little concrete external action by the EU, apart from that related to the General Data Protection Regulation (GDPR), which de facto has an extraterritorial dimension. In both the United States and

China, the GDPR is seen more as a defensive action by an EU that does not have its own digital giants than as an act of protecting fundamental right to privacy, as it is understood by European citizens. However, the GDPR is a major pillar of European digital soft power. Cyberattacks on key European infrastructure (in the fields of defence, health, media, business, etc.), digital disinformation campaigns emanating from abroad, the refusal of tech giants to contribute to European taxation and the Covid-19 crisis have all made Europeans aware that the EU must develop a digital strategy with a strong 'external action' component to protect European interests. This concern is at the heart of the current Commission's agenda. In this context, the notion of strategic autonomy has its full meaning in the digital field: it is both a matter of securing and diversifying European supplies linked to digital technology, and of acquiring the capacity to provide certain digital services autonomously, particularly in the area of data hosting.

In short, in terms of external action the EU has not fully taken advantage of its track record in sustainable development, while in the digital field it is beginning to develop what is essentially a vision based on protection. On its own this may seem too defensive and does not give the impression of a future power.

AN AFFIRMATION

The Conference on the Future of Europe is a time to affirm the EU as a digital and green power of the future.

It is important to understand the potential of current and developing digital technologies – technologies that can be used to foster a European vision for the future. For example, it is possible to imagine a transnational and multilingual European public and digital media space that allows citizens from different countries to debate with each other using their own languages and has quality non-national and pluralist sources of information automatically translated into each European language. Digital technology also enables, or greatly facilitates, the development of new political, social and health rights. In the field of health, which is of course crucial to citizens, we can now imagine a right to a biological diagnosis of equal quality for all

European citizens. In terms of security, we can imagine a right to cybersecurity for all European citizens. It is also important to highlight the need for coordination between digital policy and sustainable development policy, which should not be thought of in silos, as they are today, but as being complementary.

It is important to consider the practicalities of the EU's external action. It should take advantage of the latest digital developments, particularly in terms of personalization and automatic translation, to establish a personalized relationship between opinion leaders and the citizens of the world in their own languages. Additionally, the external action strategy should be designed in a non-autarchic way by bringing together the 'like-minded': that is, countries that share the same ethics when it comes to data and artificial intelligence.

And finally, an important proposal of the conference could be that in digital and green matters, member states make decisions through a qualified majority and not by unanimity, as is the case today. Choosing qualified majority voting for digital and green matters would certainly be a very powerful signal that the EU could give to the rest of the world.

REFERENCE

Klossa, G. 2019. Towards European media sovereignty: an industrial media strategy to leverage data, algorithms and artificial intelligence. Report, European Commission.

The EU and global economic governance
By Paolo Guerrieri

Even before the Covid-19 pandemic hit, the world economy had profoundly changed over recent years due to the decline of the multilateral order, the great power rivalry between the United States and China, and the deterioration in global economic integration. The economic and social impact of Covid-19 has made clear the extreme vulnerability of the world's population to a range of threats: from pandemics, to climate change, to digital wars, and so on. All these threats are global, and they can only be addressed and/or solved by global cooperative action. But there is a very real risk of an international systemic vacuum, with no provider of public global goods. As we have seen during the global response to Covid-19, global economic governance has never been so needed, but it has also never been so difficult.

The rebuilding of global economic governance is a key tenet of the European agenda in this age of multipolarity. The EU has been one of the great protagonists of the liberal multilateral order, and one of its biggest beneficiaries. As the largest trading bloc in the world, the EU still depends heavily on developments in the world economy. The reinforcement of a new multilateral framework – one that is able to promote economic integration and cooperation between countries – is therefore vital to European interests.

It follows that in response to the profound shifts in the international economic system the EU should strengthen its presence in the new world. What has been achieved in the past is no longer sufficient. In the words of European Commission President Ursula von der Leyen, 'it is inevitable to strive for an increasing level of European strategic autonomy'.

In concrete policy terms, developing strategic autonomy in a way that gives the EU a bigger international role could mean many things, of course, but I will limit myself to mentioning, very briefly, four priorities that the EU could positively contribute to in order to rebuild global economic governance.

EU RELATIONS WITH THE UNITED STATES AND CHINA

The first relates to EU relations with the United States and China and to the great rivalry between the two superpowers. The US–China conflict will dominate international economic relations even under the Biden presidency, and the risk of this strategic confrontation degenerating further will remain extremely high. For instance, we might see a general economic decoupling from China, which would be a policy with an extremely high cost and very low benefit. The EU risks suffering great damage from the US–China fight, and it has every interest in avoiding any degeneration that would lead to further weaponization of international economic relations.

What is required is, first, more effective management of transatlantic relations with the United States. The Biden presidency does not mean that the US–EU relationship will automatically go back to how it used to be, but it does offer Europe an opportunity to relaunch transatlantic relations, especially after the dark years of Trump.

The many ties we have with the United States – such as in the areas of common democratic values and our defence/security system – remain a crucial European asset that needs to be defended and safeguarded. With this in mind, late last year the Commission put forward a plan for the future of transatlantic relations that moves things in the right direction. The plan would see a renewal of our relations with the United States on many fronts, starting with trade, technology and the environment.

Europe must exploit this opportunity while maintaining its own identity. In this regard there is no contradiction between the relaunch of a transatlantic agenda and greater strategic autonomy for Europe. As some have outlined, they are two faces of the same coin.

Furthermore, we need to coordinate with the US when we negotiate with China, both to achieve greater bilateral reciprocity and to cooperate globally for common public goods such as those relating to climate change, pandemics and cybersecurity. It should be stressed that this approach is not at odds with the European side's full defence of fundamental rights, as the recent coordinated Western sanctions imposed on a small number of Chinese officials for their role in human rights abuses in Xinjiang have fully confirmed.

Europe should have a China policy and maintain its relative autonomy. While the EU shares many of the concerns of the United States, e.g. over security threats surrounding Beijing's nationalistic behaviour, in other areas, such as over economic integration with China and the wider Asia Pacific region, Europe's concerns are not identical to those of the United States. The provisional conclusion reached between the EU and China last December over the Comprehensive Agreement on Investment, after seven years of negotiation, has clearly demonstrated this. Nor should the EU agree to the 'decoupling' plan from China that the Trump administration vigorously pursued in recent years and that the Biden administration has, for now, only suspended.

INTERNATIONAL COOPERATION AND COMMON PUBLIC GOODS

Second, Europe should take the lead in the preservation of global public goods, such as when it comes to climate action, where the EU is already at the forefront. If a global alliance proves difficult to achieve anytime soon, the EU should favour a climate coalition between a group of countries with similar approaches, including the United States, and it should be open to other member if they commit to respecting the same goals and rules. Having already indicated its intention to introduce a Carbon Adjustment Border Mechanism (CABM), the EU should take full responsibility for the initiative. A priority is that the CABM should be WTO-compliant, in order to avoid the major risk of a protectionist conflict. More generally, the key issue is how to avoid the contentious issues of the bilateral confrontations with China, on many fronts, compromising the opportunities for multilateral cooperation on climate talks.

Of course, it goes without saying that in terms of international cooperation over public goods, there is a need in the current moment for the EU and the United States to cooperate to improve supplies of Western vaccines to the developing world, and first to Africa.

EU BILATERAL AND REGIONAL TRADE AGREEMENTS

Third, in the years to come there will not be many countries that defend openness and a rules-based world economy. The EU will need to do so, because it is in the bloc's vital interest. This means that the EU should lead efforts to reform the WTO, strengthening its role in dispute settlement and rules setting, and even confronting China in partnership with the United States and Japan in plurilateral WTO negotiations over delicate issues such as subsidies.

Furthermore, the EU needs to have an effective trade strategy at a bilateral level, as it has in recent years, to consolidate and further develop its complex and sophisticated network of bilateral and regional trade and investment agreements, all of which are complementary to the multilateral approach. In this regard, the trade integration that is already underway in the Pacific area – with bilateral agreements formed with most of the economies of the Asia-Pacific region in recent years, and with the recent regional Regional Comprehensive Economic Partnership – makes Europe's network even more strategically important.

The EU's bilateral trading agreements should also be used to promote high environmental and social standards in partner countries, to achieve 'fair trade' not simply 'free trade'.

Fourth, the emergence of a multipolar monetary regime is a very real possibility in the medium term because of the increasingly international role of the renminbi. The euro should, without doubt, be part of that new regime, so it is time to break with the EU's past neutrality on the international role of the euro and to create conditions that favour a greater international presence of the EU currency.

To this end, important choices must be made and complex reforms undertaken. The completion of banking union and the capital market union are needed, up to the creation of a safe financial asset for the eurozone. All these reforms will require quite a long time to deliver, as well as strong political support from the member states. Whatever the case, the important thing is to start the process as soon as possible.

CONCLUDING REMARKS

I mention two caveats. To maintain and further develop trade openness and to proceed with the international economic integration of Europe, we need to strengthen safeguards for workers and citizens. They want an economic system that is open, certainly, but also one that provides them with benefits and which better protects them. In this regard, social policies and welfare policies are needed to deal with the very unequal impacts of trade and technology. There is much that governments can do, but they have not made much progress in recent years. Now is the time for new policies and new measures.

Furthermore, a more autonomous and assertive global presence on the part of the EU must be based on greater unity among member states. Among the great obstacles to a policy agenda of strategic autonomy are the internal divisions that are present within the EU. Beijing has, in recent years, used a divide-and-conquer approach with national capitals to weaken the common EU front. So that we can act differently in the future, we should set up effective common decision-making mechanisms and capabilities as soon as possible. The lack of them has weakened Europe's external role in the past.

Finally, we should be fully aware that the process of European integration will never work without a strong geopolitical dimension and capability. On the other hand, the new external economic policy of the EU will be more credible if the European economy is able to return to a path of high and sustainable growth. This means accelerating the process of EU integration and internal cohesion, which can be achieved by first implementing the Green Deal strategy and the ambitious Next Generation EU programme, which will help us, in a spirit of solidarity, to overcome the dramatic crisis caused by the Covid-19 pandemic.

Defending the momentum, delivering on progress: the future of European defence

By Vassilis Ntousas

Defence policy – once the ultimate taboo domain for the EU – has experienced tremendous progress over the past few years. The unveiling of the EU Global Strategy in 2016 (which provided crucial momentum for defence-related discussions and decisions at the European level), the launch and ongoing work through Permanent Structure Cooperation (PESCO), the setting up of a Coordinated Annual Review on Defence, and the creation of an EU-funded European Defence Fund have all constituted key breakthroughs along the way. This important work continues despite the disruption caused by the Covid-19 pandemic, but it is crucial that the momentum we have achieved is carefully safeguarded and cultivated as external threats become more complex and the risks for potential renationalization of security questions become increasingly evident.

The bloc's willingness to become a stronger actor in the security arena is now in need of durable commitments and tangible delivery. This is not a fact that is recognized only around the corridors of Brussels, either: it is a growing expectation of decisive majorities of EU citizens, as confirmed by successive Eurobarometer surveys.

Starting from the simple fact that the EU cannot afford to outsource its security needs, working for a step change in deepening the policy content of strategic autonomy should be seen as a key priority (as was recently acknowledged in the February 2021 European Council). Making advances on this front is, though, fraught with difficulty, not least due to the persistence of widely divergent strategic cultures at national level, the remarkable unevenness of member states' military capacities, the different priorities that are evident across the continent, and the frequent lack of solidarity among member states. Despite the general drive to endorse its relevance, even the concept of strategic autonomy itself has become contested, with differences in the concept's understanding ranging from the policy level to a purely terminological one.

And yet, as discussions on what the concept is and what it entails unfold, it is equally important to clarify what it is not. Speaking of strategic autonomy should not be confused with autarchy. As the etymology of autonomy suggests (*auto* = self + *nomos* = law), the term simply denotes the EU's ability to decide and act according to its own rules, principles and values. The bloc's prosperity and security are tightly linked to a well-functioning, rules-based global order, so becoming more strategically autonomous therefore means becoming more resistant to undue exogenous interference. It does not, though, describe a 'Europe alone' approach.

But how do we go about unpacking the concept beyond this? Answering this increasingly urgent question requires the political will to engage in some hard internal discussions: particularly those that relate to articulating *what* the EU wants to (be able to) do in order to face *which* threats and on the basis of *which* capabilities.

This is why the work underway as part of the Strategic Compass process should be supported. This initiative, which was launched by EU defence ministers in June 2020, can make a real contribution, not only to bridging the sizeable gaps between strategic cultures across the bloc and defining what specific objectives the priorities already defined in the Global Strategy should serve, but also in forging a robust internal consensus on some key aspects that can strengthen the EU's ability to act globally. The general aim should be for unambiguous yet ambitious priorities and actions to be delineated by this process.

On the crisis management front, this requires that there is more sustained focus on how missions and operations can be engaged and operationalized more efficiently in the future. Positive developments in this area – such as the new European Peace Facility, which has been allocated an off-budget fund worth approximately €5 billion for the period 2021–2027 – are steps in the right direction. They undoubtedly enhance the EU's capacity as a global security provider.

Nevertheless, the Strategic Compass needs to provide much greater precision in how the EU meets present and future crises, not least in terms of operational readiness and its ability for force generation, and it must also provide the necessary clarity over the functional and regional focus points of its actions.

Concerning the capabilities and instruments cluster of work that is required for this to happen, emphasis should be given to defining and refining defence cooperation efforts. Despite the progress already achieved, a high degree of incoherence still persists in how the commitments that are undertaken translate into reality. Taking the well-established gaps between future ambitions and existing capabilities as a starting point, a meaningful equilibrium between the various – at times overlapping – initiatives, mechanisms and levels of capability development therefore needs to be crafted. Through the Strategic Compass, states should urgently add clarity to how they can ready, procure, produce and deliver on the necessary military and civilian capabilities as well as on pertinent operational projects in order to serve the bloc's collective objectives.

In this regard, and as tragically highlighted by the Covid-19 pandemic, efforts to boost the EU's internal and external resilience should also be placed front and centre when thinking about the future of European defence. Enhancing the bloc's ability to bounce back from crises and respond better to an evolving landscape of challenges should, however, not lead to the myopic adoption of a 'fortress Europe' approach. Rather, this calls for a much more organic involvement of specific threat multipliers – such as climate change or the digital and health emergencies – into the EU's thinking and modus operandi. Crucially, this also requires finally breaking down the barriers between siloed policy (re)actions at the EU and member state level, all the way from the planning stage to the execution stage.

Building on this, a key objective should also be that of transitioning into a more efficient model of partnering on the part of the EU. In line with what was mentioned above, a positive future trajectory for European defence relies on ensuring that greater European autonomy also means greater European responsibility, and that neither of these two concepts is taken to signify a weakening of established partnerships. On the contrary; as I have argued elsewhere regarding the bloc's bilateral relationship with the United States, the goal can and should be for a stronger Europe to translate into a stronger transatlantic partnership and footprint.

In light of this, it is clear that the Strategic Compass provides a formidable opportunity for the EU to rid itself of its complacency and conceptualize what it thinks would work in terms of the division of labour in its relationship with NATO, underpinned by a debunking of the myth that stronger European defence implies a weaker Alliance. The concomitant need to ensure coherence between any outcomes produced by the Strategic Compass and the other processes that are underway, such as NATO's new Strategic Concept, is equally clear. Similarly, and despite the decision of the UK government to leave foreign and security policy matters outside of the Brexit negotiations, it is easy to see why keeping strong links between the two sides is vital as passions calm. Nonetheless, the EU's partnership agenda should not stop there, and a full-spectrum review and analysis of existing partnerships should be carried out with a view to making sure that the bloc's external action output is coherent.

Last but not least, it is vital to underline that strengthening intra-bloc solidarity will be essential in determining the true success of not only the Strategic Compass but also all future defence initiatives. How this can be achieved is as much an institutional question – for example, through a more meaningful exploration of what the implementation of the EU treaties' mutual assistance (Article 42.7 of the TEU) and solidarity (Article 222 of the TFEU) clauses could look like in practice – as it is a political one. This is why a delicate balance needs to be struck between securing maximum buy-in among member states in terms of the decisions taken and ensuring the appropriate level of coordination and oversight by the EU institutions.

It is clear that there is no magic bullet to fix this conundrum. Doing so will require copious work and a lot of patience if the EU is to deliver on the twin task of becoming more strategic *and* more autonomous. Yet it is equally clear that the lack of meaningful, actionable solidarity and the persistence of pronounced diversity could waste the efforts of all. For a more geopolitically minded EU that wants to deliver on substantial progress in the areas of its security and defence, this is the only way through which the bloc can stand credibly in the world and be seen as defending its values in the eyes of its citizens.

REFERENCES

Lamond, J., and Ntousas, V. 2021. In our hands: progressive ideas for a renewed and repurposed transatlantic bond. Report, FEPS/Center for American Progress, January.

Ntousas, V. 2019. How can the EU learn the language of power. Expert Comment, Chatham House/World Economic Forum, December.

Pirozzi, N., and Ntousas, V. 2019. Walking the strategy talk. Research Paper, FEPS/IAI, May.

The European External Action regarding migration
By Hedwig Giusto

In the last five years we have heard over and over again how the sharp increase in the number of migrant and refugee arrivals to Europe following the civil war in Syria raised fears among European citizens who were already worn out in the wake of the recent economic and financial crisis. We have seen how migration has caused a sort of 'passing-the-buck' attitude among EU member states, precipitating a political crisis and a crisis of solidarity for the Union, and how it has helped to unleash conservative and far-right political parties' scaremongering tactics to win easy votes in the face of people's legitimate anxieties. We have seen, too, how the migration crisis has forced the EU to take increasing responsibility over an area in which member states were traditionally – and remain – the fundamental actors. And, last but not least, we have heard the stories of too many people losing their lives in the Mediterranean Sea, while too many others have endured difficulty, violence and torture in their attempt to reach a safer place and start a new life in Europe.

This well-known story had already started to take a different course by 2017 – when the inflow of migrants to Europe began to considerably decrease and the emergency mode that characterized the EU's approach for managing migration was gradually dropped – but it took another tragic crisis, the Covid-19 pandemic and the subsequent social and economic downturn, to finally (but probably only temporally) remove migration from the radars of European citizens and their governments.

And yet during this same period, the EU's involvement in the governance of migration has become an accepted feature. This has led the European Commission to attempt to develop the Union's competences in this field further: to create new European agencies and to try to finally make sense of a patchwork of European and national measures, systematizing and strengthening EU migration and asylum policy by means of a New Pact on Migration and Asylum that was presented in September 2020. The New Pact is, however, a pact in name and ambition alone, rather than in actual terms, as its components will have to be agreed by the European Parliament and the member states. Despite its aspirations, it remains an attempt to find a compromise between many distant positions, and therefore it does not go all the way to representing a significant change in EU migration policy.

As I have said, the emergency-mode approach does now seem to be behind us. Hence, instead of waiting for the next crisis to arrive, this would be a good moment to take advantage of the fact that public opinion has turned its attention elsewhere and that there seems to be a momentary 'lull' in the arrival of newcomers (a lull that the restrictions to movement introduced to fight the pandemic have naturally heightened). This might help us to overcome member states' differences and resistance and to finally shape and adopt a consistent European policy that actually fosters 'safe, orderly and regular migration' to Europe.

It remains doubtful, however, whether the EU and its member states will eventually find the political will and courage to move on from their current short-sighted approach – which, in spite of official declarations, still looks at migration mostly through a security lens – to one that, while recognizing the strategic dimension of migration, treats it as a normal, unavoidable and multidimensional human phenomenon that needs to be governed rather than stopped, and as an opportunity both for the countries of origin and for the receiving ones. We must transition from an approach that is largely based on the externalization of border and flows management to third countries, on the superficial and simplistic use of development aids and on an excessive focus on returns to one that is truly based on fair cooperation with countries of origin and transit, on evidence-based knowledge and on the values of freedom and respect for human rights that the EU promotes but does not always abide by. We also need a policy that does not put at risk the lives of those trying to reach Europe to find shelter or better opportunities.

It cannot be denied that, thus far, the strategy adopted by the EU seems to have paid off. Irregular flows to Europe have certainly decreased in recent years. But the price, in terms of the EU's credibility and in terms of respect for human rights, has been high. The existing strategy was founded on the idea that restrictive policies – mostly based on agreements with third countries, such as Turkey, who are entrusted with the task of managing borders and controlling migration flows – can stop migration and that containment is necessary in the face of an expected increase in flows, particularly from Africa. However, not only does evidence prove that restrictive policies cannot completely stop migration, but it is also doubtful that such an approach could be effective in the long term as its success depends on the state of relations between the EU and said third countries, on the latter's political stability and on the indefinite perpetuation of measures that should instead be extraordinary and temporary.

Another fundamental aspect of the current European approach to migration management is its use of development aid. Without denying the absolute importance of supporting development processes in African countries per se, the use of such instruments to control and curtail migration flows should be more carefully evaluated on the basis of available research. In fact, while popular opinion and rhetoric consider addressing the so-called root causes of migration to be one of the most important tools in reducing international mobility – primarily mobility from Africa to Europe – these views neglect a number of facts. Not only are decisions to emigrate driven by many factors – of which the economic opportunities offered by a prospective migrant's native country is just one (albeit a crucial one) – but empirical evidence proves that, up to a certain level of GDP, development increases rather than decreases emigration. Moreover, a myopic use of development aid does not take into account that exploiting aid to stop border crossing risks perpetuating an 'unhealthy' dichotomous relationship between donor countries and recipient ones or that, at the end of the day, migration also represents a remarkable tool for fighting poverty (for both the migrants and their families, and for their native countries) and stimulating development through knowledge transfer, remittances and so on. Development aid aimed at curbing migration therefore risks not achieving its primary goal, and if it is not well-targeted at the needs and conditions of the receiving countries, it risks creating obstacles to other important sources of development too.

Equally short-sighted is the idea that promoting agreements that ensure the return of irregular migrants to their countries of origin will offer a viable solution to the aim of decreasing mobility. While returns are needed in the framework of policies that open and strengthen regular migration pathways to ensure their effectiveness and credibility, placing too much emphasis on the usefulness of returns as an instrument for curbing migration is wishful thinking. Not only are returns very difficult and costly to implement, but countries of origin normally have very little interest in receiving back their nationals (whose remittances very often contribute greatly to their home country's GDP), and therefore they also have little motivation to subscribe to agreements to implement and normalize the returns practice.

The EU's future approach to migration should be based on an acknowledgement that migration cannot be stopped and that this is not a negative feature: migration is and has always been an important tool for the development of both origin and receiving countries. Given its complexity and multidimensionality, the issue of migration requires complex answers and the definition of a long-term strategy that will inevitably force the EU to find a balance between its duty to ensure the security and well-being of its territory and citizens, its moral duty to offer protection to people who need it, and the need for labour in the face of an aging and dwindling population.

Given the unsolved dilemma outlined above, then, the question of migration will certainly remain a divisive issue in the future, and defining the tools to govern it will continue to pollute relations between EU member states. And yet the fact that migration is no longer in the spotlight, at least for the time being, should be seen as an opportunity that must not be lost. Now is the time to refocus European migration policy towards a more balanced approach – an approach that combines the strengthening of regular pathways to enter Europe, with common, consistent and transparent European rules and procedures, and with more fair and equal partnerships with the countries of origin and transit. An approach in which development aid is detached from the goal of controlling borders.

Last but not least, if the EU and its member states want to stand by their fundamental values, the lives, well-being and rights of the people who are on the move should be considered to be of primary importance both in the relations with third countries and in the management of the EU's external border. In the same vein, solidarity towards migrants and between European member states should represent the guiding light for European progressives.

The European External Action and the EU constitutional system
By Diego Lopez Garrido

There is a paradox in the EU's External Action. From a legal and constitutional perspective, we see a powerful External Action in the Lisbon Treaty. The treaty introduces two innovations: stable and unified representation and leadership; and a single procedure for negotiating international agreement. There are two solidarity clauses. Article 42.7 of the Treaty on European Union (TEU) reads:

> If a Member State is the victim of armed aggression on its territory, the other Member States shall have towards it an obligation of aid and assistance by all the means in their power, in accordance with article 51 of the United Nations Charter. This shall not prejudice the specific character of the security and defence policy of certain Member States.

Article 222.2 of the Treaty on the Functioning of the European Union (TFEU) reads:

> Should a Member State be the object of a terrorist attack or the victim of a natural or manmade disaster, the other Member States shall assist it at the request of its political authorities. To that end, the Member States shall coordinate between themselves in the Council.

The treaties clearly envisage a permanent structural cooperation. Article 21.2 of the TEU says:

> The Union shall define and pursue common policies and actions, and shall work for a high degree of cooperation in all fields of international relations, in order to:

a. safeguard its values, fundamental interest security, independence and integrity;
b. consolidate and support democracy, the rule of law, human rights and the principles of international law;
c. preserve peace, prevent conflicts and strengthen international security, in accordance with the principles of the Helsinki Final Act and with the aims of the Charter of Paris, including those relating to external borders;
d. foster the sustainable economic, social and environmental development of developing countries, with the primary aim of eradicating poverty;
e. encourage the integration of all countries into the world economy, including through the progressive abolition of restrictions on international trade;
f. help develop international measures to preserve and improve the quality of the environment and the sustainable management of global natural resources, in order to ensure sustainable development;
g. assist populations, countries and regions confronting natural or manmade disasters;
h. promote an international system based on stronger multilateral cooperation and good global governance.

And Article 22.1 of TEU says:

> On the basis of the principles and objectives set out in article 21, the European Council shall identify the strategic interest and objectives of the Union.

In the TEU there are specific provisions on Common Foreign and Security Policy (CFSP). We must emphasize the following. Article 24.1 first:

> The Union's competence in matters in common foreign and security policy shall cover all areas of foreign policy and all questions relating to the Union's security, including the progressive framing of a common defence policy that might lead to a common defence.

Article 31.1 rules that decisions on CFSP shall be taken by the European Council and that the Council must act unanimously. Article 31.2 rules that the Council shall act by qualified majority when adopting (i) a decision on the basis of a decision of the European Council relating to the Union's strategic interests and objectives (Article 22.1), (ii) a proposal from the High Representative of the Union for Foreign Affairs and Security Policy presented following a specific request from the European Council, or (iii) a decision defining a Union action or position. And Article 31.3 defines the so-called passerelle clause. This is a highly relevant norm that permits the European Council to unanimously adopt a decision stipulating that the Council shall act by qualified majority in cases other than those referred to in Article 31.2.

In my view, there has been a 'silent constitutionalization' in the EU since its foundation: the Treaty of Rome, the Maastricht Treaty and the Treaty of Lisbon. The main pillars are the free market, the primacy of European law, and 'strategic autonomy' within the framework of the 2016 Global Strategy for the European Union's Foreign and Security Policy.

An example of this silent constitutionalitation is the NextGenerationEU programme. This €750 billion pandemic recovery fund offers the possibility of consolidating the European project and Europe's capacity of act.

Nevertheless, in practice, the External Action of the EU is not hugely powerful. Difficulties arise from the fact that member states have their own interests. Interests that differ from those of the EU as a whole, mainly in relation to foreign policy and defence policy.

The EU is a formidable power in trade business regulation, but it suffers from a lack of coherence when it comes to foreign policy. In this respect, as President Macron has said, Europe is 'on the edge of a precipice'.

The EU needs to develop a military force of its own. It has to act as a political bloc, with policies on technology, data and climate change. And it must build up its structured cooperation and a defence fund, which are only in their early stages.

Many countries are too embroiled in domestic woes. The EU does not have a clear and predictable strategy on its relations with Russia, or with North Africa, China or Turkey, or one with the United States after its huge internal polarization that delivers 'foreign policy self-destruction', without consensus in the American scenario.

The EU's market is strong but it is weak in other dimensions of its External Action (e.g. health and technology). There are obstacles to the bloc speaking with one voice: it has five Commissioners, all responsible for different areas of European foreign policy, as well as European Council President Charles Michel and European Commission President Ursula von der Leyen. The Union's strategic priorities are therefore not consistent enough.

PROPOSALS

- Europe should be subservient neither to the United States nor to China (while remembering that the United States is a democracy).
- Europe has to come together to build a place for itself in the space between Washington and Beijing.
- Europe should have a bold External Action over issues like industry, the digital economy (e.g. 5G), infrastructure and education.
- It should take progressive multilateralism as its guide. These goals are only positive within the framework of strong multilateral institutions (e.g. the WHO, the Paris Agreement, the UN) and strong cooperation with international partners (e.g. the adoption of a Europe–Africa agenda, through concrete joint initiatives).
- A new transatlantic agenda – one not based on US dominance and a subordinated Europe, but instead focused on health, trade, sustainability and security (and on a European pillar within NATO) – is needed. There should be an EU–United States summit this year.
- During the Portuguese Council presidency, there should be efforts to abolish the death penalty.
- We need a strong Conference for the Future of Europe. One that is open to organized civil society, think tanks and European citizens, and that updates its constitutional framework.
- We should strive for non-proliferation of nuclear weapons.
- We should activate the foreseen *passerelle* clause (Article 31.3 of the TUE). In that case, treaty reform is not necessary.

- World tax harmonization and the abolition of tax heavens are needed.
- There should be a new European asylum agreement, to counteract the fact that the flow of refugees and the recent economic crisis have fuelled the rise of far-right and populist political parties.
- We need European strategic autonomy to protect the values of peace, solidarity, cooperation, the rule of law and democracy, which are the bedrock of Western culture.
- The idea of a European Security Council should be explored.
- Europe needs more foreign policy independence (e.g. it should develop its own technological capabilities), and it should roll out military operations outside of NATO.
- Europe should do more to defend itself, and it should be able to define its own global position in geopolitical terms. Geopolitics is back.

The EU is, and should remain, a normative power, exporting liberal democracy.

PART III
Economic Governance for an Empowered European Union

PART III

Synthesis of the debate

By Robin Huguenot-Noël

Economic governance means very different things to the various EU observers and actors. Since the neoclassical revolution of the 1980s, economic governance has often been used as a way to highlight a 'soft-touch' regulatory approach to market developments. Here, the EU's role is primarily understood as that of a 'referee' enabling market integration. The deepening of the single market should serve a process of 'negative integration' and help remove obstacles to the 'four freedoms': the free movement of people, goods, services, and capital. Governance of the Economic and Monetary Union (EMU) focuses on implementing rules that keep member states' public finances in check and ensure (impose) fiscal coordination.

An alternative approach views economic governance as a system always linked to the social and political environment in which it evolves. Based on the demands of policymakers and the public, (EU) institutions act as policy entrepreneurs, contributing to shaping the path to economic development. Here, the purpose of economic governance is less about achieving a market equilibrium than delivering on common aspirations shared by EU citizens. Obviously, moving to such a kind of 'positive integration' in a Union of twenty-seven member states comes with its own challenges. But it also has the merits of relentlessly seeking new ways to define what European public goods are about.

In the context of the Future of Europe debate, the nature of the economic tools at the disposal of the EU institutions will surely be heatedly discussed. Contributions will assess the merits of EU fiscal and monetary policy, and (hopefully) those of better-coordinated industrial and social policy in reviving economic growth. But we must be wary of putting the cart before the horse. The debate should first serve the purpose of clarifying what role heads of state and governments are ready to allow the EU institutions to play in everyday economic policy-making. It is clear that today – considering that the need for strong state intervention has come back to centre stage – EU institutions will need to come up with something more ambitious than just small safeguards of the market economy.

The remainder of this chapter sheds light on the insights of the expert group into what the aspirational goals of a new EU economic governance framework should be, what challenges stand in the way, and which institutional and policy reforms are needed to overcome them.

THE EUROPEAN FRAMEWORK FOR ECONOMIC GOVERNANCE

The economic governance of the EU in the last decades has been marked by an attempt to govern by rules and to rule by numbers – with the wrong rules and numbers. Surprisingly enough, this approach has not worked. The 3 per cent deficit and 60 per cent debt rule was decided on the back of an envelope. EU and other domestic 'debt-break' rules resulted in meagre investment levels and subdued growth, and yet they also heightened macroeconomic divergence, especially between the eurozone's core and its periphery. At the same time, global economic integration went unregulated, leading to growing discontent among EU citizens feeling left behind. A political backlash ensued, with the rise of Eurosceptic and nationalist parties, triggering heightened pressure on the EU integration project and, ultimately, leading to Brexit. Many factors were in play, including structural ones such as the unregulated flow of capital and political divisions between government leaders. EU decision-making processes were also to blame: unanimity rules in the area of taxation paradoxically led to unfettered tax competition and the erosion of fiscal resources, ultimately undermining welfare provisions.

Economic development in the EU was hence durably impacted by the ideological framework in vogue at the time of the signature of the Maastricht Treaty. The ordoliberal doctrine negatively impacted investment and growth prospects by scaremongering about the impact of deficits and debts, praising the benefits of austerity and setting its own criteria to say how macroeconomic stability should be defined. Neoliberal ideas also ran high, with countries across the EU following doctrines of lower state intervention, supply-side structural reforms and labour market flexibility, regardless of their impact on individuals and their social structures.

To what extent have recent evolutions, including the Covid-19 pandemic, affected this reality?

The Covid-19 pandemic has led to a sea change in both economic thinking and policymaking at EU and member state level. At long last, governments are considered as part and parcel of the solution to the pandemic, rather than the problem. This trend also reflects more structural trends. The global economy is marked by profound structural change, be it in terms of climate change, digitalization and artificial intelligence, or soaring inequalities. Finally, with Brexit, the meaning of Europe has changed to an extent, which we fail to fully appreciate yet. Both new challenges and new opportunities will arise in terms of the EU's relationship with its borders, the civil service, services, taxation, etc. All these developments not only created new pressures on governments to act; they also revealed the need for better-coordinated action at the supranational level to address challenges of a global nature.

Besides, the current context of permanent uncertainty provides an opportunity for new ideas to be taken up about how to deal with an economy that is increasingly vulnerable to pandemics, economic shocks and the wider consequences of climate change. There is now a relative consensus over the need for governments to conduct the necessary investment for the decarbonization and digitalization of the EU's industry. At the same time, there is also growing recognition of the importance of providing more effective social protection safety nets to limit the impact of shocks on individuals and societies.

How should EU institutions transform themselves to bring economic governance closer to citizens' concerns?

Today, there is a mismatch between the goals we set ourselves in the context of the Sustainable Development Goals (SDGs) and the

EU's economic governance framework, which provides the means according to which such objectives should be pursued. The first step should be to agree on the 'first principles': that is, the vision underlying the EU's economic governance framework. Economic instruments are tools, not ends. Trying to make European countries agree on a development strategy will assuredly continue to face resistance among bureaucracies who are willing to pursue economic governance 'by rules' as they knew them. This is where political leadership should come in and set the tone, as was recently done with the adoption of the European Pillar of Social Rights (EPSR) and the corresponding Action Plan.

We also need to improve democratic accountability in the EU decision-making process. Too often there is a tendency to involve many political actors only at the approval stage. This is particularly valid for economic governance in the EU, where decisions in areas with low salience but high socioeconomic relevance are taken among like-minded finance ministry officials as they escalate through the decision-making process. In the end, a choice between limited policy options is made – in ECOFIN, say, or in the Governing Council of the European Central Bank. This approach should evolve and allow for issues as critical as the EU's overall fiscal stance or European Central Bank (ECB) policy to be more regularly discussed in the European Parliament, thereby helping to reconcile 'policy with politics' in the EU's economic governance.

THE ROLE OF EUROPEAN ECONOMIC COORDINATION

European integration in the fields of economic and social policy has been asymmetric from the beginning. EU governments certainly hold important prerogatives over how they wish to regulate their economy, e.g. over taxation, industrial policy or wage negotiations. And yet EU monetary and fiscal integration has considerably deepened since the adoption of the Maastricht Treaty. Monetary policy is now in the hands of the European Central Bank, which sets the tone for nineteen member states. EU institutions also have considerable responsibility as far as economic integration is concerned, including in areas related to the single market, competition policy and trade policy. By contrast, employment and social policies largely remain a national prerogative. Indeed, EU welfare state regimes widely differ in terms of pension rights, access to health care, the labour market and education policies. And whereas the Lisbon strategy demanded that equal attention be provided to both competitiveness and social cohesion, the 'soft-law' coordination mechanisms that are supposed to boost the latter have lost traction since the mid 2000s. Above all, austerity became the biggest game in town during the Great Recession, with social cohesion and material deprivation often being relegated to secondary concerns.

How should the coordination of national policies (e.g. in the European Semester) be redirected to support a long-term development strategy?

The sovereign debt crisis has been a game changer for the coordination of national policies by EU institutions. Years of austerity in the eurozone's periphery have been associated with the rise of nationalist and Eurosceptic parties. At the same time, concerns have arisen that downward competition between welfare regimes will create a new race to the bottom, undermining the sustainability of welfare provisions. The adoption of the EPSR, which can be seen as a response to these developments, is incontestably a promising avenue with regards to the EU's long-term development prospects. Yet imbalances remain between the social and economic governance frameworks. The new coordination tools implemented during the eurozone crisis (including, notably, the Fiscal Compact and the Macroeconomic Imbalance Procedure) essentially strengthened the EU's macroeconomic surveillance prerogatives. Accordingly, the dominance of budgetary rules led to increasing power in the hands of the ECOFIN Council, reinforcing the governance of the EU's economy by rules and numbers only.

Public support for effective welfare provisions across the EU has reached new heights in the wake of the pandemic. This strengthens the need to put social rights on the same footing as the four economic freedoms in EU policy coordination. On the political level, the EPSR should be incorporated into the EU Treaties by means of a Social Protocol. Governance should also be revised: objectives and benchmarks should be set for all coordinated policies from the European Semester and the Annual Sustainable Growth Strategy (ASGS). Benchmarks could start with minimum standards that grow over time to take account of the specific context in each EU member state, as per the example of the minimum wage proposed in the EPSR Action Plan. Monitoring should include socioeconomic impact assessments, facilitating policy learning. Finally, institutional reform will be needed, assigning greater power to those who make social policy and making the coordination cycles more democratic. At EU level, joint meetings between ECOFIN and EPSCO in the Council should become common practice in the European Semester, as should an annual Macroeconomic and Social Dialogue in the European Parliament. At the country level, governments should be mandated to discuss country reports and country-specific recommendations in the parliament and to systematically involve regional partners in the design of development plans involving EU funds.

Should different rules and processes apply to eurozone and non-eurozone EU members?

Being a member of the eurozone has consequences for economic and social policy at the national level. In the euro area, monetary policy is run by the European Central Bank, which sets a common interest rate for all of its members. When an external shock hits, countries generally rely on a devaluation of their currency to restore their competitiveness. This mechanism no longer applies to countries in the eurozone. The same holds when the national currency is pegged to the euro, as is the case in Denmark today. It is not the case in Sweden, though, which operates under a floating exchange rate. Sweden can therefore rely on a wider toolkit to deal with unfair competition arising when euro area countries engage in tax or social dumping. Euro integration obliges further solidarity among its members. The rise of (youth) unemployment rates in Southern Europe during the Great Recession should provide impetus for fiscal and social policy to be considered equally in the management of the eurozone. Completing the EMU is hence key in this respect.

Does this mean that countries who are not members of the euro area should not be included in initiatives such as the European Pillar of Social Rights? The inclusion of all EU members in the EPSR shows that promoting an ambitious socioeconomic agenda for all member states does not have to stand in the way of completing the EMU. Structural pressures – be it decarbonization, digitalization, demographic change or the rise of the platform economy – are largely the same in all EU member states. Welfare protection regimes do not only reflect centuries of battle for social citizenship.They can also be an opportunity for improving the resilience and the economic performance of the EU as a whole if we manage to ensure that these are also designed in a way that is fiscally sustainable. Challenges stand in the way. Politically, the scepticism of the 'frugals' to agree on a common EU debt issuance mechanism suggests that fiscal solidarity remains hard to achieve. Democratic constraints, expressed, for instance, in the repeated challenges presented by the German Constitutional Court, will also need to be duly appreciated. And yet, as the adoption of the Fiscal Compact during the Great Recession highlighted, there is no reason why these barriers could not eventually be overcome. The strong support of the European public for effective welfare provisions ultimately obliges us to consider their contribution to the sustainability of the European integration project.

THE EU'S ECONOMIC, FISCAL AND MONETARY POLICIES

Immense progress has been made in recent months with the adoption by the ECB of the Pandemic Emergency Purchasing Programme (PEPP), agreement being reached over the Next Generation EU and SURE programmes, and the temporary suspension of the Stability and Growth Pact. The risk that the EU's overall response may be too limited macroeconomically remains, but as things stand, the EU's economic governance is much better equipped than it was before the pandemic. Today, instruments that had been debated for years are on the table and, importantly, there is also broad consensus in policymaking and academic circles that the EU's economic framework has to evolve to become more responsive to a wide range of challenges. The challenge now is to ensure that this shift in macroeconomic thinking is sustained and also that it trickles down to the realm of EU monetary, fiscal and industrial policy.

What roles should monetary and fiscal policy play?

The ECB monetary policy has proven to be a crucial asset for safeguarding the euro against financial market pressures over the last decade. The institution has managed to surmount the challenge posed by the different risk exposures faced by sovereign countries, acting as a de facto fiscal authority and widening the (otherwise very restricted) fiscal space of some euro area governments. While the Pandemic Emergency Purchase Programme has been helpful during the pandemic, debt levels have soared in many member states and more permanent mechanisms, such as the creation of an EU 'safe asset', should be considered to avoid the possibility of some governments restraining their spending efforts during the recovery phase. As of now, the eurozone's monetary policy remains more conservative than that of the United States Federal Reserve, whose chairman, Jerome H. Powell, recently recognized the need to increase the focus on boosting employment, albeit at the expense of some overheating of the economy. Due attention should clearly continue to be given to the negative social consequences of overheating the economy, but in the current environment, marked as it is by low inflationary pressures and high labour market disturbances, targeting full employment should be put on a par with fighting inflation. Looking ahead, we need to consider how the ECB could take action to stop the purchase of 'brown assets' and move to the exclusive creation of green bonds that support EU climate mitigation objectives.

EU fiscal policy is also in dire need of an overall. The deal that was struck on Next Generation EU does conjure up a historical breakthrough for the EU, but now we need to transform temporary tools such as the Resilience and Recovery Plans (RRP) and the SURE programme into permanent mechanisms. Priorities in this regard would be to provide the EU with a long-term debt issuance capacity and with an unemployment reinsurance fund.

As far as national policy is concerned, the EU's response to the pandemic also proved more flexible than it did during the Great Recession as it provided EU countries with additional fiscal space in a *countercyclical* manner. A trap we now face is to fight only for such 'escape clauses' when what is needed is a new set of rules that are better adapted to the macroeconomic environment we face today. Issuing debt always comes with consequences: interest rates on government bonds tend to benefit wealthier households, while debt reduction is often performed through tax increases or spending cuts that asymmetrically impact the economically worst off. Yet debt and deficit *rules*, as they stand, are by essence unable to manage important contingency situations. To remedy this, fiscal *standards* would be more appropriate to assess sustainably in context. Such standards should only apply to expenditures that fall outside public investments that are deemed to benefit future generations. The latter would be subject to a 'golden rule' that incentivizes investments in infrastructure and social investment programmes. This debate on the definition of what constitutes sustainable expenditure would also allow us to revise our conception of the way we define debt sustainability (singling out debt servicing costs, for example) and propose differentiated debt reduction pathways.

But EU economic governance requires a rebalancing that goes beyond the creation of new macroeconomic stabilization instruments. Not only do we need to ensure that countries with limited fiscal space do not end up in a debt overhang that would threaten the EU's economy as a whole, but we must also ensure that those with fiscal space actually invest in the assets that Europe needs to address its challenges. Today, the European Commission is too often discussing fiscal issues with individual countries on the basis of technical rules. For the EU to become the 'growth engine' it once aspired to be, EU governments should be provided with a common space to debate what a desirable fiscal stance would be. Having an annual Macroeconomic and Social Dialogue in the European Parliament would allow for this aggregate fiscal policy stance to be regularly adjusted. Appropriate mechanisms would be associated with this procedure to allow for reducing the risks of moral hazard but also to take appropriate account of those economies most adversely affected by the aggregate stance.

How should industrial policy in the EU evolve?

Completing the EMU should also clearly involve designing a new strategy, comprised of clear objectives and tools, for European industry. In recent decades, EU institutions have primarily focused on boosting industrial competitiveness, in line with the restrictive provisions of the EU Treaties. Accordingly, most official EU publications focus on the issue of the technological frontier. Currently, the rules that govern the single market serve as a pan-European mechanism for regulating European industry by creating a level playing field for companies. The EU's trade and investment agenda aims to guarantee economic openness at the global level. Besides, both the European Semester and EU cohesion policy have increasingly been used to incentivize reforms aimed at transforming national economies in line with new global trends. The priorities of the Resilience and Recovery Fund should be understood as a continuation of this agenda.

Looking ahead, the EU yet clearly needs a more comprehensive industrial strategy. Setting a *direction* for industrial change is essential. A proper industrial policy should be based on a shared vision and appropriate tools to support the decarbonization and digitalization of industry, to promote the creation of 'good jobs', and to tackle growing geographical and social disparities. A first step would be to define the major strategic and priority areas. The Covid-19 pandemic revealed that Europe must organize itself to meet its own needs and tt cannot depend on the rest of the world for all of its goods and services. Appeals to autarky are unrealistic and irresponsible. Equally, though, as the Commission itself once claimed, globalization needs to be 'harnessed' by appropriate EU rules and standards, in the spirit of the Paris Agreement or the General Data Protection Regulation (GDPR). We also need to build on and improve the European Green Deal by stepping up efforts on our climate mitigation ambitions and devoting the necessary means to them, including through a transformation of the European Investment Bank to become the world's main financier of climate action. For the EU to act as a 'policy entrepreneur', a shift in the priorities of the European Semester will be required: away from fiscal discipline and towards long-term development targets. Existing fiscal boards should be replaced by industrial policy advisers, and the competitiveness councils by industrial policy councils. Equally, the design of the National Resilience and Recovery Plans (NRRPs), conceived as bottom-up exercises, should be seen as an opportunity to decentralize the planning process, further engage lower levels of governance (such as regional and local authorities) and increase the involvement of social partners and civil society actors.

How should the European budget and the tax system be updated to address new challenges and benefit from new sources?

The EU's fiscal capacity remains very limited. In the United States, government spending at the federal level represents 20 per cent of total US Gross National Income (GNI). By contrast, the EU budget amounts to around 1 per cent of European GNI (or less than 3 per cent if we consider intergovernmental spending as a whole). Overall, EU spending hence represents only about 2 per cent of the total of public expenditures in the EU. The deal reached by EU governments on the 2021–2027 Multiannual Financial Framework (MFF) and on Next Generation EU represents a major step forward in this context. Firstly, the agreement on joint borrowing constitutes a leap forward in terms of European integration. It also crystallizes a paradigm shift in terms of the role of investment and the public sector in both the crisis resolution and the recovery phases. The plan will finally incentivize member states to devise development or recovery plans, thereby adding purpose to the largely static definition of budgetary priorities often witnessed in EU budgetary negotiations. There are, nevertheless, some shortcomings with this decision, starting with the temporary nature of the plan, which is scheduled to be phased out in 2026. There are also risks that the governance and fragmentation of the funds will lead to slow disbursement, mitigating their expected impact. Finally, the extension on the rebates secured by the 'frugals' leaves a bitter taste as it sets a long-lasting precedent that we might have hoped would have died out with Brexit.

Negotiations over Next Generation EU also brought the issue of the EU's own resources back to the fore. Changing the structure of EU own resources should not be understood as automatically leading to the EU raising new taxes, and nor should it be equated to an increasing tax burden for EU citizens. Rather, it should be seen as an opportunity to reconsider the composition of resources and to identify synergies between EU and national resources. Furthermore, by considering new revenue streams beyond the EU's own resources, this debate provides an opportunity to abandon the *'juste retour'* logic and allow the GNI-based share of the EU's own resources (which has considerably increased since the 1990s). Instead, the new structure for the EU's own resources should be designed to support EU policies in key areas of EU competence, helping to strengthen climate action or reduce the fiscal heterogeneity of the Union.

Several proposals are now on the table. Green taxes benefit from the highest level of political support, with taxation of unrecycled plastics waste receiving most support of all. Its yield to the EU budget is expected to be limited, though, with revenue also diminishing over time. Ensuring that a high percentage of this tax revenue goes to the EU budget should be considered a minimum requirement for the EU to maintain the ambitions it set itself for the European Green Deal. Other proposals include a tax on goods imported from non-EU countries that have low standards in terms of climate friendliness, and an extension of the CO_2 emission trading system to the aviation and maritime sectors. We should not see these proposals as alternatives but as a good policy mix for the wider purpose of climate mitigation. Beyond climate issues, a final issue for concerns relates to the corporation tax gap. This is the revenue loss that we estimate to be occurring due to tax avoidance by tech firms. The tax gap is thought to be €100 billion per year, or about two-thirds of the EU budget. Given the resistance of the United States to addressing this problem, tackling the issue would have been seen as impossible a year ago, but recent declarations by the Biden administration improve the chances of an agreement being reached in OECD/G20 negotiations. Short of a wider deal, the prospects for a digital tax or a single market levy would improve. Overall, it should be kept in mind that the EU may most benefit from agreeing to limited but *long-lasting* contributions to its own resources.

THE INSTITUTIONAL ARCHITECTURE OF THE EU'S ECONOMIC GOVERNANCE

What would a republican framework for EU economic governance look like?

Res Publica is about the effective governance of *public goods*: that is, the services made available to all members of the society. The construction of the European project has, by and large, occurred gradually, according to a logic of 'spillover effects', with integration in some areas (the single market) incentivizing the pooling of common resources in others (monetary policy). This process led to the creation of essentially two types of EU public goods.

First, 'club goods' are accessible to all European citizens. These are *inclusive* public goods, and they create incentives to cooperate and consent. For such types of goods, an agent may be needed to ensure that members play by the rules and to reduce asymmetric information. The four freedoms of the single market, which essentially require the Commission to act as a referee, are a good example.

Second, 'common resources goods' depend on scarce resources and constitute *exclusive* public goods. Member states have no incentive to cooperate – in fact, they have some incentive to compete. For instance, in the case of monetary policy, one member of the eurozone may be tempted to engage in excessive borrowing (lending) at the cost of interest rates increasing (falling) for others. Here, a single authority is required to enforce the optimal option, while relying on the collective choice of all individuals who are affected by these externalities.

Making intergovernmental governance work in spite of the absence of incentives for cooperation is a complex task for European institutions in the context of the E(M)U's economic governance. The option of forcing cooperation through rules has not proven to be effective and has hampered economic growth in the last decades. As a matter of fact, exclusive European public goods require the central agency to play a more proactive role than in the case of inclusive public goods. Such conditions are met in the case of the ECB, which can rely on the appropriate amount of leeway to define the EU's monetary stance. The same cannot yet be said for fiscal policy. In theory, for EU economic governance to prove both effective and legitimate, the definition of the aggregate fiscal stance should be moved up to the EU level while being controlled by the European Parliament as the only institution that directly represents all European citizens.

Besides, the EU *sui generis* model invites us to appreciate additional dimensions in the definition of public goods. First, given the multidimensional nature of policymaking in the EU, legitimate decision making suggests that the nature of public goods should be differentiated based on the policy communities involved in a given policy area. Second, given the multilevel governance framework of the EU and its attachment to the subsidiarity principle, control at different levels of governance is key to further legitimizing this process. Here, a distinction should be made between actors having a *vote* and those having a *voice*, as is sometimes done in the context of debates on EMU integration involving non-eurozone EU members.

What can we learn from federal experiences in other countries about the distribution of competences in EU economic governance?

The European Union today may look like a federal system comparable to that of the United States or Germany. According to the definition of 'fiscal federalism', though, several elements are missing for the EU to be considered a federal entity. Unlike the United States, the EU lacks the coercive power to enforce its laws, largely relying on sticks and carrots that have little impact on the economies of the larger member states. National governments also have the exclusive power over amending the treaties of the EU. And finally, spending and tax powers at the EU level are limited. In short, the EU system is closer to the 'cooperative' German model in institutional terms. But the central level here has neither the legal competencies nor the financial resources of the German federal government. At the same time, the EU's strict budgetary rules also contrast with the regime in place in highly decentralized federal systems such as that of the United States or Switzerland, where federal government has little control over state budgets. Today, by combining strong fiscal decentralization with centralized fiscal rules, the EU in fact provides a model largely inconsistent with any model of fiscal federalism.

How could EU's economic governance be rebalanced to allow for a more effective system? Institutional reforms could go in one of two directions. A first option would be for the EU's economic governance to become more federalized by centralizing and integrating additional spending and taxation powers. To achieve this, the EU would be given further regulatory powers to directly provide public goods and it would be authorized to raise the necessary revenue to fund these activities. An alternative option would be to keep most stabilization, distribution and allocation responsibilities in the hands of EU member states but to free them from the shadow of fiscal austerity, thereby providing them with more discretion to invest in, say, infrastructure and welfare provision.

Today's EU economic governance framework combines elements of both options. In the wake of the Great Recession, which revealed flaws in the original design of the EMU, EU institutions favoured an approach of *fiscal coordination*. As the Covid-19 pandemic hit, the issue of the *stabilization capacity* of the E(M)U was brought back to the fore, while the issue of redistribution also made its way onto the Council's table. In the same vein, EU initiatives such as the ECB's Outright Monetary Transactions programme, the European Stability Mechanism and Next Generation EU have played a crucial role in addressing macroeconomic imbalances. Meanwhile, the imposition of tight fiscal *rules*, originally trespassing on long-fought-for national welfare protection regimes, eventually backfired. Fewer rules with more flexibility may ultimately be what EU economic governance most critically needs.

Aspirations: empowering progressive ideas in the EU's economic governance by matching 'policy with politics'

By Alvaro Oleart

For far too long, issues related to the economic governance of the EU have mostly been discussed in technocratic terms, removing the political dimension from the policy- and decision-making processes. These depoliticized discussions over economic policy at the European level – which mean that political decisions are presented as if they are 'technical' or 'administrative' choices, and as if there are no alternatives – explains why Vivien Schmidt (2006) has conceptualized the EU's policymaking as 'policy without politics'. The depoliticization of EU-level political discussions contrasts with the 'politics without policy' that exists at the national level, in which heated politicized discussions over economic policy have a relatively minor policy impact because most important decisions are taken at the European level by national governments in intergovernmental settings.

On the rare occasions on which we have seen EU economic governance being politicized, it has tended to take place by pitting EU member states against one another. The single most important episode of politicization took place during the eurozone crisis, in which EU member states were set against each other, resulting in a heated conflict that peaked when most EU member states, as well as the Troika, opposed the attempts of the Greek government, led by the left-wing party SYRIZA, to restructure the country's debt. This type of politicization, led by national governments against other national governments, mirrors the intergovernmental processes that continue to drive EU economic governance.

Alternatively, in contrast to depoliticization and a rather antagonistic type of politicization, it is possible to imagine and build an

EU economic governance institutional framework that facilitates transnational politics within the EU – one that matches 'policy with politics'. As the Covid-19 crisis has emphasized, EU member states are inextricably linked to one another. The political–economic processes in one member state have a direct influence on other member states. As all EU member states are in the same political–economic boat, the time has come for national governments to open the cabins of national politics and bring non-executive actors into the various streams of European political debate. Such institutional change would embolden the formation of transnational coalitions, which facilitate politicization along transnational lines, rather than pitting 'frugal' countries against 'Southern' ones, 'creditor' against 'debtor' countries, or 'Western' countries against 'Eastern' ones. Instead, matching 'policy with politics' will be accomplished by encouraging the formation of pan-European coalitions of progressive actors that oppose conservative or neoliberal coalitions.

Progressive ideas and movements already travel beyond national borders. Movements such as #MeToo, Fridays For Future and Black Lives Matter illustrate the increasingly transnational flow of politics. However, in a context in which transnational politics in the EU is more necessary than ever, the current institutional set-up of the EU's economic governance does not support the channelling of this energy. In order to make society more feminist, more environmentalist, more antiracist and generally more equal, it is necessary to address social justice from a transnational perspective, not an intergovernmental one. This mismatch between the increasingly transnational flow of progressive ideas in the EU and the rather intergovernmental EU institutional structure and dominant technocratic discourse is likely to cause further dissatisfaction if the EU is unable to address it.

The Multiannual Financial Framework 2021–27 and the €750 billion Next Generation EU recovery package, both of which were agreed during the European Council summit of July 2020, offer a particularly good opportunity to democratize EU economic governance. As it has been acknowledged that the Covid-19 crisis is a European one – one that requires a policy approach that goes beyond the nation-state, as illustrated by the unprecedented European mutualization of debt – EU economic governance structures should adapt accordingly. A possible way of boosting 'policy with politics' in the EU's economic governance structure is to increase the weight of the European Parliament at the expense of the Council and to bring national parliaments into the EU policy- and decision-making processes in such a way that national political parties and civil society organizations are given incentives to pay more attention to the European level. This would contribute to bridging the divide between European and national politics. A likely consequence of this move would be the creation of transnational alliances between national parties and civil society across borders, thereby energizing transnational politics rather than pitting EU member state governments against one another.

Not only would matching 'policy with politics' at the European level democratize EU economic governance, but it would also affect its power relations. This was the case when the Transatlantic Trade and Investment Partnership (TTIP) was defeated by the pan-European mobilization of a coalition of progressive political parties, civil society organizations and trade unions (Oleart 2021). As neoliberalism is unlikely to be defeated through technocratic discourse and intergovernmental processes, fostering the democratization of EU policymaking, transnational activism and bridging the divide between EU and national politics are preconditions for bringing progressive ideas into the EU's economic governance.

REFERENCES

Oleart, A. 2020. *Framing TTIP in the European Public Spheres: Towards an Empowering Dissensus for EU Integration.* Palgrave Macmillan.

Schmidt, V. A. 2006. *Democracy in Europe: The EU and National Polities.* Oxford University Press.

European economic governance: key issues to assess its recent past and its desirable evolution

By Vivien Schmidt

In the decade preceding the Covid-19 pandemic, but also even before that, the EU's economic governance suffered from a range of problems. Eurozone crisis governance involved governing by rules and ruling by numbers – with the wrong rules and numbers. Ones that did not work. The result has been too little investment and low growth, as well as continued macroeconomic divergence. Globalization also went too far, leaving the EU vulnerable to breakdowns in global supply chains when it needed them most, to digital platforms that control content and avoid taxes, to deindustrialization in Europe, and to citizen discontent. Such discontent has had a range of socioeconomic sources, as workers increasingly felt left behind, suffered from stagnant wages, from bad jobs with bad benefits, from increasing poverty and rising inequalities (gendered and otherwise), and from diminishing opportunities (especially for the young). The discontent has also manifested itself in sociocultural concerns, in particular about loss of social status, and has engendered political pushback, including the politics of 'taking back control', the decline of mainstream parties and the rise of Eurosceptic anti-system parties and movements.

Blame these problems on what you will: the structure of capitalism and the driving force of the market; political divisions between EU actors; the institutions and laws that make positive-sum decision making so difficult. But do not lose sight of ideas: ordoliberal ideas about macroeconomic stability, the dangers of deficits and debt and the benefits of austerity – to the detriment of investment and growth; and neoliberal ideas about the need for ever freer markets and a smaller and smaller state, the glories of competitiveness and the advantages of labour market flexibility – ignoring increasing social precarity and insecurity.

Importantly, things have changed since the Covid-19 pandemic. There is now a recognition of the need for new ideas about how to deal with a European economy that is being challenged not just by health and economic disasters but also by climate change. We need to rethink the European Economic Governance Framework beyond the old ideas, to repair the damage wrought both by the management of the euro crisis and by unmanaged globalization. New ideas call for an enhanced role for the state as entrepreneur: to promote growth and provide investment to meet the challenges of the green transition and the digital transformation while ensuring greater social equity with more democracy.

So how do we get from here to there? To assess the desirable evolution of the European framework for economic governance, we need to consider how to change the policies and procedures while also enhancing democracy. In what follows, I suggest some pathways we might take.

MONETARY POLICY AND MACROECONOMIC COORDINATION

There are many ideas about what the European Central Bank (ECB) could do to further enhance the EU's economic prospects through its role in monetary policy and macroeconomic coordination – ideas beyond its already ambitious Pandemic Emergency Purchase Programme (PEPP). First and foremost, the ECB should move from an almost exclusive focus on the primary objectives set out in its charter to the secondary objectives. This could mean giving itself a target of full employment on a par with fighting inflation, of ending 'neutral' bond-buying while creating green bonds for the environment, or even of providing so-called helicopter money that offers direct support to households in need. Finally, it could create an EU 'safe asset' while solving the problem of national debt overhang by having the European Stability Mechanism buy up a portion of the sovereign bonds held by the ECB.

Importantly, in making any such moves, the ECB would benefit from enhancing its accountability and transparency while democratizing the process. One way of doing this would be to increase ECB accountability to the European Parliament: through formal requirements for ECB–EP dialogue, say. Another would be to create venues for more democratic debate and deliberation about EU macroeconomic governance. Let us call this the 'Great Macroeconomic Dialogue' and have a yearly conference to outline the grand economic strategies for the coming year, making space for dialogue between the ECB and other actors – not only with the European Parliament but also with the Commission and the Council, as well as with representatives from industry, trade unions and civil society from across Europe.

INDUSTRIAL POLICY AND THE EUROPEAN SEMESTER

The EU has also made great strides forward with its temporary Resilience and Recovery Fund as part of Next Generation EU. But this kind of industrial policy needs to be reinforced through the development of permanent EU-level debt. Think of this as an EU sovereign wealth fund that issues debt on the global markets and uses the proceeds to invest, through grants to member states, in education, training and income support, in greening the economy and digitally connecting people, and in big physical infrastructure projects. The fund could also be used to invest in EU-level cross-border endeavours as well as for redistributive purposes in a range of innovative EU funds: an unemployment reinsurance fund, a refugee integration fund, an EU fund for just mobility, and a poverty alleviation fund.

The next question, then, is how to ensure that such new industrial and social policies succeed. For this, the European Semester would be the ideal vehicle for oversight and assistance, but only if we rethink both its purpose and its rules. The eurozone's restrictive deficit and debt rules clearly need to be changed to meet the new circumstances and goals. The rules should be permanently suspended and replaced with, say, a set of 'fiscal standards' to assess sustainability in context. These would apply to any expenditure that falls outside public investment that is deemed to benefit future generations (the golden rule). Moreover, public debt itself should be ignored with regard to public investment if it is sustainable (meaning the government can borrow at a rate lower than the average rate of growth of GDP). One of the lessons of the past decade is that you cannot cut your way out of public debt through austerity; the only way out is through growth. In this vein, another initiative should be to eliminate the debt brake from national constitutional legislation, which was a hindrance not only for those without the 'fiscal space', who could not invest, but also for those who had it and did not invest.

European Semester procedures also need to be reimagined. The Semester provides amazing architecture for coordination, but for what purpose? At the inception of the eurozone crisis, it was converted from a soft-law coordinating mechanism (akin to the 'open method of coordination') into a top-down punitive mechanism of control. But it subsequently came to be applied with greater and greater flexibility even as it became the object of increasing politicization within and between EU institutional actors. Today, in light of the pandemic response, the Commission's mission has changed completely, with a new focus on the National Resilience and Recovery Plans (NRRPs) as bottom-up exercises by member states' governments.

The question now is what is the best way to exercise coordinating oversight while decentralizing and democratizing the process? For overall assessments, one way would be to replace the Macroeconomic Imbalance Procedure, which ended up mainly as a discussion between the Commission and individual member states, with a more coordinated approach via something like a new macroeconomic dialogue, possibly as part of the Great Macroeconomic Dialogue mentioned above. As for individual member states, more fine-tuned assessments of where they are in the business cycle, of their growth outlooks, and of their prospects of meeting their investment targets could help inform Commission recommendations. Also of use would be to transform the existing fiscal boards into industrial policy advisers, and to turn the competitiveness councils into industrial policy councils, while decentralizing the planning process for NRRPs to regional and local levels while democratizing it by bringing in social partners and civil society actors. Moreover, while national governments should take their plans to their national parliaments for approval, the EU should involve the European Parliament much more at different stages of the European Semester while also linking it more fully to the Social Dialogues in the context of the European Pillar of Social Rights.

INTERNATIONAL TRADE AND COMPETITION POLICY

The question of how to manage globalization going forward is also of great importance. It has become clear to everyone that, while global value chains should continue, European and national supply chains need to be recreated and relocalized through the inshoring of a portion of Europe's manufacturing capability. The EU needs to think globally about promoting European champions, and it needs to think locally about protecting infant industries where they do not endanger the single market. Moreover, if the EU continues with single market rules on competition that demand a level playing field, then it should revise state aid rules upwards, to allow member states to invest much more heavily in national industries in critical areas. Finally – and this should go without saying – the EU should deal once and for all with tax justice issues. It should abolish tax havens and distortive taxation practices within the EU, and it should ensure that member states collect the taxes they are due from corporations (and, for that matter, from their citizens).

SOCIAL AND LABOUR POLICY

Finally, the EU needs to revitalize its approach to social and labour policy. At the very least, the EU needs to move from labour market flexibility to more labour market security, particularly through ensuring that part-time, temporary and gig workers have the same social rights and protections as full-time workers. It should also facilitate unionization to ensure upward pressure on wages through bargaining; it should create common European unemployment reinsurance schemes; and it should set a minimum wage (or equivalent) to ensure against unfair competition and a race to the bottom in compensation. Finally, how about providing universal benefits, such as a guaranteed (basic) minimum annual income, funded by the digital dividend? (That is, by having digital platforms pay for licensing our data.)

CONCLUSION

In summary, there are lots of ideas out there about how to improve the European Framework for Economic Governance. Now is the moment to implement them to establish more managed globalization with a more proactive and democratized 'state' at the EU level. One that is able to respond to citizens' needs and demands; to ensure their economic well-being and their social rights while enhancing their political participation. Only in so doing can we hope to counter the siren calls of national populism.

REFERENCES

Schmidt, V. A. 2020. *Europe's Crisis of Legitimacy: Governing by Rules and Ruling by Numbers in the Eurozone.* Oxford University Press.

Avgouleas, E., and Micossi, S. 2020. On selling sovereigns held by the ECB to the ESM: institutional and economic policy implications. *CEPS Policy Insight*, PI2021-04, March.

Longergan, E., and Blyth, M. 2018. *Angrynomics*. Newcastle: Agenda.

Blanchard, O., Leandro, A., and Zettelmeyer, J. 2021. Redesigning EU fiscal rules: from rules to standards. Working Paper WP 21-1, February, Peterson Institute for International Economics.

A European economic policy mix to support the European project in the long term

By Michael Landesmann

Thus far, at least, monetary and fiscal policy have worked better together, and in a more timely manner, during the Covid-19 crisis than they did during the financial crisis, but it is still early days (at the time of writing, it is only one year since the Covid-19 shock hit). The real test of the willingness to tackle the important deficiencies in the macroeconomic policy setup that are present at the EU/eurozone level is still to come.

From an intellectual standpoint, there is now widespread awareness – following the experience of the financial crisis – that there have to be major changes/reforms to the way macroeconomic policy is conducted at the EU/eurozone level. This awareness has existed for quite some time among academics and economists, but over the last decade it has also trickled down to the general public as well as affecting the views of a wider set of policy-makers. This intellectual shift has been further strengthened during the current crisis.

There has also been a shift with regard to the need for an industrial policy and, to some extent, also with regard to the development of a strengthened social policy pillar at the EU level: witness, for example, the generally warm reception that the SURE programme has received.

WHAT SHOULD WE FOCUS ON?

In this chapter I intend to relate some of the main themes of a forthcoming FEPS report ('Completing the European recovery strategy:

fiscal, monetary and industrial policy' (FEPS-IEV)) that a group of us has been working on.

The basic idea that guided the authors of the report was the importance of confronting the major 'centrifugal forces' present within the EU/eurozone at the intercountry level and also within member countries. How can reforms of the EU/eurozone policy framework be made more successful at countering these 'centrifugal forces'?

Firstly, what were/are these centrifugal forces? Figure 1 presents a rather well-known 'stylized fact' about the impact of the 2008/9 financial crisis: the rather dramatic widening of the income gap between the 'euro area south' and the 'euro area north'. Most of the thinking regarding reform of the EU/eurozone policy framework is directed towards avoiding a repeat of this experience in the wake of the Covid-19 crisis and also to tackling the longer-term structural problems of the European economy. These are what create such a widening of economic experiences, with all their detrimental social and political impacts.

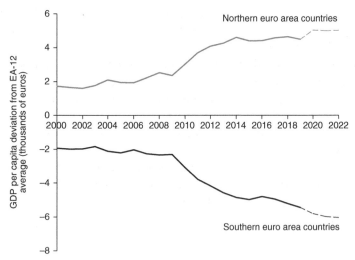

Figure 1. Population-weighted GDP per capita for northern versus southern euro area countries (difference to EA-12 average). (Data source: AMECO. Own calculations. Northern EA: Belgium, Germany, Netherlands, Finland, Austria. Southern EA: Greece, Spain, Italy, Portugal.)

THE MACROECONOMIC POLICY SETTING

I will not delve deeply into possible reforms of the monetary policy setting of the eurozone below: firstly, because I am not an expert on this; and secondly, because this is an area in which the expertise of the European Central Bank (ECB) – and the institution's track record in terms of both the development of its arsenal of instruments and the extent and timing of their use – has developed rather well. However, I will point to an important contribution from Willem Buiter: he sees the Eurosystem as a de facto currency board system with nineteen different profit centres, and the main issues he discusses are the dangers of differential risk exposure at the national central bank levels and of sovereign default risks within the Eurosystem. This lies behind both the vulnerability of the EMU set-up and its periodic testing by financial markets, which can pose (and at times has posed) an existential threat. His reform suggestions all aim at risk reduction for the Eurosystem as a whole and for the different national entities within it. His analysis fits well with ours in this report.

Let me move on to fiscal policy.

The fiscal framework that is in place, which relies on specific fiscal rules, was revealed to have a strong pro-austerity bias in the course of the financial crisis and during its aftermath (and would have again during the Covid-19 crisis if the rules had not been suspended). The rules were designed with an asymmetric view of 'externalities': a strong weight was put on the 'moral hazard' that countries would misuse fiscal policy space, thereby placing a burden on the Eurosystem as a whole (through the interest rate channel, and through a de facto reliance on a bailout); whereas little weight was put on the other 'externality', i.e. that in the case of highly interdependent economies (with strong intercountry multipliers) there would be suboptimal fiscal expansion by individual countries. This is what created the argument for much stronger fiscal policy coordination and for joint spending programmes at the EU level.

We of course welcome the initiatives that were taken during the Covid-19 crisis: the new fiscal instruments that were set up at the European level, the most prominent of which is the Recovery and Resilience Facility, but also various other new initiatives such as the

SURE programme, support for SMEs, and also increased funding for EIB-sponsored investment. All of these measures (and, of course, the rather decisive intervention by the ECB) had an important impact on the major issue that is capable of causing a potentially highly differentiated impact of the crisis: namely, the uneven 'fiscal space' that is available to different member countries.

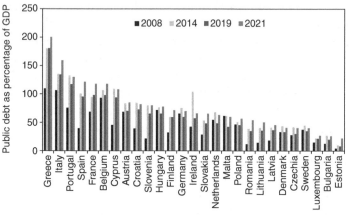

Figure 2. Public debt (as percentage of GDP). (Source: AMECO (Autumn 2020). The public debt:GDP ratio for 2021 is a forecast.)

In principle, the 'fiscal space' for the eurozone as a whole is not different from that available to the United States: the eurozone is a very large economic entity, with a trusted monetary authority, and it is unlikely, were it to issue collectively much more debt, that this would encounter major adverse reactions by financial markets. The issue of uneven 'fiscal space' arises because the ECB cannot be regarded as a 'lender of last resort' to the individual member states (in fact, it is prohibited from being one by its constitution), and fiscal authorities in those member states are therefore under differentiated pressure. Uneven debt levels (see figure 2), and the basic parameters that determine debt sustainability in the longer run (i.e. prospective trend growth of national income, and the interest rates at which countries can borrow to cover fiscal deficits), are basic determinants of whether a country can embark on sufficient fiscal spending in periods of crisis and therefore support a sustained recovery. Hence, without coordinated fiscal policy arrangements and collective support, different member states would be in very uneven positions with regard to implementing fiscal policy programmes that could adequately counter the impact of the crisis. This unevenness would then generate a number of spiralling feedback processes in some of the member countries (negative fiscal multiplier effects affecting incomes, detrimental impacts on the balance sheets of banks and credit conditions and, in turn, on state finances, contracting private and public investment, etc.) that would lead to growing disparities in growth, employment and social conditions, all of which we observed after the financial crisis.

The issue of providing sufficient and more balanced 'fiscal space' has thus been the main issue addressed by EU- and eurozone-level initiatives. The strong actions taken by the ECB were, of course, vital to keep fiscal space open to all member countries and avoid a potentially disastrous spiral of uneven sovereign risk and escalating costs of fiscal policy actions in individual member states. However, more needed to be done.

Regarding 'fiscal rules', it was correct to suspend them during the crisis. The big issue now is when, and in what form, fiscal rules will be reimposed. It is manifestly clear that they cannot be reimposed in their current form: the high increases in debt levels during the current crisis make it completely unrealistic to return to existing rules. Further, the current and likely future scenarios regarding the relationship between prospective rates of interest and prospective longer-term growth rates have changed. Olivier Blanchard, Alvaro Leandro and Jeromin Zettelmeyer (2020) have discussed this change in future scenarios and they argue that we should move away from fiscal rules altogether and instead adopt 'fiscal standards'. This is a more radical proposal than ours, but it deserves serious consideration.

However, we limit ourselves here to proposing wide-ranging reforms of the fiscal rules, mostly because we think that the proposals by Blanchard, Leandro and Zettelmeyer have less of a chance of being realized quickly enough politically and it is essential that reforms of the existing fiscal framework are implemented quickly during the course of the recovery from the Covid-19 crisis.

Firstly, therefore, in line with other economists we favour an 'expenditure rule' rather than the current 'fiscal deficit' rule. It is well known that an expenditure rule is less likely to have procyclical effects. Secondly, our proposal comes with an important addition: it should be combined with a widened interpretation of the 'Golden Rule'.

Under the Golden Rule for public investment, government net fixed (and human) capital investment would no longer be included in the relevant deficit measures for calculating the 'structural' fiscal balance, which would provide additional space for public investment. It would not only serve to loosen the constraints imposed by fiscal rules but would also encourage countries with fiscal space to run more expansionary policies where this is appropriate to ensure a more balanced economic expansion across the eurozone.

In our proposal, we extend the Golden Rule so that the notion of 'investment' should include education and training expenditure. This will be especially important during the recovery and post-recovery phases of the current crisis as long-term technological trends (digitalization), associated changes in work organization and structural policy changes (the Green Deal) will shape and reshape the demand for labour.

On top of this, one has to tackle the hysteretic effects of the current crisis: the fall in the participation rates of the young and of women, and compensation for skill erosion and losses of education and training during the pandemic, which have had differential impacts on different social groups (people with different family backgrounds, minorities, recent migrants and refugees whose integration process was seriously interrupted, etc.).

The application of the Golden Rule will also be important for another reason: there was already a widespread deficiency of investment over a decades-long succession of business cycles. This must be counteracted at national level but also at the EU level, with a sustained investment programme in genuinely European public goods. Obvious areas for such a programme are public health (taking note of the lessons of the pandemic) and transport and energy infrastructure (see the companion paper by Creel *et al.* (2020), which outlines details of such a programme). Such investment programmes could be financed in the same way as Next Generation EU, with the Commission raising money on behalf of the EU, with the debt serviced by payments out of the EU budget, ideally in the form of new EU own resources.

We also emphasize the need to expand social pillar measures such as the SURE programme, but extending it to joint schemes on youth unemployment and training, as well as to the joint unemployment reinsurance schemes that have long been advocated. They can act as important Europe-wide automatic fiscal stabilizers and would therefore also lift fiscal constraints during periods of crises and contribute to widening the social legitimacy of the EU policy framework.

REFERENCES

Blanchard, O., Leandro, A., and Zettelmeyer, J. 2020. Redesigning the EU fiscal rules: from rules to standards. 72nd Economic Policy Panel Meeting, Bundesministerium der Finanzen.

Buiter, W. 2020. *Central Banks as Fiscal Actors: The Drivers of Monetary and Fiscal Policy Space*. Cambridge University Press.

Creel, J., Holzner, M., Saraceno, F., Watt, A., and Wittwer, J. 2020. How to spend it: a proposal for a European Covid-19 recovery programme. Policy Notes and Reports 38, IMK (Macroeconomic Policy Institute).

Gräbner, C., Heimberger, P., Kapeller, J., Landesmann, M., and Schütz, B. 2021. The evolution of debtor–creditor relationships within a monetary union: trade imbalances, excess reserves and economic policy. IFSO Working Paper 10/2021, Johannes Kepler University/wiiw.

Landesmann, M. 2020. Covid-19 crisis: centrifugal vs. centripetal forces in the European Union – a political economic analysis. *Journal of Industrial and Business Economics* 47(3), 439–453.

Landesmann, M., and Székely, I. P. (eds). 2021. *Does EU Membership Facilitate Convergence? The Experience of the EU's Eastern Enlargement* (two volumes). Palgrave Macmillan.

Next Generation EU public finances

By David Rinaldi

The average government spending within the EU is more or less in line with that of the United States, at around 45 per cent of GDP. Central and Eastern Europe member states have lower expenditure than the EU average, while Nordic and other western member states spend more than the United States. What changes dramatically from one side of the Atlantic to the other is, of course, how that public spending is carried out and which level of government is involved. In the United States, about half of total public expenditure is covered by the federal level, with state and local levels responsible for the other half. In Europe, Union-level spending amounts to little more than 1 per cent of EU GDP, or 2 per cent of total European public expenditure. It is this disparity – 2 per cent of European public spending versus 50 per cent of US public spending – that marks the difference between a truly united federal world power and the ongoing European trial.

There is little doubt that if Europe wants to move forward, gain relevance and drive transformation in any field – whether it is strategic autonomy; the green transition; the digital revolution; health, security and industrial policy; etc. – a complete rethinking of, and a big boost to, European public finances is a necessary step.

Now, if we look at the development of the EU budget since its inception, it is eminently clear that we will not achieve something that looks like US federal budgetary firepower anytime soon. The EU moves slowly, with incremental steps. From a budgetary standpoint, in fact – and despite EU enlargement, the global financial crisis, the eurozone crisis, the migration crisis and the climate emergency – the ceiling for the Union's budget in the last two decades has remained capped below 1.3 per cent of European GNI.

The 'doing more with less' strategy has become the norm, with blending and financial instruments trying to leverage scarce public investment as much as possible. Another trend we have witnessed is the creation of other intergovernmental, or temporary, or off-budget solutions. For instance, if we include some intergovernmental spending (e.g. the European Stability Mechanism or the Facility for Turkey) and the temporary €750 billion of Next Generation EU funding, the EU share of European public sector spending increases, but not massively: we may get from roughly 2 per cent of European public spending to approximately 4 per cent. There is still a long way to go to get to the 50 per cent US federal level, but it would at least mean a doubling of the EU financial arm if such tools were made permanent and moved under Community Law.

Interestingly, the initial debate about the creation of Economic and Monetary Union (EMU) that began at the end of the 1960s with the Werner Report (1970) was very much linked to the idea of a big community budget with automatic stabilizers and interregional transfers. When, instead, the Maastricht Treaty came out twenty years later, the focus of EMU had shifted to monetary matters and their connection with fiscal policy, with little to no attention paid to EU budgetary matters.

Now, another thirty years on, we continue to discuss, plan and design the future of our Union with the serious risk of neglecting once again the relevance of taking the EU's public finances to the next level.

NEXT GENERATION OWN RESOURCES

If it is true that, at least from the spending side, some steps forward have been realized, the revenue side has not exactly developed in the direction that the previous Commission had hoped for. First, the relevance of GNI-based own resources is still too sizeable to expect member states to approach budgetary negotiations without that net-balance logic in their minds – logic that is very detrimental to the design of truly functional European expenditure. Second, the statistical VAT own resources have not been reformed; they remain complicated from a computational viewpoint and very limited in terms of magnitude. Third, despite Brexit we have not been able to get rid of rebates, which actually came back onto the agenda of the

Council during the last Multiannual Financial Framework and Next Generation EU negotiations. Austria, Denmark, the Netherlands, Sweden and, to a lesser extent, Germany managed to negotiate decreases in their contributions to the EU.

Most of what should be done towards designing new own resources can be drawn from the research conducted by a Commission-led High-Level Group on Own Resources chaired by Monti in 2014–16, which concluded that: (a) reforming own resources should impact the composition of resources, not necessarily the volume of the EU budget; (b) with higher synergies between EU and national resources, increasing EU resources can be done without increasing the fiscal burden on citizens; and (c) the design of new own resources should 'support EU policies in key areas of EU competence: strengthening the Single Market, environmental protection and climate action, energy union, and reducing the fiscal heterogeneity in the Single Market'. Plus, of course, (d) rebates should be abolished and (e) the GNI-based share of own resources should be reduced, to abandon the net-balance approach – but we already know that political compromises took us in other directions.

The novelty of the July 2020 Council conclusions, in line with point (c), was the opening of a political process to relaunch potential new own resources.

New own resources based on non-recycled plastic waste

This is a new own resource of the Union introduced in January 2021. Typically referred to as the EU plastic tax, it is actually a national contribution by member states to the EU budget based on the weight of non-recycled plastic packaging waste that they produce (€0.80 per kilogramme) – with caps and rebates, of course. This is useful to incentivize member states to put forward concrete action plans on reducing plastic waste, but from a public finance viewpoint it is definitely not a game-changer. Firstly, it may not produce additional fiscal resources unless member states introduce national plastic taxes. Essentially, it is just a shift of resources from national coffers to European ones. Secondly, the resulting contribution to EU own resources is slight and temporary. The optimistic estimates of the

Commission refer to approximately €7 billion per year being raised, amounting to 4 per cent of own resources; national contributions are supposed to remain stable for about five years but will then decrease as plastic waste is minimized.

A Carbon Border Adjustment Mechanism (CBAM) and a reform of the Emissions Trading System (ETS) scheme

As with the national plastic contributions, the objective of these measures is primarily environmental and linked to the implementation of the EU Green Deal. Nonetheless, in this case the impact on EU own resources could be sizeable. The revenue potential of a CBAM (Krenek, Sommer and Schratzenstaller 2019) ranges from €27 billion to €84 billion per year, and it is not expected to phase out as fast as the plastic waste contribution. On top of that, a reform to the ETS that incorporates the aviation and maritime sectors could raise additional revenues of between €3 billion and €10 billion per year across Europe. Various interests are at stake, though: there are geopolitical considerations for the CBAM, and the strategic and sensitive aviation sector also happens to have been rather badly affected by the Covid-19 pandemic.

A digital levy linked to the single market

The 2018 Commission proposal for a Digital Service Tax was a missed opportunity. First, EU leaders failed to find swift agreement, and several member states have now introduced, or are about to introduce, their own national versions of a digital tax, making it more difficult to establish a truly European levy that shifts revenues from national budgets to the EU budget in the near future. Second, when this new tax was proposed, it was not even designed as a potential own resource. Chapter 4 of the 2018 proposal for a Council Directive on the Digital Service Tax reads: 'The proposal will have no implications for the EU budget.' A new consultation is ongoing and a revised proposal will soon be launched, but at this stage this option looks like a sort of plan B for if the G20 negotiation on the OECD proposal for a minimum effective corporate tax rate does not go through.

A financial transaction tax (FTT)

First discussed in 2011 in the aftermath of the global financial crisis to make the financial sector pay its fair share, the FTT has not yet come to life. It was initially estimated to generate €57 billion per year if applied to all transactions in all EU countries. The scope of application and the number of countries has since shrunk so much, though, that expected revenues have now been set at €3.45 billion per year.

Social democrats have been able to get this issue onto the political agenda of the Union again, and the proposal of the German Finance Minister Olaf Scholz does now have a chance of proceeding. Unfortunately, even here the establishment of a new tax, even at the European level, does not necessarily imply a new source of money for the EU budget. European progressives have to make two miracles happen: firstly that the FTT is introduced and secondly that it is levied at the European level.

SOME IDEAS TO INFLUENCE THE DEBATE

In an open process of consultation in which citizens are also involved, it is worth trying to test some innovative and/or radical policy ideas that have not yet made their way onto the political agenda. Although they might initially seem rather politically unfeasible, they have a chance of prompting debate and opening spaces for consensus on a more progressive premise.

A European net wealth tax

Confronting both the Covid-19 and climate emergencies requires an unprecedented volume of public resources. The ability of the wealthiest households to contribute is much higher than was previously thought. Data show that the richest 1 per cent of Europeans hold 32 per cent of Europe's total net wealth, while the poorest half of all households only hold about 4.5 per cent (Kapeller, Leitch and Wildauer 2021). Addressing these growing inequalities while financing transitions and transformations that will benefit everybody could bring a double dividend. Top tax scholars – Piketty (2020), Saez and Zucman *in primis* (Landais, Saez and Zucman 2020) – have been rather vocal about this. A recent FEPS study investigating the revenue potential of an EU net wealth tax confirms that even with a restricted focus on the top 1 per cent of Europe's wealthiest households there could be a sizeable amount of tax revenue raised, even taking tax evasion into account (Kapeller, Leitch and Wildauer 2021). The revenue potential of a European net wealth tax lies between 1.6 per cent and 3.0 per cent of GDP annually. A highly progressive tax model, such as the wealth cap model proposed by Piketty, would have a revenue potential of up to 10 per cent of GDP.

Combining clever design choices with high thresholds and no exemptions, and with a small amount of investment in infrastructure from the EU's tax authorities, would make a European net wealth tax feasible.

A common withholding tax at the EU border

After long debates over the Common Consolidated Corporate Tax Base since the Commission's first proposal in 2011, European countries still have to find consensus about what the base for corporate tax should be. And with the debate on corporate tax shifting towards the G20 level with the recent OECD proposal, there is room to devise other corporate-related taxes that are specific to the EU and its internal market. FEPS has put forward a proposal for a common withholding tax on outgoing dividend, interest and royalty flows at the common border of the EU for intrafirm payments (Lejour and van't Riet 2020). This would be a direct tax on the profit of multinationals being transferred outside the EU. It would not apply on transactions between member states. Such a measure would curb both tax avoidance and tax competition, and, by putting a common floor in the taxation of passive income, it would remain in line with the OECD/G20 discussions on minimum taxation. As is the case for tax receipts on import tariffs at customs borders, this new tax would be levied at the EU border and it is therefore a natural candidate for a truly European own resource.

An EU just mobility fund

Internal devaluation and intra-EU mobility are the available automatic adjustments within the euro area in the case of shocks. Indeed, mobility is low within the EU, and it should be enhanced, but not all mobility flows – particularly if they are protracted over time – are a good signal for the European project. Constant outflows create youth and brain drain, giving rise to dangerous vicious circles: countries in a downturn lose human capital and tax revenues while better-off countries receive a skilled workforce, income taxation and a boost to their internal demand thanks to inflows. From a public finance standpoint, the problem is that the countries of origin have made substantial public investment in the education of the workers that they lose – from early childhood to tertiary education. Net of small remittances, the returns on that investment are enjoyed by the countries of destination. The sustainability of the public finances of the countries of origin are endangered by diminishing contributions to the pension system and smaller income tax revenues, and – constrained by debt/GDP and deficit/GDP rules – these countries have few resources available to unlock the investment necessary to redress the economic imbalances and create the economic activities that could prevent further 'economic' mobility.

In the future our Union will need to be equipped with a fund to which member states contribute according to how many inflows of residents they get from other Europeans countries and from which they receive funding according to how many outflows they have in a given year. In short, resources for the EU budget generated by contributions by the countries that are benefiting most from intra-EU mobility should be used to target investment and industrial policy in areas that, without EU intervention, would risk serious divergence and impoverishment.

Bye bye unanimity

The most radical measure, though, is not a new policy or a new potential tax generating EU own resources. The most radical proposal for the future of Europe in regard to next generation public finances is a procedural – and highly political – matter: moving from unanimity to qualified majority vocting on tax issues. That would be *the* great step towards European integration, and it could unlock several potential developments.

In addition to the general *passerelle* clause that the Commission is planning to employ, and on top of the enhanced cooperation that has already been authorised for the FTT, the Treaty on the Functioning of the European Union (TFEU) offers two options to bypass unanimity. Qualified majority voting can be the way to go under specific circumstances: (i) for measures of a fiscal nature in the environmental field (Article 192); and (ii) to eliminate distortions to the functioning of the single market (Article 116). The former is likely to be employed for the sustainable taxes mentioned earlier in this chapter. The latter, never used so far, is still waiting for politics to realize what is obvious: that many different tax practices in the twenty-seven European tax jurisdictions are distorting competition within the EU and preventing the proper functioning of the European single market.

REFERENCES

Hemerijck, A., Francesco, C., Rinaldi, D., and Huguenot-Noel, R. 2020. Social investment now! Advancing social EU through the EU budget. FEPS Policy Study, 31 January.

Kapeller, L., and Wildauer, A. 2021. European wealth tax for a fair and green recovery. Policy Study, March, FEPS/Renner Institute.

Kotanidis, S. 2020. Passerelle clauses in the EU Treaties – opportunities for more flexible supranational decision-making. European Parliament Study, December.

Krenek, A., Sommer, M., and Schratzenstaller, M. 2019. Sustainability-oriented future EU funding: a European border carbon adjustment. Working Paper 587, August, WIFO.

Landais, S., and Zucman, A. 2020. A progressive European wealth tax to fund the European covid response. *voxeu.org*, 3 April.

Lejour, A., and van 't Riet, M. 2020. A common withholding tax on dividend, interest and royalty in the European Union. FEPS Policy Brief, September.

Núñez Ferrer, J., Le Cacheux, J., Benedetto, G., and Saunier, M. 2016. Study on the potential and limitations of reforming the financing of the EU budget. Report, Centre for European Policy Studies, June.

Piketty, T. 2020. *Capital and Ideology*. Cambridge, MA: Harvard University Press.

A European budgetary capacity to support the European project in the long term

By Peter Bofinger

WHY DO WE NEED A EUROPEAN BUDGETARY CAPACITY?

There are two main arguments for having a strong European budgetary capacity: to enable fiscal stabilization during severe economic crises and to stimulate long-term sustainable economic growth by providing sufficient funds for government and private future-oriented investments. In this chapter I will demonstrate that the lack of a sufficient budgetary facility puts Europe at a severe disadvantage in the global economic contest, especially with regard to the United States and China.

MACROECONOMIC STABILIZATION: INSIGHTS FROM FUNCTIONAL FINANCE ('MODERN MONETARY THEORY')

The Covid-19 pandemic has highlighted the weaknesses in Europe's institutional structure. According to the OECD's March 2021 forecast, economic output in the United States in 2022 will already be 6 per cent above the 2019 level. In contrast, gross domestic product in the euro area, as well as in Germany, will only exceed the pre-crisis level by 1 per cent in 2022. In Spain and Italy, which have been particularly hard hit by the pandemic, economic activity is actually expected to be around 1.5 per cent lower in 2022 than it was in 2019.

The main factor in the performance of the United States is its fiscal policy. According to IMF calculations, Covid-19-related fiscal support measures (both the additional expenditure and the foregone revenue) since January 2020 have reached 25.5 per cent of GDP in the United States. The equivalent figure for Germany is 11.0 per cent, while in Spain and Italy it is just 7.6 per cent and 8.5 per cent, respectively.

At the start of the pandemic, proposals were made to create joint financing possibilities for crisis management. The European Council responded to this and adopted the Next Generation EU solidarity-based reconstruction fund. However, at only 3 per cent of GDP, the volume of direct grants from this fund is modest compared with what we see in the United States. In addition, the funds have not yet been distributed and they are not conceived of as a stabilization instrument.

The moment for modern monetary theory

The lack of a joint eurozone-wide or EU-wide macroeconomic stabilization facility is a severe drawback for Europe compared with the United States or China. It implies that the strategy of 'functional finance' developed by Abba Lerner (1942), which is nowadays presented as 'modern monetary theory', cannot be fully applied in Europe.

Lerner presents the key messages of functional finance as follows:

- 'The ... responsibility of the government ... is to keep the total rate of spending in the country on goods and services neither greater nor less than that rate which at the current prices would buy all the goods that it is possible to produce. If total spending is allowed to go above this there will be inflation, and if it is allowed to go below this there will be unemployment.'
- 'Any excess over money revenues, if it cannot be met out of money hoards, must be met by printing new money.'

The macroeconomic strategies followed by most major countries during the Covid-19 pandemic coincide with the logic of modern monetary theory. Fiscal policy plays the leading role in stabilization policy. By purchasing government bonds, in principle without limit, central banks ensure that no financing bottlenecks arise for fiscal policy.

In a hearing in the UK's House of Lords, Charles Goodhart put this as follows:

> We are in a very weird world where we are actually undertaking helicopter money; we are following exactly the precepts of modern monetary theory, otherwise known as the magic money tree; and at the same time, we are claiming that we are not doing it. We are doing what we claim we are not doing. I find this situation absolutely weird.

The recipe of functional finance has also been used in Europe, with the European Central Bank (ECB) having been willing to finance the whole of the euro area's deficit. However, as demonstrated by the limited stimulation measures, especially in Italy and Spain, countries with high debt levels did not dare to test the limits of macroeconomic stabilization.

The specific insolvency problem of euro area member states

This can be explained by a fundamental problem of membership of the EMU. For large economies such as the United States or Japan, the problem of insolvency for the state is absent, since it is indebted in its own currency. If private investors are no longer willing to buy government bonds, the central bank always stands ready with bond-purchasing programmes.

The situation is different for EMU member states since their debt is denominated in euros. A loss of confidence by private investors can therefore lead to the insolvency of the government. As the euro crisis in 2010/12 has shown, EMU member states are then dependent on the willingness of the other member states to arrange a rescue programme with strict conditionality.

This risk can only by avoided with the establishment of a joint European stabilization fund whose debt is not counted as being debt of the individual member states.

FINANCE AND GROWTH: A SCHUMPETERIAN PERSPECTIVE

The need for a European budgetary facility goes beyond macroeconomic stabilization. The challenges of climate change and digitalization require massive public and private investment. While President Biden has announced a massive investment programme totalling about 10 per cent of US GDP, the grants that make up Next Generation EU total only 3 per cent of the bloc's GDP.

The lack of public funds available for investment is aggravated by the rules of the Stability and Growth Pact, which do not take public investment into account. This contradicts the 'golden rule' according to which governments are allowed to finance investments with credit. Europe therefore suffers not only from the lack of having a federal level, but its room for manoeuvre is additionally curtailed by a flawed fiscal framework.

The role of credit-financed growth is emphasized in the development theory of Joseph Schumpeter. *Mutatis mutandis* this theory can also be applied to governments that are financed by their central bank. China is a prime example of such a credit-led growth model, which can be regarded as a dynamic version of modern monetary theory.

THE NEED FOR AN ENHANCED EUROPEAN BUDGETARY FACILITY

Compared with China and the United States, Europe's lack of a federal budgetary facility financed by its central bank is an obvious drawback. It prevents effective macroeconomic stabilization and it constitutes a brake on growth. In order for Europe to reach a level playing field, far-reaching integration of fiscal policies would be required, but as this would imply a major transfer of national fiscal policy responsibilities to the European level, such a change in regime is unlikely for the time being.

Revising the Stability and Growth Pact in an investment-friendly manner

What intermediate solutions might be possible? A relatively easy measure would be to revise the Stability and Growth Pact to allow the debt financing of public investments in line with the 'golden rule'. This would reduce the need for a common budgetary facility.

But this would also require a revision of the debt reduction rule, according to which an annual reduction in debt by one-twentieth of the difference between the actual debt level and the 60 per cent threshold must be reached. For Italy, with a debt level of about 160 per cent of GDP, this would leave no space for major debt-financed public investment.

A 'Hamiltonian moment'?

Therefore, for countries with high debt levels, financing solutions at the European level are the preferred solution. In this regard, the Recovery and Resilience Facility, which is the centerpiece of Next Generation EU, was definitively a 'Hamiltonian moment', as Olaf Scholz, the German finance minister, put it. For the first time in its history, the EU was entitled to raise a significant amount of debt. At this stage it is still an open question whether this paradigm shift will pass the scrutiny of the German Constitutional Court, which has been asked to check the compatibility of the funds with EU law. In the case of a positive ruling, though, the funds could set a precedent for further joint initiatives to foster the green and digital transitions.

EUROPE AT A CRITICAL JUNCTURE

With President Biden at the helm, the United States is now embarking on large-scale investment projects. In China, the government has traditionally strongly supported new technologies directly or indirectly through the large state-owned banks. In neither country are these activities restricted by deficit rules or rules about the allowed level of debt. With its current institutional framework, Europe is at a serious disadvantage compared with its main competitors for global technological and economic leadership. What is more, it will be very difficult to design the green transformation in way that is both effective and socially acceptable.

While the need for more financial power is obvious, it will be difficult to overcome the resistance from member states against more competencies being transferred to the European level. The Next

Generation EU funds are therefore an important test of the potential for enhanced budgetary competencies. If this fails, Europe will not face a bright future. The only hope then would be for member states to change the treaty and be brave in order to achieve more fiscal integration.

REFERENCE

Lerner, A. P. 1941. Functional finance and the federal debt. *Social Research* 10(1), 38–51.

What can we learn from federal experiences around the world?
By Tanja Boerzel

THE EU – A FEDERAL SYSTEM *SUI GENERIS*

The relationship between federalism and European integration has long been strained. For many, federalism and federation are 'f words', synonymous with centralization and the creation of a European super state. In the early days of European integration, federalism was indeed a political vision or programme for the constitution of a sovereign European federation. But as a social science theory, federalism provides a constitutional language for analysing and discussing the dividing and sharing of sovereignty in a multilevel system of governance.

Without suggesting that the EU is, or should become, a federal state, it does share most of the features that define a federation according to the literature. The EU has a system of governance with two orders of government, each existing under its own right and exercising direct influence over the people. At the same time, it is not easy to determine the particular nature of the EU's federal system. In some areas, the EU is much less like a confederation (security, defence), while in others it is a quasi-federal state (monetary policy). As the EU is a federal system *sui generis*, what can we learn from federal experiences around the world? I will argue that it is precisely the differences between the EU and other federal systems that reveal the key challenge – if not the outright deficiency – of the EU's economic governance.

EU ECONOMIC GOVERNANCE: A FEDERAL OXYMORON

The EU today looks like a federal system, and in many areas, it works like a federal system too. At the same time, it is not a federal state and is unlikely to become one any time soon. First, the EU lacks the coercive power to enforce its laws. The effectiveness of EU law ultimately relies on the willingness of member states to comply with it, and to make others comply. Second, member states remain the 'masters' of the treaties, i.e. they have exclusive power over amending or changing the constitutive treaties of the EU. Third, the EU has no spending or taxing powers to speak of.

The EU can rely on the enforcement authorities of its member states to ensure compliance with EU law. Amending the EU treaties is as cumbersome as changing national constitutions, particularly in federal states. The key difference between the EU and any other federal state lies in its fiscal system, i.e. the division of spending and taxing power between the EU and its member states.

In principle, we can distinguish two federal models. The first is cooperative or intrastate federalism, of which Germany is almost a prototype. This system is based on a functional division of labour between the different levels of government. While the federal government makes the laws, the states are responsible for implementing them. The vast majority of competences are concurrent or shared. The sharing of spending responsibilities is backed by a sharing of tax revenue in a joint tax system. Federal government and the states share the most important taxes. The allocation of joint tax revenue allows for horizontal and vertical fiscal equalization payments to reduce inequalities between states with regard to their capacity to generate income.

The second model is dual or interstate federalism. This model, to which the United States most closely corresponds, emphasizes the institutional autonomy of the different levels of government, aiming for a clear vertical separation of powers (checks and balances). Each level should have an autonomous sphere of responsibilities. Competences are allocated according to policy sectors rather than policy functions. The institutional autonomy of each level of government presupposes a fiscal system that grants the states sufficient resources to exercise their competences without the financial intervention of the federal government. This should be ensured by the power of states to levy their own taxes in order to have an independent source of revenue to sustain their spending responsibilities. Federal grants provide for some fiscal equalization.

The EU federal system looks more like the German cooperative model than the US dual one., but it does not follow the fiscal system of either model. The responsibilities for stabilization, distribution and allocation still lie with the member states. The EU is a regulatory federal system. It has neither the legal competencies nor the financial resources to effectively reduce unemployment, stimulate economic growth, redistribute income or directly provide public goods and services, such as public health and education. This is different from highly decentralized federal systems (the United States, Switzerland, Australia), where the federal level has substantial spending and taxing power. At the same time, those federal governments have little control over state budgets. The EU's strict budgetary rules, by contrast, severely constrain the member states when it comes to fulfilling their stabilization, distribution and allocation responsibilities.

Strong fiscal decentralization in the shadow of centralized fiscal rules is inconsistent with fiscal federalism and explains why the EMU has failed to effectively balance European unity and national diversity.

REBALANCING EU ECONOMIC GOVERNANCE: LESS MIGHT BE MORE

Federalism is a balancing act between federal (supranational) and confederal (intergovernmental) principles for organizing power in a multilevel system of governance. The EU needs to rebalance these principles to make economic governance more effective and legitimate. This rebalancing can go in one of two opposite directions.

EU economic governance could be federalized by centralizing and integrating spending and taxation power. The EU would obtain substantial legislative competencies to create jobs and economic growth, reduce social inequality and directly provide public goods and services of transnational scope, such as those relating to digitalization or vaccination. To fulfil these responsibilities, the EU would be authorized to raise the necessary revenues in the form of EU or joint taxes.

Alternatively, stabilization, distribution and allocation responsibilities could remain decentralized, but with economic governance being freed from the shadow of fiscal austerity, granting member states more fiscal discretion to invest in public health, education, infrastructure and social security.

For many pundits and EU scholars alike, this is a make-or-break moment for the bloc. If it misses the opportunity for the ultimate leap towards fiscal union – if not towards a federal state – disintegration, possibly even demise, will be unavoidable. But are we really facing a 'Hamiltonian moment' in which member states are ready to mutualize debt? They might be willing to grant the EU more responsibilities related to economic governance, but will they agree to beef up the EU's spending power accordingly? The recovery fund and the multiannual financial framework constitute the largest budget the member states have ever agreed on. To help raise the €1.8 trillion involved, the EU has been authorized to borrow funds on behalf of the Union on the capital markets. For the first time, member states are engaging in collective borrowing. Unlike Eurobonds, all member states will be liable. To repay these joint debts, the EU will receive new own resources in the form of a tax on non-recyclable plastic waste, a digital levy, a carbon border adjustment mechanism, a financial transaction tax and an extension of the EU emission trading scheme.

And yet even if the member states agreed to make such arrangements permanent, the financial resources raised for Next Generation EU are a drop in the ocean compared with what member states, such as Germany, have pumped into their economies in the form of loans, grants, bonds and securities. Moreover, it remains to be seen whether the German Constitutional Court will be persuaded by the EU's new approach of not leaving it solely to the European Central Bank (ECB) to stabilize the eurozone. The required consent by the European Parliament and the national parliaments ensures democratic legitimacy, something that the ECB and the European Stability Mechanism have previously lacked. In any event, the transfer of fiscal powers to the EU is likely to be opposed by at least some member state parliaments and constitutional courts.

If a United States of Europe is not on the cards, then loosening the EU's grip on the expenditure of member states is the way to go. Not only does restoring fiscal autonomy appear to be politically more feasible, but it would also increase the effectiveness and legitimacy of EU monetary policy. The EU needs fiscal rules to minimize the risk of moral hazard and its destabilizing effect on price stability. At the same time, rigid rules are not an end in themselves. Debt-financed government expenditures and budgetary deficits are not a problem per se: at times, they are unavoidable to stabilize the economy, reduce social inequality and ensure the provision of basic public goods and services.

The European Commission, the ECB and the member state governments have bent EU rules time and time again to provide the necessary flexibility, particularly in times of crisis. And yet these decisions tend to be biased towards the interests of big and fiscally conservative member states. They have helped to manage financial and economic crises. In the long run, however, the European Stability Mechanism, the Outright Monetary Transactions of the ECB and Next Generation EU do little to foster social cohesion within and between member states. On the contrary, fiscal divergence, economic differentiation and social inequality have been increasing in the EU.

We need fewer rules with more flexibility. As long as the EU remains a regulatory federal system, its capacities to engage in stabilization, distribution and allocation are extremely limited. Its regulations not only have to grant member states the necessary autonomy to stimulate economic growth, provide assistance to poor households and safeguard the provision of public services; they also have to make sure that member states use their fiscal autonomy to invest rather than consume. More autonomy, finally, comes with greater transparency and democratic accountability. Member state governments will no longer be able to blame Brussels for poor health care systems, job losses and insufficient network coverage.

REFERENCES

Börzel, T. A. 2005. What can federalism teach us about the European Union? The German experience. *Regional and Federal Studies* 15(2), 245–257.

Börzel, T. A. 2016. From EU governance of crisis to crisis in EU governance. Regulatory failure, redistributive conflict, and Eurosceptic publics. *Journal of Common Market Studies* 54(S1: Annual Review), 8–23.

Börzel, T. A., and Hösli, M. 2003. Brussels between Bern and Berlin. Comparative federalism meets the European Union. *Governance* 16(2), 179–202.

A republican framework for EU economic governance

By Stefan Collignon

Through its institutional arrangements, European integration has generated a large collection of European public goods affecting a growing number of European citizens. The European Coal and Steel Community led to the European Economic Community with a Customs Union, and the Common Agricultural Policy laid the foundations for the single market and the single currency. The freedom for people to travel and work anywhere within the bloc required new forms of safeguarding for domestic and foreign security. Standards of social fairness and justice have created transfers and social policies, and the Covid-19 pandemic has revealed that even public health issues can no longer be confined to local communities. All these institutions have created public goods.

This extraordinary progress of 'ever closer union' had its own inner logic. Transnational cooperation in one sector created strong incentives for further policy integration in other sectors in order to fully capture the intended benefits. These positive spillover effects drove Jean Monnet's 'community method' of gradual integration – a method that proved more successful than Altiero Spinelli's ideal of a supranational European federation of states because it anchored the unification of Europe in the daily practices of governments and citizens and did not rely on a popular movement for adopting the noble ideas of fraternity and peace.

However, Monnet's gradual integration has encountered its own difficulties. Progress stalled when the collapse of the Bretton Woods system destroyed the economic stability on which the postwar economic recovery had been founded. The creation of the single European market in 1986 set up a new framework for economic development and political management with 'four freedoms' – the free movement of goods, services, capital and persons – at its core. The single market required the abolition of national regulations and their re-regulation at the European level. This set the agenda for intensified intergovernmental cooperation within the European Council. Nevertheless, this new regime was only sustainable within a European Monetary Union, and the creation of the euro fundamentally changed the dynamics of European integration.

Public goods are services that are made available to all members of a society. Because they are consumed and produced collectively, the market mechanism cannot ensure their efficient allocation. Public goods therefore need public institutions for their management.

We distinguish between two classes of European public goods. The first are 'club goods': these are accessible to all European citizens, while non-Europeans can be excluded. Overcoming such exclusion has been a strong incentive to join the EU. The four freedoms of the single market are clearly club goods. Citizens of the EU benefit from increased market opportunities, economies of scale, better economic growth, higher employment and increased prosperity. The governance of these public goods is in the hands of member states. Like the members of a sports club, they cooperate to provide the best possible service for everyone. This improves the standing of governments with their voters and generates legitimacy for further integration. For this reason, club goods are *inclusive* public goods, which generate cooperation and consent. Blockages due to asymmetric information can be overcome by the European Commission, which facilitates the flow of information and ensures that all members play by the rules.

The second class consists of 'common resource goods'. These depend on scarce resources to which everyone has open access. This implies that if one party consumes them, the possibility of consumption by other parties is reduced. There is therefore no incentive to cooperate – rather, there is one to compete. I therefore call these goods *exclusive* public goods. An example of competition over scarce public resource goods was the rush to buy Covid-19 vaccines during the pandemic, although the European Commission was able to guarantee a balanced distribution of the supplies that were secured. More generally, money is, by definition, a scarce resource, so all policy issues related to the distribution of money face the same problems as exclusive public goods. The central bank provides money in line with stable prices, a prerequisite for any successful currency, and the euro has become a hard budget constraint for all member states. This has transformed the incentives for cooperation in many policy areas. Money flows where it finds the highest return, and there is competition for where it goes; some regions or sectors benefit, others do not. The most salient example is fiscal policy. Excessive borrowing by one member state would provide additional resources for one country but would push up interest rates for all. Policies that benefit one member state may therefore damage all others. The absence of incentives for cooperation makes intergovernmental governance dysfunctional for all common resource goods.

There are two ways to solve this dilemma. One is to impose strict policy rules and follow them up by binding sanctions in the case of misbehaviour. This was the purpose of the Stability and Growth Pact. However, experience has shown that strict rules are not necessarily always optimal. For example, the management of macroeconomic aggregates often requires discretion in response to shocks, while the imposition of strict budget rules hampered economic growth during the euro crisis. Fiscal policy therefore requires at least some degree of discretion. Because it is the function of governments to provide different amounts of collective action in variable situations, exclusive European public goods – but only these – must be governed by a single authority. We could call this a European government, and it would be logical to transfer competencies for governing exclusive European goods to the European Commission, which has the necessary administrative infrastructure. Such a government would play an important role in designing and enforcing the optimal policy mix between government spending and monetary policy. The Maastricht Treaty correctly assigned the competencies for a coherent monetary policy stance to the European Central Bank (ECB), but its equivalent for fiscal policy is absent. This means that the policy outcome is suboptimal, and the ECB easily becomes overburdened in a crisis.

However, such centralization of the governance of European public goods is unthinkable unless it is matched by democratic legitimacy. Because the access to public goods is free to all and the external effects on their lives are unavoidable, citizens in a democracy must have the right to choose how they want their common goods to be administrated. These choices can be made by member state governments for inclusive public goods when the incentives for their provision generate cooperation, but in the case of exclusive public goods this is not the case, and non-cooperation leads to government failure. Legitimacy for these exclusive goods can only be generated by the collective choice of all *individuals* who are affected by their externalities in the EU. This means that democratic control must be exercised in the last resort by the European Parliament, for it alone represents all citizens. The Council should have a voice with respect to the effects of the implementation of these goods for and by national policies.

Again, fiscal policy is a good example of how this assignment of competencies could work. We know that macroeconomic stability is a result of appropriate interaction between monetary policy and the aggregate fiscal stance in a given economic situation. The European government must therefore define the aggregate euro area deficit (or surplus) but, given the limited size of the EU budget, most of the spending will be done by national governments and budgets. In dialogue with the ECB and the Council, the European Commission would define the aggregate fiscal stance and assign budget shares to member states. The European Parliament would deliberate and ratify the macroeconomic budget law and member state governments would subsequently execute their budgets.

Our analysis has a clear message: the nature of European public goods must determine how they are best administered; it should not be decided by member states bargaining over their partial interests. European public goods are citizens' *res publica europea*. They constitute the European Republic, and this republic is already the reality of citizens' daily lives. The republican approach to European integration does not therefore reflect a distant utopia. Its originality comes from how it internalizes the externalities of public goods and assigns the double requirements of the efficiency and legitimacy of their governance: by giving individual citizens the right to choose policies at the European level, it generates input legitimacy; by putting a single authority in charge of exclusive public goods, the efficiency and welfare of the Union are improved. This creates a democratic culture of debate, deliberation and responsibility. This is what it takes to make European integration sustainable in the long run.

PART IV

The EU and the Next Democratic Transformation

PART IV

Synthesis of the debate

By François Balate

> 'The Union is founded on the values of respect for human dignity, freedom, democracy, equality, the rule of law and respect for human rights, including the rights of persons belonging to minorities.'
> Article 2 of the Treaty on European Union

Democracy has been discussed, debated and defined over many centuries. One central element of it is that citizens make the decisions.

As a founding value of the European project, the question of the democratic organization of the EU has always triggered reflection, research and analysis. Looking at the legal and constitutional framework of the EU, we can see that the Union is founded on representative democracy (Article 10, TEU), i.e. citizens decide on their representative. But it is also hardwired in, to try to ensure the broadest possible engagement of citizens and civil society organizations in a transparent and consultative manner (Article 11, TEU), i.e. citizens can decide to organize themselves to further engage in the political debate. The entire political system of the EU is then built on these principles: from elections to the balancing of power, from public consultations to technical policymaking.

In May 2021 (as this book is published), more than a year after its announcement and after long interinstitutional debates, a large-scale democratic experiment is about to be launched within the EU. The Conference on the Future of Europe is being presented as 'a unique opportunity for all European citizens and our civil society to shape Europe's future, a common project for a functioning European democracy', to use the words of David Sassoli, the president of the European Parliament.

According to a recent pan-European survey (*Eurobarometer*, March 2021), a vast majority of EU citizens want to have their voices heard more when it comes to the future of the EU. While voting – the means of representative democracy – remains a central method of contributing to this, citizens envisage other avenues as well: public consultations, citizens' assemblies, online dialogues, petitions, citizens' initiatives, civil society activism, engagement with political parties and trade unions. This clearly shows that democracy is a dynamic process – one that is constantly being transformed.

In this chapter we will look at the main elements of this democratic transformation and their impact on the European project, its political system and its institutional architecture.

THE EVOLUTION OF THE EUROPEAN POLITICAL SYSTEM

When one considers the democratic transformation of the EU, one needs to look first at the evolution of its institutional and electoral frameworks.

The EU political system has changed since its early days. Key milestones – such as direct elections to the European Parliament, the institutionalization of the European Council and the successive treaty changes – have changed its dynamics and its power balance.

Long-time trends in the evolution of the EU political system that are essential to understanding its future include the increasing power of the European Parliament, the politicization of the European Commission, the emergence of a European public space, the linkages formed between the European and national political scenes, and, last but not least, the increasing polarization of European politics.

These trends have created many assumptions and given rise to much debate. Is the European Commission an independent agency or a government? How should we elect the president of the European Commission? Should the European Council play a more central role? What role do European political parties play in the work of the European Parliament? And there are many more questions too. All of this highlights the fact that, while the EU political system has already seen great development, it could still mature further.

Before looking into possible future developments of the EU political system, one main conclusion can be drawn from these debates: the EU remains a *sui generis* and hybrid political system.

What key changes should be introduced into the European political and electoral systems?

Successive treaty reforms and electoral contests have brought many new features into the European political and electoral systems: the direct election of Members of the European Parliament; new legislative processes and roles for the co-legislators (i.e. the European Parliament and the Council); the election of the president of the European Commission via the so-called *Spitzenkandidat* process (i.e. leading candidate or *tête de liste*); as well as many other more subtle or technical evolutions.

In 2019, during the latest European electoral contest, we witnessed a reverse in the decreasing turnout that has been a feature of all EU elections since 1979, with half of Europe's voters going to the polls. While this could be explained in a variety of ways (from the role of European political parties, to the investments recently made by Europe's institutions, or to the issues at stake, such as climate change or social inequalities), some lessons can be drawn. Furthermore, the aftermath of the election – with a fragmented European Parliament and the bypassing of the *Spitzenkandidaten* process by the European Council, which led to the election of Ursula von der Leyen as president of the European Commission – has several implications for the future of the European political and electoral system.

First, there is a need to further institutionalize the principle of the *Spitzenkandidaten* process. After it was first formally used in 2014, with the election of Jean-Claude Juncker as president of the European Commission, the system suffered from a bit of a backlash in 2019, with none of the candidates appointed by their respective political families managing to reach a majority in the European Council (even though Frans Timmermans, the candidate of the Party of European Socialists (PES), came closest to doing so). Until there is a clear understanding among member states, political parties and institution officials, the idea of there being a leading candidate for the presidency of the European

Commission will never be clear enough to voters, and it will not therefore be seen as a straightforward and legitimate process. Large amounts have been written about this topic without anyone managing to show a clear correlation between the personification of the electoral contest at the European level and a higher turnout, but the absence of an established procedure clearly does not help.

Building on the question of leading candidates, we could also further explore the nomination of members of the European Commission (something that is currently in the hands of member states). The potential candidates could be known ahead of elections, or even be part of a party ticket (with all of them running for seats in the European Parliament), and gender balance could be ensured. The candidates could then act as a shadow cabinet (in the British tradition) should they not end up as part of the College of Commissioners.

A second key development concerns the transnational lists. Until now, Members of the European Parliament (MEP) have been elected within their national constituencies by national constituents: German voters elect German MEPs, Finnish voters elect Finnish MEPs, and so on. How can we build a pan-European electoral environment, then, if the elections are seen through a national lens (with candidates too often running on local issues and not looking at the broader European picture that they would (ideally) need to embrace if elected)? The main idea here is to create transnational lists with a pan-European constituency: those German and Finnish voters could now vote for candidates from across Europe.

Rejected by a vote of the European Parliament in 2018 (with strong opposition from conservative parties), the idea of transnational lists raises many operational questions about their implementation, mainly over the harmonization of electoral systems (i.e. the types of lists, the weighting of votes) and national representation (i.e. how to ensure proportional representation for countries with lower populations). Some argue that a test run could be undertaken with a list of 'super candidates', i.e. ones who could then claim an executive position within the European Commission. This process would, of course, be led by the *Spitzenkandidat*.

Third, in order to further develop the EU political and electoral system, European political parties should be empowered to play strong roles. They need to improve their direct engagement with national parties, citizens and activities, including with civil society and youth organizations, to develop their electoral manifestos (here it is worth noting the great work done in this area in 2019 by the PES, who worked closely with civil society and youth organizations) and define their lists of candidates, including the leading ones. They should also invest further in the potential of digitalization to bring about more inclusive and participatory campaigns. (They must avoid falling prey to the 'digital divide', though, which might give them a distorted picture of their engagement, and they would also need to ensure protection against undesirable foreign interference.)

European political parties also have a key role to play in strengthening gender equality (in collaboration with their women's associations, such as PES Women) and increasing diversity among the political representatives of EU institutions. Along the lines of the 1998 Charter of European Political Parties for a Non-Racist Society, a Charter for Gender Equality could be considered not only when establishing candidate lists but also when it comes to choosing the leading candidate.

Fourth, we need to look into interinstitutional dynamics, and especially the relationship between the European Parliament and the Council. While the European Parliament has seen its prerogatives and powers increase since its creation, there remains an imbalance of power with the Council (both the European Council and the Council of the European Union). By giving the right of initiative to the European Parliament (i.e. the capacity to initiate legislative proposals – currently limited to the Commission) and by considering the Council as a true second legislative chamber (similar to those found in many federal and non-federal systems), this would already correct this imbalance.

Furthermore, the European Parliament should be more involved in certain policy areas in which its role is still limited in comparison with the role of the Council or the European Commission. For example, it should be more central to the field of economic governance: is it normal to hear more from the European Central Bank chief than from the president of the European Parliament – who is never invited to stay for the entire meeting of the European Council

– when it comes to matters relating to taxpayers? This would help to strengthen the link with citizens, who have a direct link with the European Parliament by virtue of the election of their representatives.

A final element when it comes to interinstitutional relations is the question of the 'government programme'. We need clarity and streamlining to move beyond the multitude of 'agendas' we currently have – whether they come from the leaders of the European Council, the Commission Work Programme or, more recently, letters from parliamentary group leaders to the member states and the European Commission – to define the political programme of the legislative term to come. The EU would benefit greatly from clarity in its institutional organization.

Many questions flow from this broad picture of the desired evolution of the EU political system. Questions over voting age (several member states, such as Austria and Malta, have lowered it to sixteen), citizenship education, the funding of European political parties, the role of European political foundations, and many other similar issues will be at the heart of the Conference on the Future of Europe, and will also be deeply debated by the European Parliament during its current term (i.e. reforming both the European electoral act and the status of European political parties and political foundations).

THE MEGA-TRENDS OF THE DEMOCRATIC TRANSFORMATION

Democracy is a dynamic process. It is not static. It evolves with society and its technology. However, it does rely on fundamental principles: equality before the law, the accountability of political officials, access to public office, and government for the people.

Throughout history we have seen our democratic societies evolve, but these principles have remained central: more people have been enfranchized and have been granted rights, new ways of engaging with citizens have been developed, the media landscape has evolved, new counter power has emerged, and the transparency of the decision making has increased.

Our democracy is currently facing new 'mega-trends' that are shaping its functioning: the digital transformation, the changing media landscape and increasing youth participation in democratic life.

As the EU institutions debate the key legislation on these matters (i.e. the Digital Services Act, the Digital Market Act, the Media & Audio-visual Action Plan and the Democracy Action Plan), it is hugely important to look at the impact of these mega-trends on democratic life in Europe.

What is the impact of digital transformation on our democratic lives?

The digitalization of our societies has been underway for several decades now, with a range of impacts on our daily lives. Information and communications technology – such as computers, email and smartphones – has profoundly transformed our personal and professional interactions while speeding up the circulation of information and knowledge. Global communication has contributed to the blurring of natural borders – relating to both time and geography – and to huge scientific achievements in various fields: medicine, education, transport, etc.

When it comes to the impact of digitalization on democratic life, several positive aspects can be outlined. As briefly touched upon above, digital technologies have brought with them new knowledge, which has contributed to increasing the overall education of the wider population. Via the internet, the new technologies have improved access to information for many: a more informed citizenry is better able to play a positive role in democratic life. Consequently, they have also allowed more people to become directly involved in debates about daily decisions and societal matters. The democratic base has been broadened.

Another positive impact that can be underlined is access to services. Indeed, the digitalization of our interfaces with public authorities have reduced our administrative burdens and improved our access to public services, from our daily administrative needs to entirely different ways of engaging with society (through volunteering, social activities, entrepreneurship and so on).

While it would be possible to list many more positive impacts of the digital transformation, the negative ones are also worth noting, especially when we consider what they might mean for our democracies.

Digitalization contributes to inequalities, not only through unequal access to its benefits (due to huge discrepancies in access to digital infrastructure, reflecting already deep socioeconomic inequalities) but also through the economic distortion it creates. By blurring the borders between states and between spheres of regulation, tech corporations have contributed to an erosion of the tax base (by using various methods of tax avoidance). By doing so, they have harmed the capacity of public authorities to harness the benefits of growing economies to serve the people, not just the interests of the corporate world.

Another key negative impact of digitalization surrounds the question of cybersecurity. Indeed, a new field of threats and foreign interference has been created, which can have a devasting impact on democratic life (the manipulation of elections via fake news, deep fakes, and other problems exacerbated primarily through social media) and can also affect access to basic infrastructures (e.g. when health data is hacked by terrorist groups, thereby threatening access to urgent treatment).

Digitalization might have many positive impacts, but the detrimental effects of the negative ones are outweighing the positive ones.

There is a risk that democracies will actually just fade away, because of manipulation and other types of cyber threats. As a democratic system normally relies on its citizens having access to fair, transparent and pluralistic information and being able to participate via trusted processes, digital threats can put all of that at risk (as has been seen in many recent examples: the Brexit campaign and the 2016 and 2020 US elections, for example).

As a consequence of the economic distortion caused by big tech corporations and of their concentration of data, the worth of this information and the capacity to act upon it are no longer in the hands of the public authorities who are accountable to citizens via democratic means. Instead, these things are in the hands of private entities that answer to no one except their shareholders and the fluctuations of the market.

And finally, building on the previous concerns, access to a pluralistic media landscape – a key foundation of democracies – is under threat because of an absence of control and regulation over the private companies that run social media platforms (Google, Facebook, etc.). As the vast majority of citizens now access news items via social media, serious doubts are raised about the concept of a fair and pluralistic media environment.

How can we use digital transformation, a changing media landscape and further youth participation to renew our democratic contract?

Looking at both the challenges of digital transformation and the potential it offers allows us to reflect on how to harness these new technologies to reinforce our democracies. To these considerations, we should also add a need to increase youth participation.

First, digitalization allows us to bring more citizen participation into our policymaking and societal debates. Indeed, as highlighted below, a much larger range of citizens can be involved in consultations, online dialogue and other types of public engagement. Furthermore – and this is particularly relevant in the European context, with its twenty-four official languages – technology allows us to provide immediate translation nowadays. Not only is this true when it comes to different spoken languages, but it would also allow us to be more inclusive for people with visual, hearing or speaking impairments.

There is a lot of research that has suggested further ways of using artificial intelligence (AI) to improve policymaking and increase the efficacy of our administrative and judicial systems. But conversely, there are also many studies that have shown that processes involving AI technologies, or ones that are based on algorithms, have a tendency to reflect human biases, including deeply rooted discriminatory behaviours (racism, sexism, etc.). This is why, if we want to embrace digitalization to reinforce our democracies, we also need to work on fixing the imperfections of our societies to make them more inclusive while also ensuring the security of the data we collect and preventing cyberattacks.

We need to put the European values that we discussed in our introduction at the heart of the development of a new democratic algorithm.

In that regard, we could look to the 'We Europeans' survey, which ran between 2018 and 2019 and managed to reach out to 38 million citizens, collecting 70,000 unique contributions, using twenty-five languages across twenty-seven countries. It gathered citizens' views about the priorities of the next European Commission. While this happened outside any kind of 'institutionalized' process, we can imagine the potential such an initiative could have if larger resources were invested and if it was structured as part of regular democratic debate. The upcoming Conference on the Future of Europe, and the digital platform it will use, will be an experiment to watch closely.

Second, bringing together the question of digital transformation with the changes undergone by the media landscape offers great opportunities. First and foremost we need to end the monopoly of big tech over access to information and ownership of personal data. We have already mentioned that the vast majority of citizens access their news via social media and on the internet, but it should also be noted that only a small percentage of people actually trust this news. This demonstrates a deep failure and a great threat to the foundations of our democracy. There is a great risk to a pluralistic and accessible media landscape.

We need to ensure the necessary level of investment in technological developments to support our media and news companies so that they can become less reliant on the big platforms, such as Google, Facebook and Twitter (who all happen to be based outside Europe). Harnessing the power of technology and the translation capabilities we have already referred to could also be part of strengthening the European public space and of a broader cultural democratic movement.

Third, we need to talk about youth participation. Over the past decade it has often been said that young people are apathetic, or uninterested in politics. Is that really the case, or is it simply that they felt like they were facing the closed door of an outdated system?

Youth participation should not be understood through traditional, if not conservative, lenses for political parties. It has been repeatedly demonstrated that young people engage with and care about political issues, just in different ways. We must look at Fridays for Future, at mass engagement on social media, at the mixture between cultural and political content, and at many other examples if we are to really understand the incredible power of young people and youth organizations.

But beyond these acts of self-organization, there is a need for structured and institutionalized engagement with young people. Youth turnout might have increased during the 2019 European elections, but the average age of a member of the European Parliament is still above fifty years old. We need to move beyond the current situation in which institutions call for more youth participation while all the positions of power and the real decision-making processes are in the hands of an older generation.

The institutions of the EU should also explore institutionalized mechanisms to put young people at the heart of the political debate, building on successful experiments such as the 'co-management system' in the Council of Europe (where youth representatives sit on equal footing with ministers in discussions and decisions on policy recommendations). Recently, UN Secretary General António Guterres and the EU Commissioner for International Partnerships Jutta Urpilainen have surrounded themselves with youth advisory/sounding boards to help them with their work. Is this the way to go?

Finally, on youth participation, it is important to note that the young should not be consulted only in a few policy fields, such as those relating to education or mobility. Young people have a holistic vision for society, and it should not be ignored. This is how we strengthen our democratic contract.

As we talk about the future of Europe, we cannot leave young people out of the decision-making process. Doing so would risk deepening the existing generational divide and creating long-lasting consequences for the European project. Youth participation is the best way to make the European project future-proof.

Ultimately, we need to go back to the founding principles of democracy and keep trying to strengthen them: involve more citizens, make public authorities more accountable, increase countervailing powers. Ultimately, we need to keep filling the engagement gap between electoral contests to make democracy a right and a duty for every day.

THE ARCHITECTURE OF THE EU

The political and institutional architecture of the EU is defined in great detail in its founding treaties. The latest – the Treaty on European Union (TEU) and the Treaty on the Functioning of the European Union (TFEU) – were adopted in Lisbon in 2007 and entered into force in 2009 (after the failure of the European Constitution in 2005). You will find the ways in which Europe's institutions are organized in the treaties, as well as how they interact and what the policy competences of the EU are.

Today, more than a decade after the last reorganization of the EU's institutions and policies, and after successive crises (from the financial crisis, to the sovereignty debt crisis, to the current Covid-19 pandemic), it is right to ask if the current institutional framework is the most appropriate one possible. There have been several calls to improve the way the EU works, even from within the Union's institutions (e.g. there was a 2018 communication on the principles of subsidiarity and proportionality that called for increased involvement from national parliaments and for the further involvement of regional authorities). Too often have member states played deaf in the Council.

Institutions, governments and assemblies, and not only those within the EU, need to answer questions about both their input and output legitimacies. We need the right democratic arrangement to deliver the most efficient policies that improve people's well-being. The Conference on the Future of Europe is the ideal opportunity to ask these questions: what do we do together, as a Union, and how do we do it?

First, what can be done within the framework of the Lisbon Treaty?

Whenever a crisis looms in the EU, many voices call for Treaty change, as if it were the silver bullet for all problems. While some longer-term and much-needed changes would require reform of the EU's constitutional framework, a lot can be done within the remit of the current treaty (i.e. the Lisbon Treaty).

Indeed, this treaty, built on the extensive work of the European Constitution (which started with the earlier Convention on the Future of Europe in Laeken with years of negotiations and preparation), has a lot of unused potential. Too often, a lack of political action is justified by the fact that the treaties do not allow it. But is that correct?

In times of crisis, political ingenuity often manages to overcome this mental blockage over the Treaties. If we look at the financial crisis of ten years ago, many of the actions that the European Central Bank took were initially thought to be impossible, or against the treaties. And more recently, as part of the response to Covid-19, the recovery plan ('Next Generation EU'), which relies on collective borrowing by the EU on the financial markets, was also possible within the current constitutional boundaries. Many of the political developments referred to earlier in this chapter regarding the *Spitzenkandidaten* process were also made possible through interpretation of the treaties.

The rule of unanimity within the European Council (and, as a consequence, the threat of a veto) is often seen as one of the main obstacles to the EU having efficient policies and actions. The Lisbon Treaty states that decisions should be made by unanimity in a range of policy fields (e.g. external action, international agreements, breaches of fundamental rights) or as part of a special legislative procedure, as opposed to the ordinary legislative procedure that puts the European Parliament at the heart of the process (which is therefore considered to be more democratic). However, the same Treaty has a special procedure, called the *passerelle clause*, that allows the way decisions are made in all policy fields covered by a special legislative procedure (Article 48 of the TEU) to be changed. Unfortunately, this fact is too often overlooked, and the EU's actions in these fields is therefore still ruled by the unanimity of member states.

What is the next step for the EU's political architecture?

The Conference on the Future of Europe gives us the opportunity to think beyond operational fixes to the EU's constitutional treaties.

We have a chance to give new impetus to the European project as a political, societal and cultural force – one that has real meaning for its citizens. We have an opportunity to redefine the engine, the paradigm on which European integration is conceived.

When the Single Market was built under the leadership of Jacques Delors, a new horizon was presented to all Europeans: we build a single market, we get a common currency, and it will be in all citizens' pockets by 2002. But can citizens *fall in love* with the market? We need to provide a more engaging goal for citizens now. A common European ID card? A common social security system? A common sustainable energy framework? We need to let the Union's citizens decide on a clear outcome – a clear change to their daily lives – and then it is the role of public authorities to create legal convergence in order to reach this horizon.

Earlier in this chapter we expressed the need to also redefine the democratic matrix of the EU, ensuring the right balance is struck between representative democracy and new forms of direct participation. One important level of power – in the sense of its capacity to make an impact on citizens' daily lives – is that of regions and cities. This level is often overlooked in the current EU political context. Currently represented via the Committee of the Regions, regional and local authorities have barely any say in the legislative debate, but they often have the primary responsibility over implementing the decisions that are made – decisions made by the 705 members of the European Parliament and the twenty-seven member states, represented by their respective ministers. Every day, a million local and regional elected officials across the Union are acting on and implementing measures that are often taken far away from them. As Karl-Heinz Lambertz, the former president of the Committee of the Regions, has said: 'It's unfortunate that, in practice, our European democracy attaches so little importance to the largest number of elected representatives.' As we rethink the architecture of the EU, we need to ensure sufficient space is made for regional and local authorities.

To conclude, the EU has a great opportunity to take the next step in its political history. It should embrace another democratic transformation, one that sees it bring more citizens into its processes, one that sees it become more efficient, and ultimately one that contributes to the increased well-being of all of Europe's, and the world's, citizens. The Conference on the Future of Europe is a first step, and an opportunity that should not be missed.

Aspirations: the EU's next democratic transformation

By Lora Lyubenova

Democracy has been a core value of the EU since it was established. The European democratic process of decision making is very complicated and unclear for European citizens, and as a result the majority of voters at European elections do not understand how their votes go towards shaping European politics. The European political process has to regain citizens' trust in democratic decision making.

From *Spitzenkandidaten* to president of the European Commission: the process of election versus the process of appointment

The introduction of the *Spitzenkandidaten* process should make clearer to European voters to whom their votes are going, not only when electing members of the parliament but also when it comes to the head of the EU executive body (the European Commission). Voters need to know which leader their votes are going to and what kind of political values she or he represents. So far, on paper 'what became known as the "*Spitzenkandidaten* process" is a procedure whereby European political parties, ahead of European elections, appoint lead candidates for the role of Commission President, with the presidency of the Commission then going to the candidate of the political party capable of marshalling sufficient parliamentary support' (European Parliament Research Service 2018).

Unfortunately, the implementation of the idea of European political parties having a 'leading candidate' fell at the final hurdle in 2019 (after the last European elections). The European political parties did nominate their leading candidates, but the links between the leading candidates and a concrete political programme at the national and European level remained unclear to voters. Moreover, the outcome of the elections did not guarantee that the leading candidate from the European political family that won the most seats in the European Parliament was going to be appointed as president of the European Commission. In 2019 the leading candidates were nominated by European political parties and campaigned as candidates for the position of 'President of the European Commission', but despite all their efforts another candidate was eventually appointed behind closed doors, to be approved by the European Parliament, after the elections. The election process for the leading candidate would be more correctly titled, then, if it was labelled an election for the 'misleading candidate'! For voters, the entire democratic process of elections for European political representation, based on political programmes and values, seemed to have shifted over the course of one night, with their views not really taken into consideration.

In order for citizens to get involved in the European democratic process we should make sure that European citizens trust the process and believe that their votes are going to matter in the political decision-making process. In the first instance, the EU must include citizens in the process of nominating the leading candidates of European political parties. The democratic process has to be transformed, building a clear link between leading candidates, European and national political parties, and their political programmes and priorities.

European transnational lists for members of the European Parliament

The election process of having a leading candidate for each political family should have a clear link to the candidates for Members of the European Parliament. In practice, the current election process for European elections sometimes puts together controversial national political programmes for the campaign at European level. It happens that elected members of the European Parliament from the same political group inside the European Parliament, but who come from different member states, can have completely different views (even pre-election rhetoric may suggest that they are opposed to each other). It remains unclear for the voter at the European level which political agenda the elected members of the European Parliament will follow: the political programme represented at the national level during the campaign or the political agenda of the political group to which they belong inside the European Parliament.

The democratic election process in the EU must build a transparent link between national and European political agendas. In order to do this, European elections have to proceed via competition between European transnational lists that represent the political programmes of their European political parties. The transnational lists have to equally represent candidates from different geographic regions and backgrounds, and they must also guarantee gender equality in representation in the European Parliament. We wil not be able to achieve gender equality in any parliament if we do not introduce a gender balanced list of candidates.

I believe that by combining the idea of leading candidates with European transnational lists (including a zip system for gender balanced lists), we can encourage voters to be actively engaged in the political process, starting with voting and continuing by following up on the implementation of the political proposals. In other cases, citizens' trust in the European democratic process is insecure. The democratic processes that form the EU have to be progressively developed in order to regain the trust of voters and to ensure that European institutions are strong and that they are able to safeguard democracy and the implementation of the rule of law.

REFERENCES

Lyubenova, L. 2017. Better inclusion of young refugees in education, labour market and society. Report, Friedrich-Ebert-Stiftung, Sofia.

Lyubenova, L. 2020. The application of European Pillar of Social Rights' principles during the Covid-19 pandemic. Report, Sofia University and Friedrich Naumann Foundation, Sofia.

Sociedade e Trabalho. 2016. Centenary of the Ministry of Labour, Solidarity and Social Security: Conference the Future of Work. Lisbon: MTSSS/GEP.

Key changes to be introduced in the European political system
By Olivier Costa

Effective reflection on the key changes to be introduced in the EU political system for the next phase of the European project needs to be based on three observations.

First, it must be remembered that the EU regime has, since its origin, been shaped by long-term trends. We need to identify those trends and assume they will continue: it is virtually impossible to swim against those trends, and if they are to be successful, reforms will have to surf on them.

Five main tendencies can be distinguish in this respect, and all of them are to some extent intertwined. The first is the empowerment of the European Parliament. This trend has been ongoing since the 1970s, and it continues treaty after treaty, day after day. The second is the politicization, governmentalization and presidentialization of the Commission, mostly as a result of internal changes and the involvement of the European Parliament in its appointment. The third trend is the emergence of a supranational political space in which European political parties and their representatives interact over various ideas and programmes for the EU. The fourth is the increasing connection between national politics and EU politics and the growing interest of citizens in EU affairs. And finally, we need to consider the increasing polarization between anti-Europeans and pro-Europeans, both at the level of each member state and within the main institutions of the EU (the European Parliament, the Council of the European Union, and the European Council).

The second of our three observations is that there is a need for meaningful reflection about the EU political system if we are to avoid any taboo. We must consider the EU as it works concretely today, and not as it is *supposed* to work. For instance, the College of

Commissioners is still described as an independent and non-political organ by the treaties and by those who oppose its politicization. However, it obviously is a political body, and has been for quite some time. It is closer to being a government than an agency or an independent administrative authority, and it is composed of politicians, acting as politicians. Some also refuse to consider the Council as a high chamber because it is a peculiar body that also has executive functions and that can sometimes simply be an arena for debates between member states. But its main function today is to act as a high chamber and this should be accepted.

The third observation is that any democratic political system should be understandable by its citizens. We cannot evaluate the degree of legitimacy of the EU if we only assess the rules on which it is based and the way those rules are implemented, or by measuring its capacity to take into account citizens' expectations and to provide them with public good and sound policies. We need to also consider the subjective perceptions that citizens have. In this regard, the EU system obviously needs to improve its transparency, clarity and readability: values that are key to the propensity of citizens to acknowledge that a system is legitimate.

For instance, people believe in national institutions if there is a simple narrative about the way they are designed and function that is known. This is not the case for the EU political system, which is seen as being too complex and obscure. Massive reform is therefore needed, to make it simpler and more coherent, and further politicization and a more central role for European political parties are required.

At the national level, most citizens do not have detailed information about given initiatives of their government, but they nevertheless have opinions about them, because parties have them. In most cases, they align with the position of their preferred party or political leader, either to support or to oppose it. We need a similar process of identification at the supranational level, allowing citizens to position themselves according to the various activities of EU institutions. To achieve this we need to continue the process of parliamentarization of the EU by increasing the centrality of EU elections, the European Parliament and European parties. Doing so will increase the readability of the EU political system. Strong mobilization will be required to achieve this goal because 'parliamentarization' competes with two alternative approaches to the functioning of the EU.

The first of these alternatives is intergovernmentalism, which has regained much relevance since the Treaty of Lisbon and during the crises that have hit the EU since its adoption. The European Council has been institutionalized and has become the main actor in the EU's management of crises. It also plays a key role in setting the agenda – something that was not expected. There is also a new decentralized and intergovernmental approach to EU policymaking, based on the contribution of national administrations.

The second alternative is the Community method. It is praised by actors who wish to retain the status quo: they oppose further parliamentarization of the EU, and they dislike the idea of further renationalization. They believe in the central role of the Commission, and they propose that we focus on improving the existing treaties: via the Better Regulation strategy, by searching for 'evidence-based policies', through the generalization of impact assessments, by consulting with stakeholders, and so on. Some also recommend a process of 'agencification' of the Commission: they suggest the transformation of some of its Directorates-General in charge of policies – like competition or trade – in executive agencies, acting in an independent way, like the Commission was doing before its politicization.

Both the intergovernmental approach and the 'Community method' of EU governance fail to pay attention to the issues of democratization and citizen participation. Parliamentarization does address these issues. The objective is not to transform the EU into a parliamentary system: some specificities of the EU need to be preserved because the EU is not integrated and homogeneous enough to function as a federation. We need to preserve the hybrid nature of the existing political system, and its virtues, especially when it comes to favouring the emergence of a consensus at various levels: among the member states, within each institution, and then between them. Six reforms could nevertheless be considered in order to clarify the overall design of the EU polity, to increase the level of participation of citizens, and to formalize the role of European political parties in the Union's functioning.

The first one is the institutionalisation of the *Spitzenkandidaten* (lead-candidates) procedure. In its current form – an informal procedure that may or may not be implemented – it is highly problematic. It has demonstrated its capacity to mobilize citizens and to give them the sense that European elections have a major impact – by contributing to the choice of the President of the Commission and the definition of its programme – but a codified procedure is needed.

The second reform is very much connected with the first: it is about the creation of transnational lists for EU elections and the reinforcement of the role of European parties in this matter. It would help if campaigns focused on EU issues and on the programmes of European parties in this matter. It would also give more visibility to the lead-candidates, who would, by definition, draw up those lists. Transnational lists would also be a symbolic affirmation of the existence of an EU polity, and they would constitute a step forward for EU citizenship.

The third reform is the generalization of primaries. As the lead-candidate of the party that wins an EU election would automatically become President of the Commission, it is crucial for that person to be perceived as having been chosen by a large number of people, and not just by the board of their party. Primaries are also key to creating real political debate within each party, fueling exchanges within the European public space around the main political issues and better involving citizens and activists in the lives of parties. This would show people that EU policies are not solely the result of intergovernmental negotiations, the adjustment of private interests or debates between experts, but of political choices expressed by the different European parties and, within them, by the candidates competing in the primaries.

A fourth reform would be to acknowledge the right of the European Parliament to initiate legislation – which is currently a privilege of the Commission. While this may be less important than it seems, as most legislative texts are drafted by the executive power in all advanced democracies, it is important symbolically because most citizens do not understand why the European Parliament is deprived of such a basic right when it is the central institution described by the treaties.

A fifth reform would be to constrain the Council to behave and work as a high chamber. Today, it is partially described as such by the treaties, but it does not really deliberate as a legislative body. It still does not play the game when it comes to transparency or politics. The Council is mainly a place for intergovernmental negotiations and not for political deliberation, and it tends to leave every key decision to the European Council.

Finally, our sixth reform would be to clarify the relations between the European Parliament and the European Council. The latter is a kind of collective head of state – one that has to escape the control and pressure of the European Parliament – but the current situation is not democratically satisfying: the European Council has become a major actor in EU policymaking but it is not accountable in any way. It is totally disconnected from citizens' representatives.

All of these six changes would make more sense if they were decided upon at once. These institutional reforms require a global approach if the permanent institutional tinkering is to stop and if we are to avoid the unintended consequences of half-baked modifications. The Conference on the Future of Europe is the right place to undertake such a reflection – even if it has not been encouraged to do so. It is also crucial to link any institutional reform with further developments in EU competences. Reforms that were focused solely on institutions would probably – like the Constitutional treaty – fail to be approved by citizens because of an insurmountable communication hurdle: justifying the necessary reforms would require explaining that the EU's current institutions are not democratic enough, thereby proving the Eurosceptics right. If the institutional reforms instead saw further development of EU policies – as was the case for the Single European Act and the Treaty of Maastricht – they could be justified through the requirements of deepening European integration.

REFERENCES

Caunes, K., Costa, O., Garben, S., and Govaere, I. (eds). 2021. Special issue on the Conference on the Future of Europe. *European Law Journal* 27, forthcoming.

Costa, O., and Brack, N. 2018. *How the European Union Really Works*, 2nd edition. Routledge.

Costa, O. (ed.). 2019. *The European Parliament in Times of Crisis: Dynamics and Transformations*. London: Palgrave.

The new prospects for the European electoral and party systems

By Ania Skrzypek

The Conference on the Future of Europe has already been both widely praised and roundly criticized. On the one hand, for three years various prime ministers have been appearing in front of the European Parliament or lecturing at the podiums of renowned universities to spell out the trajectory that they think the EU should pursue. They have spoken about the need to bring Europe closer to its citizens, whose voices and votes should matter most. On the other hand, the much-anticipated process of involving diverse stakeholders in the debate has seen its launch delayed and its format placed in rather a tight institutional straitjacket. There is concern about the outcome being subject to the deadline of the next EU elections, which may prevent longer-term debate, as that process may also be hijacked to serve a specific EU presidency or national elections. In the midst of all this, progressives should be the ones feeling extraordinary responsibility when it comes to making sure that the Conference remains a historical turning point – one that will see citizens empowered through a strengthening of the participatory and representative features of European democracy.

MOVING ON, MOVING FORWARD

There is a need to examine the state in which the European and electoral party systems find themselves. The reference point here is the last European elections, which saw a number of encouraging developments. The turnout rose for the first time since 1979. The traditional, pro-European parties did not perform as badly as expected, with the social democrats enjoying solid results, potentially benefitting from the 'Timmermans effect'. The outcome suggested that the institution of the top candidate started having a greater impact, and also that the European parties played a greater role in the campaign. In 2019 there was more of a fierce competition between them. Following the vote, greater attention was paid to the need to secure gender equality among the top jobs. The negotiations saw the further consolidation of some political families, including the social democrats, on whose behalf Prime Minister Pedro Sanchez led the talks. And once the name of the Commission's candidate for president was announced, several European parliamentary groups, including S&D (the Socialists and Democrats Group in the European Parliament), composed letters to spell out their respective groups' political demands vis-à-vis the Commission's work programme, making their support conditional when it came to signing up to a specific agenda. The newly elected College of Commissioners became the first in the EU's history to be that highly politicized, as the representatives of the respective political families inside of it started working in factions.

Nevertheless, there were also regrettable setbacks. The newly elected European Parliament is the most fragmented there has ever been, and it continues having to recompose itself. Though Frans Timmermans was clearly favoured to be the Commission's president, he was blocked by the veto of just two countries. The unexpected nomination of Ursula von der Leyen provoked the newspaper headline: 'Who killed the *Spitzenkandidaten* system?' And finally, despite trying to make the debate first and foremost about the issues, in the end, groups such as S&D faced a divisive strategic choice. Not voting for von der Leyen could mean her getting elected with votes from the right-wing, and extreme right-wing, parties.

These reflections leave us with much to ponder. But although implementing ideas such as top candidates has proved challenging since 2009, the progressives should not abondon them. Instead, they should reiterate their commitment to enhancing the transnational dimension of EU politics.

HARD LAWS AND EVEN HARDER POLITICAL WILL

With that acceleration in mind, the European Parliament is currently working on two reports: one about reforming the European electoral system and one about reforming the European party system. These should be seen as supplementary to the Conference on the Future of Europe (CoFoE), providing a solid reason to use the CoFoE Declaration clause stating that there would be 'no treaty changes unless…' and in the future demand a change.

The report on the electoral system should argue for ending the Lisbon Treaty's ambiguity regarding the relationship between the top candidates (as presented by the European political parties) and becoming the Commission's president-elect. It should also strive to start debates about several other issues, such as the lowering of the voting age, voting in this age of digitalization and civic digital rights, mechanisms to protect elections from foreign and corporate influence, and finally redefining the parameters of European campaigns. The existing provisions fall short of setting guidelines for what became a pan-European campaign, with features such as televised debates between the leading candidates, extensive use of social media and an eagerness by activists to campaign across national borders.

Additionally, there is a need to return to a discussion about transnational lists. This proposal failed during the previous legislative period, despite there seeming to have been a window of opportunity when British MEPs sadly vacated their seats. Calculations showed that the mandates that were thereby freed up could have been reallocated and attached to elections via transnational lists in a way that would have meant that the electoral principles of proportionality and representation could still have been upheld. Consequently, even if the idea of resurrecting transnational lists might seem risky, succeeding in making them happen would require taking an even greater risk, as it is impossible to consider transnational lists as a stand alone issue. They have to be linked with a number of other questions. For instance, should transnational lists be seen as an indispensable step in upgrading political union and adding a fifth: allowing transborder votes? What kind of parliamentarism would allow the Union to improve representative democracy and the efficiency of the decision-making processes? Should the EU aim for the bicameral system? Should the leading candidates be required to run on transnational lists when the existing statistics show that the absolute number of votes cast may see a European party other than the one with the most seats winning the bid for the Commission's president?

These questions, and several others, show that the debate about reform of the electoral system is inseparable from deliberations about how to strengthen the institutional system. That is a healthy link, since both issues connect with the mission of making the voices and the votes of European citizens matter more. All of this connects with the second of the above-mentioned reports – the one that looks at the future of European political parties.

This will certainly bring some clarification at the organizational level. But while it is being drafted, the European parties should look to go beyond what is currently on the debating table. They need to prove that they are still able to be the protagonists of change. Change that happens not because of hard laws but because the political will to innovate can be even stronger.

To begin with, the 2019 election proved that it is possible to think differently about the function of a political platform in the European context. European political parties should consider revising the internal processes that they have that lead to formulating political proposals. They may want to explore differentiation between their fundamental programmes, their electoral programmes, their manifestos and their programmes for governing. Doing this could be seen as a bridge between pan-European and national debates, as well as being a way of closing ranks with the European Parliament groups that were established after the 2019 elections. There is also a need to look at the function of other documents – statements and reports – to see how their drafting could provide a way to open up internal networks and create more inclusive thematic forums. If they could be opened up to the public, they could engage diverse audiences in consultative process and exhibit strong political differentiation at the EU level.

Then, regardless of the decisions made at the EU level about transnational lists and leading candidates, European political parties should not give up on them. Instead, they should look at ways of making improvements to them. First, there needs to be clarification about the internal procedures (from nomination to selection), the timelines and also the relationship between the top candidate and the election platform. It should ideally be the same as the manifesto of the europarty that backs her/him up. Second, consideration needs to be given to whether the leading candidate should have a team of running mates – colleagues who, if possible, would be the Commissioner-nominees after the elections, or who would serve as a kind of shadow cabinet inside of the European political parties. This would allow the process of forming the Commission to become even more transparent, and European political parties would be even more involved in it. And third, there are strong reasons to recommend that discussion takes place about making the nomination process for the leading candidates more inclusive. Here, a double candidacy option would be an idea to consider.

GENDER EQUALITY AS A PRINCIPLE AND A PRACTICE

As already mentioned, while there were many disagreements about the nominees for the top jobs after the last European elections, there was clear acceptance of the fact that, overall, the list should be gender balanced. This has had a clear effect on the public sphere, but there is much to be done to improve the inclusiveness of European politics.

To begin with, while drafting the report on the European political parties, recognizing their political women's organizations could be considered. Many of these have existed as long as the European political parties themselves, often in the form of inner-party committees. But if they could be elevated to have the status of organizations, they could perhaps apply for additional funding if additional provisions were created inside of the European political party envelopes.

Second, before the European elections the European political parties could consider signing some kind of Diversity and Equality Charter. In the 1990s a similar idea was proposed. It focused on prudence in dealing with public funds and it succeeded in setting good standards. Nowadays, European political parties could consider making common pleas and sharing best practices, promoting inclusiveness and diversity on their own lists.

Third, while the double-candidacy idea has already been touched upon, there would have to be stronger demand for it to ensure that not only the top posts, but also the entire Commission and the parliamentary bodies (the presidium, the committees, etc.) were gender balanced. The member sstates should be obliged to always nominate gender balanced duos. And europarties could anticipate the process of Commission formation by introducing a mechanism of 'running mates' and ensuring a gender balanced pool of candidates to become Commissioners. Should a member state fail to provide a gender-balanced duo of nominees, the right to nominate the second person would by default go to the European Parliament.

IT COULD BE YEARS, OR IT COULD BE A MOMENT

Political reforms are undoubtedly complex processes. To succeed, they need to rely on the willingness of stakeholders to pursue change and alter political culture. In the case of the complicated European institutional and political system, it has long been accepted that compromises, and hence transformations, take time. But while the necessary debates could take years, so many of their aspects could be clarified straight away, in the heat of the current moment. Progressives should not miss the chance to increase citizens' involvement and confidence in the EU.

REFERENCES

Skrzypek, A. 2020. Solidaristic, social and sensible – reflections on progressivism for today and when tomorrow comes. *Social Europe Journal*, April.

Skrzypek, A. 2021. Compassionate and visionary leadership. Key lessons of Social Democratic governance in Covid-19. In *FEPS Progressive Yearbook*, edited by L. Andor, A. Skrzypek and H. Giusto. FEPS/Astra Warszawa.

Skrzypek, A., and Thissen, L. 2020. Weibliche Regierungsscheffinen im Umgang mit der Pandemie. In *Virenregime. Wie die Coronakrise unsere Welt verändert. Befunde, Analysen, Anregungen*, edited by Th. Schmidinger and J. Weidenholzer, pp. 292–314. Vienna: Bahoe Books.

The digital revolution and our democratic lives: meeting the challenges

By Gerda Falkner

THE BENEFICIAL EFFECTS OF DIGITALIZATION ARE ABUNDANT BUT THEY HAVE MADE US DEPENDENT

Digitalization has brought numerous benefits to our lives and our societies. Ever-faster computers and the internet now connect people with each other and (more recently) also with 'smart' objects such as household machinery, sports gadgets and children's toys. Groundbreaking research and innovation are possible thanks to ever-faster communication and calculation: see, for example, the speedy development of vaccines to combat Covid-19!

Alongside such gifts (which I do not discuss further here for reasons of space) have come challenges for the democratic functioning of our modern societies. Overall, the fact that our individual, societal and political *dependency* on the workings of digital infrastructure has grown must be considered a negative facet. Almost nothing can function nowadays without computing power and electricity – all the way down to food delivery and our water supply. Although digital infrastructure is therefore 'too crucial to fail', increasingly dangerous cyberattacks have become an almost daily occurrence – attacks on individual users, but also on major service providers and even institutions such as parliaments and national banks.

The number 1 challenge of our times is therefore to *balance security and innovation*. Meeting this challenge is all the more difficult considering that digitalization progresses almost 'naturally', driven by individual enterprises and consumers. In contrast, cybersecurity needs political decisions to be made and coordinated actions to be taken on top of decentralized ones. The stakes are high: a devastating cyberattack could ultimately disrupt even digitalization itself in affected areas or societies, possibly to the benefit of undemocratic powers. And stakes are even higher where democratic infrastructure, such as public administration or even elections (as in Estonia), has already gone online.

DIGITALIZATION AND THE FOUNDATIONS OF DEMOCRACY

The internet's great ability to facilitate fast and cheap communication is omnipresent these days, and most citizens enjoy that benefit on a daily basis. By contrast, it is much less evident that specific implementations of that same technology *threaten to disrupt democracy*.

Consider that digitalization affects all essential elements of democratic life, from the economy to voters and politics.

The economy

Our economies form the crucial bedrock for democratic governance. Alas, they lean towards more inequality than ever before – inequality between businesses and between individuals.

Present-day capitalism is characterized by so-called network effects, favouring domination by a small number of enterprises. Internet platforms such as Amazon and Google attract business because they are big and offer more options than their competitors – a self-reinforcing mechanism. Furthermore, digital giants tend to diversify, integrating both horizontally (i.e. offering more types of business to their customers) and vertically (i.e. taking over parts of the production chain to gain even more control and increase profits). Existing competition law procedures are not a good fit for the speed of the digital economy and the open borders we find in our globalized world. Unfortunately, it is well known that markets that tend towards a few quasi-monopolistic players do not bode well for democracy.

Moreover, the internet giants thrive when it comes to the most precious resource of the digital age: data. Buying things or searching online produces computerized information about consumers. This resource is essentially free for the internet giants to exploit, with or without the de facto *un*-informed 'consent' of the users. Firms use it not only to improve their services but also, most importantly, to produce computerized calculations about and representations of their users and their users' contacts. Such information is sold to advertisers and used to 'nudge' users towards staying online to read or buy more, leaving additional data traces. Among other things, the digital giants use this information to develop artificial intelligence, which will make them even more influential in the longer term, just as Shoshana Zuboff's book on 'surveillance capitalism' warns (Zuboff 2019).

Many people argue that this form of oligopoly-driven market economy could also make consumers and workers ever more unequal in the absence of any pushback. Uber and businesses like it tend to undermine traditional employment relationships, and in any case, digitalization could make many human jobs superfluous, thereby producing ever-mounting fears among those few who are still employed. These are all conditions that are known to make democratic societies less stable.

The individual

Such potential effects of digitalization connect the economy with yet another pillar of democracy: the individual.

Democracies need voters to express their free will in regular elections, all based on a political discourse in which arguments are publicly weighed against each other. Relevant intermediaries between citizens and the state's institutions are political parties and the media. They both perform essential functions, but these functions are increasingly in danger because of online misinformation and hate-mongering (see below).

Moreover, we may witness a decline in autonomy, and possibly even the 'end of the individual', if digitalization proceeds unabated. Algorithms maximize people's time online via attention-grabbing headlines and by provoking strong emotions like hate (Vaidhyanathan 2018). Psychologists warn that ever-more screen time leads to the unlearning of truly discursive communication and favours psychological dependency on receiving 'instant gratification' online. In the long run, constant 'nudging' by digital giants who know our preferences and weaknesses might engender outright manipulation of individuals: see, for example, the Cambridge Analytica scandal. Individuals would then no longer possess any personal 'will' to speak of, and genuinely free elections might become a thing of the past.

Public administration and politics

Finally, public administration and politics are faced by digitalization's innovative potentials and by its looming dangers as well.

Information and public services can be offered more efficiently via the internet, at least to those who are digitally connected. New models of wide-scale citizen involvement in politics are technically feasible. Democracies could even run elections digitally, as some states in the EU are already testing (i.e. Estonia). However, faster and cheaper services do not come without costs and risks, e.g. regarding confidentiality and, potentially, even the secrecy of votes. A paper ballot can be counted on site with witnesses in a controlled setting and then destroyed forever. Digital data can be intercepted or multiplied while barely leaving a trace. As soon as public administration, or even elections, move online, not only will they become potential targets for cyberattacks but they will become even more prone to real or perceived forgery and data leaks. The manipulation of elections is now both a real danger (it is highly probable that Donald Trump would not have been elected to the US presidency without Russian cyber trolls) and a dangerously delegitimizing factor for democracies (even the mere possibility of manipulation is harmful). And the misuse of sensitive election data could extend far into the future, when new powers might be interested in the past political choices of individuals or groups.

Unless our societies somehow manage to achieve a situation of highly reliable cybersecurity, caution in realizing all that is technically feasible seems warranted: balancing security and innovation is a major challenge nowadays, both in basic infrastructure and in democratic and economic infrastructure (see above).

What is more, in this digital age politics is being replaced with something that only faintly resembles what it once was. So-called social media replaces in-depth journalism from specialized teams, meaning that the fourth power in the democratic system of checks and balances fades away. Furthermore, election manifestos will soon be replaced by tailor-made political advertisements that are micro-targeted to specific individuals. In combination, these messages may be not simply incoherent but possibly actually conflicting. In other words, consistent parties might soon be obsolete, and political candidates may soon be at the mercy of internet platforms – but democracies depend on the trustworthy representation of values and meaningful debates about political options (e.g. Bartlett 2018).

A WAY OUT? ACT NOW, OR DEMOCRACY MIGHT FADE OUT FAST

Fortunately, scholars of the 'digital revolution' have thrashed out a wealth of options that will allow us to reap the benefits of new technology while still securing the basics of democratic life. We need decisive action far beyond existing EU provisions and exceeding the latest ideas proposed by the European Commission. Among the most promising options are the following.

- More and better *rights for citizens*: e.g. the right to *effective data protection* (not simply the right to being able to 'sign off' for supposedly free services without practical choice) and, since aggregated data is usually more valuable, *group* rights regarding group data as an economic resource; the right to *personal integrity* (i.e. not being subjected to addictive software or online 'behaviour modification' via inadvertent nudging) and to *reinforced privacy* (i.e. not being subject to ubiquitous tracking online or in public places; the right to disconnect).
- Innovative *public digital services and infrastructures* for consumer empowerment and to secure public discourses that favour compassion over aggression; the non-commercial use of new tech and digital common goods, e.g. open-source software and public interest platforms; data governance models outside private

business, run by public and/or civil society bodies; and the adaptation of educational and welfare systems to digital times (public investment seems worthwhile, considering that the future of democracy is at stake).
- Much stricter *regulation of online platforms*: specific and speedy anti-trust procedures; platforms treated as publishers and taxed appropriately, to ensure fairer competition with the real economy and with professional journalism; effectively forbid whatever is illegal offline from happening online; guarantee a basic requirement of interoperability for all novel online formats so that providers can be changed easily, as is already the case for email and internet access; extend labour laws to the 'gig economy'.
- A greater focus on *resilient design* and *digital sovereignty* seems key to upholding citizens' rights and democracy in the digital age. This is a major task when one considers the existing supply chains and global competitors' pressures, but it might be a case of now or never.

REFERENCES

Bartlett, J. 2018. *The People vs Tech – How the Internet is Killing Democracy (And How We Can Save It)*. New York: Dutton.

Vaidhyanathan, S. 2018. *Anti-Social Media: How Facebook Disconnects Us and Undermines Democracy*. Oxford: Oxford University Press.

Zuboff, S. 2019. *The Age of Surveillance Capitalism: The Fight for a Human Future at the New Frontier of Power*. New York: Public Affairs.

What are the potential and the limits of the Lisbon Treaty?

By Mercedes Bresso

The Conference on the Future of Europe should try to be as effective as possible. Exploiting the maximum potential of the present post-Lisbon treaties represents the quickest way to an 'ever closer Union'.

The Conference could propose to the EU institutions that they use the treaty provisions to accelerate reforms that are suggested by the Conference itself, thereby avoiding the biggest problem that the Union suffes from: the very long time it needs to undertake reforms.

It is clear that for some reforms a treaty change will be necessary, but we can change our Union in a really significant way simply by using the treaties we already have.

We should demonstrate that Europe can be profoundly reformed without embarking on a long procedure of treaty modifications. This was done during the financial crisis by the European Central Bank (ECB) under Mario Draghi and during the Covid-19 pandemic by the Commission President Ursula von der Leyen. Something similar could be achieved by the Conference, acting with the support of European citizens and asking for a stronger EU in the world, quickly recovering from crisis, realizing a strong, social and green market economy, achieving what it has been decided.

All legislative acts of the EU must clarify its legal bases. Very frequently, these are found in the single market regulation: the EU's main competence.

To avoid this ambiguity, the Conference should clarify what kind of Europe it wants by addressing the following questions.

- What competencies should be conferred on the EU (that is, which ones should only the EU manage) for which a formal transfer of

sovereignty is needed (foreign, defence and security policies, the single market policy, EMU, the EU budget and fiscal capacity, etc.)? Some of these would require treaty changes, but in many other cases it could be enough to simply specify the extent of the attribution.
- What competencies should be shared, for which the Union can realize a coordination and approve the common framework for national laws: environmental regulations, harmonization of social measures, coordination of economic and fiscal policies, and so on?
- And finally, what competencies should remain with, or be returned to, the member states (and their regions), leaving the EU to intervene only when requested or for coordination?

The Conference should also consider the following question.

- What tools could the EU use to decide and produce results, rapidly and effectively, in the field of its competencies? Here, institutional reforms will be needed. Some of these can be made using the provisions of the Lisbon Treaties; others will require treaty changes.

One of the Conference's main results could be a strong request to member states to accept qualified majority voting in the Council and in all legislative procedures, putting the European Parliament on the same level as the Council, as a legislator. This would bring a real revolution to the decision-making process, which is actually the real *'maillon faible'*, clearly perceived by citizens and observers, who ask very frequently why the Union is so long, when able to decide. This change would be possible using the *passerelle* clause or an inter-institutional agreement, or simply through strengthened cooperation.

A treaty is a toolbox for action, not an objective in itself. But no reform can be done without the appropriate tools.

I will now present some examples of reforms that we could realize using the present treaty provisions. The same approach should be used for foreign, defence, migration and security policy.

INSTITUTIONAL REFORMS

The Parliament

We could create a parliamentary subcommittee on EMU matters, exclusively for MEPs elected in euro area countries, which would have the power to discuss questions concerning the euro and euro-zone economic policy. Decisions could be taken by a super-committee, acting like a plenary, composed of all euro area MEPs or, alternatively, by the European Parliament. This differentiation might be possible without treaty change, i.e. with an inter-institutional agreement, and it could allow better coordination between euro area MEPs and the Eurogroup.

We should reform the relevant electoral law and introduce the same rules for all members states and for the transnational lists – headed by their *Spitzenkandidaten* – that are presented by European political parties. We should define a procedure for a common candidate for a coalition and for negotiations if any candidate has a majority in the European Parliament.

We could develop forms of online direct democracy or improve the European Citizens' Initiative.

The European Council

The European Council should 'curb' its interference in the legislative process and use the *passerelle* clause to allow the Council to migrate to qualified majority voting and ordinary legislative procedures in all the fields allowed by the treaties. Differentiated forms of integration (i.e. a multitier Europe) could be realized when some member states refuse to enlarge the competencies of the EU using this enhanced cooperation.

The Council

The Council should act on an equal footing with the European Parliament, using qualified majority voting and the ordinary legislative procedures. It should reduce the number of Council configurations, which should act as parliamentary committees, open to Parliament representatives, and it should create a unique Legislative Council, acting like a European Parliament plenary session and thereby improving the transparency of its decision-making processes.

The Commission

The introduction of the *Spitzenkandidaten* process for choosing the president of the Commission will require a decision from the European Council and the approval of an inter-institutional agreement with the European Parliament. The agreement should define a procedure for selecting candidates and allow alliances to be formed between political parties, and it should be clear about what should be done if the winner is unable to reach a qualified majority in the European Parliament.

Member states should propose at least two candidates for the Commission, with gender equilibrium. The number of Commissioners should be reduced in accordance with what is possible in the the treaty.

The Commission should represenst the eurozone at the International Monetary Fund and the World Bank and represent the EU in international organizations in which it has the competence to do so.

Economic and Monetary Union (EMU)

A new legal framework for economic policy coordination could be established by better using the available instruments (Article 136 of the TFEU).

- The EMU should be completed through a set of commonly agreed benchmarks in the following areas: the labour market, competitiveness, tax policy, and environmental and social standards. Respect for these standards could allow members states to participate in a shock-absorption mechanism. Respect for the Stability and Growth Pact could be improved through use of incentive mechanisms.
- The Union should be given the capacity to borrow money (i.e. through eurobonds) for strategic investments (thereby

- stabilizing the mechanism used for both the Recovery Plan and the Juncker Plan).
- A budget should be established for the eurozone, based on fiscal capacity and own resources. This could be created using an internal agreement.
- The *passerelle* clause should be used to introduce qualified majority voting and co-legislation in all economic matters. Use Article 48(7) of the TEU and Article 312(2) of the TFEU to switch from unanimity to qualified majority voting for the adoption of the Multiannual Financial Framework regulation, reducing its terms to five years.
- A permanent instrument to finance reforms or provide countercyclical assistance should be created. (Eventually, we should look to have a euro area stabilization function under enhanced cooperation.)
- A European Treasury should be created, with the capacity to issue debt. It should be accountable to the European Parliament.
- The European Parliament's role in the European semester process should be strengthened, and environmental and social benchmarks should be introduced.
- A Financial Union should be created, completing the Bank Union and the Capital Markets Union.
- A Fiscal Union should also be created (i) to establish the exchange of information between national tax authorities to avoid tax planning, base erosion and profit shifting, and (ii) to create a common consolidated corporate tax base, with a minimum rate. There should be coordinated action to fight tax havens.
- An Energy Union should be created.
- The European Parliament's role should be widened, extending the ordinary legislative procedure to all economic and fiscal affairs using the *passerelle* clause or enhanced cooperation.

Social Europe

Competence over social affairs was not attributed to the EU by the treaty, but using its competence for the single market the Union's action in this field has been enlarged. An example of this is the approval of the European Pillar of Social Rights (which demonstrated that the Lisbon Treaty could be interpreted in an extensive way). But the implementation of this instrument, which is fundamental for our citizens, risks being blocked by conflicts of competencies. It would be better if the status and limits of EU intervention in social matters was clarified, including over health services, where the necessity of coordination has become evident during the Covid-19 pandemic.

We could develop the social aspects of the EMU, guaranteeing the rights of workers in terms of mobility, promoting the introduction of a minimum wage (as a percentage of the median national wage) and a minimum welfare system, stabilizing the common unemployment insurance scheme that was created during the pandemic period, and introducing an employee's mobility directive.

A set of social criteria should be established for the evaluation of national economic performance in the realization of structural reforms.

Ecological transition

An Environmental Act should be established to summarize, clarify and enhance all environmental regulations, particularly those relating to climate change. The act should define the 'ecological transition' – the legal basis for action – and all the policies concerned. It should also clarify the European, national, regional and local competencies in this field.

After the pandemic: a republic of Europe – what would it mean?
By Ulrike Guerot

'À coup sûr, cette chose immense, la *République européenne, nous l'aurons.*' — Victor Hugo, Paris, 1872

EUROPE AND ITS FORGOTTEN CITIZENS

The Covid-19 pandemic is the latest in a series of crises that have alienated Europe from its citizens. More than ever, the EU is under pressure to reform its institutions and to reconnect with its citizens. In addition to the problems caused by Covid-19, the political environment has been darkened by Brexit, the questions of Catalan or Scottish independence, the rise of populism nearly everywhere in Europe, and serious problems with the application of the 'rule of law' – to name just a few of the problems we face.

Roughly a third of European citizens – the so-called populists – want to retreat to their nation states or to the autonomy of regional 'subs'; another half wants a *different* Europe. Civil society, especially young people, are becoming more and more passionate about renewing the old structures of the EU and its so-called institutional 'trilogy', which fail to appropriately represent the will of Europe's citizens. The European Council, especially, as a rather opaque and barely accountable political body, is coming under increasing pressure. The representation gap with the current structures of the EU is obvious.

European citizens – their voice and their wishes – were largely forgotten during the setting up of the EU's institutions, over the first seventy years of its history (from 1950 to 2020). The EU's institutional trilogy includes a parliament that has no real legislative power, only the power to take decisions alongside the Council, no accountability and no control of the budget or the executive power of the EU. The so-called 'democratic deficit' has become ever more apparent in recent years. During the banking crisis a decade ago, European citizens rebelled against many policies pursued by the EU. For the first time they vigorously, and very loudly, asked to participate in European policymaking. They called for transnational lists and truly European parties. And around the time of the 2019 European Parliament elections, two such pan-European parties emerged out of these social movements: VOLT on the liberal side and DiEM on the more progressive side.

The 'sovereignty question' – who makes decisions in the EU: the citizens or the European Council? – became a widely discussed topic and finally led to the inception of the Conference on the Future of Europe, a promise made by Ursula von der Leyen after she had been designated president of the European Commissions in the autumn of 2019 despite not having been the *Spitzenkandidatin* herself. Seldom had the European system let European citizens know so clearly that while they can always vote, they have no power. As a reaction to this – Ms von der Leyen probably felt the urgency herself – some 300,000 European citizens are supposed to discuss their future in citizens' hearings directly within the next two years. The Commission has been busy designing the form and format of these hearings for the last year, as well as their content and context. The real issue is to guard against the whole exercise – however well intended it is – ending in yet more citizen disappointment: we do not need another evasive report about the flaws of the European policy system that has no ambition and no suggestions for radical change that tilts the system towards real sovereignty and power for citizens.

THE PRINCIPLE OF GENERAL POLITICAL EQUALITY

The core problem is that the Conference on the Future of Europe wants to consult European citizens – but European citizens, if the term is taken literally, do not exist. If the conference had one – just one! – goal that would trigger system change, then it would be to *make* real European citizens before consulting them. The definition of what European citizenship will mean in the future must be the cornerstone of the conference!

As things stand, von der Leyen will, at the end of the day, be interviewing Danish or Greek citizens, or Dutch or Portuguese ones, as nobody has a European passport. National passports are only wrapped in a Bordeaux-red European cover. Although they are called 'European citizens', they are de facto still living in 'national law containers' (Ulrich Beck). In his famous book of 2003, which raised the question *Sommes-Nous des Citoyens Européens?* ('Are we really European citizens?'), the French Philosopher Etienne Balibar answered with a clear 'no'. This answer is still valid in 2021!

One of the most imminent problems of the EU's democratic deficit is that European citizens are not equal in front of the law: they have different voting systems, different taxation, different access to social rights in their reciprocal countries, etc., in their respective countries. And yet in a democracy, citizens do not compete with each other when it comes to voting, taxation or social treatment. They obey the same rules, and that is precisely what makes them citizens of the same state.

An essential, but not sufficient, condition of any democracy is that all citizens are equal. If Europe wants to become a democracy, it must therefore make all of its citizens equal in the eyes of the law in *all* its facets. For now, there are three facets to the 'European' existence of EU citizens. First, there is their 'market citizenship': for example, they share the same regulations when it comes to consumer protection and roaming fees. Second, there is their capacity as a worker or an employer: they benefit from free movement of persons and can take on work in, or workers from, any European country. When it comes to the third facet – what citizenship really means: common voting procedures, taxation and social access – Europeans ultimately remain *national* citizens.

Classically, 'one person, one vote' is the key requirement of a democracy, giving rise to a single electoral body that then decides on a budget and social distribution. This corresponds to the famous saying 'no taxation without representation'. In the words of the French sociologist Marcel Mauss, it is not origin or identity that makes a nation, but a body of citizens deciding together over a budget, taxation and the social question. If citizens agree to do so, these citizens create the foundations for a republic, as they submit to the same laws, and above all the same laws with respect to voting, taxation and social access. General, secret, direct and equal elections thus constitute '*Le Sacre du Citoyen*': the 'sacredness' of the citizens (Pierre Rosanvallon). European citizens today miss precisely this 'sacredness' of their citizenship. This is what they need to fix during the Conference on the Future of Europe!

In current European discussions, the notion of *citoyen* ('citizen') often alludes to the sharing of values or to 'feeling European'. And yet citizenship essentially means *having the same rights* – even when the same values are not shared! In this respect, the current notion of European citizenship, which was granted in 1992 through the Maastricht Treaty, has remained normatively incomplete. European citizens share roaming fees … but not a voting system. They can go to the same consulate, in Kinshasa say … but they do not share the same system of taxation. They can take jobs in various European member states … but they do not get the same unemployment pay, child allowances or retirement benefits. In short, there is permanent segregation based on nationality. This must become a focus for Europe after the pandemic.

Formally, the EU offers 'four freedoms': the freedom of movement of people, goods, capital and services. And yet, until now, the EU has had a hybrid law community. If Europe wants a game changing 'reboot' after the pandemic, European law will need to go from 'hybrid' literally down to earth, where the citizens (or the 'political subjects' of European unity) live: legal equality must encompass them all in all aspects of their lives. Applying the general principle of equality for all European citizens would mean embedding the European single market and the currency into a common European democracy, because a currency union *is already* a social contract, as Jean-Jacques Rousseau put it. That would represent a quantum leap from an internal market and a currency project towards real European political unity.

The same European rights and regulations within the EU's legal framework are applying to goods in the legal frame of the single market; to capital within the euro-governance; or to work/services, meaning to the 'economic factor' of European citizens, who are yet not considered equal in their legal integrally. All three of these things

– goods, capital and work/services – benefit from legal equality throughout Europe. It is only European citizens who are facing legal discrimination. Oilcans and light bulbs are 'equal' under European legislation across the EU; citizens are not.

Another question is whether European citizenship has permanent status. A case (C-252/29) submitted to the European Court of Justice in August 2020 will need to decide whether British citizens lose their European citizenship after Brexit. The Maastricht Treaty is a 'Union of States' and a 'Union of Citizens'. European citizenship has been granted by the EU as an individual right. The question is whether the 'state entity' of the United Kingdom can take away these individual rights of European citizens – among them the British – only because it is leaving the EU under Article 50. If the European Court of Justice decides that European citizenship has *permanent status* – independent of the state affiliation of those citizens – this could become a political entry door to shifting sovereignty in Europe: from states to citizens.

UTOPIA IS SOMETHING THAT WE MAKE

Citizens who join in a political body based on equal rights (*ius aequum*) establish a republic. If European citizens were to agree to the principle of political equality, they would de facto have founded a European Republic. This would represent a paradigm shift from a United States of Europe based on the *integration* of nation states towards a European Republic based on the sovereignty of European citizens – citizens who would become the main actors of European progress. The #CTOE alliance (www.CitizensTakeOver.eu) – a group of European citizens that take the form of a citizens' assembly – already has two-hour Zoom meetings every Wednesday with the aim of writing a European Constitution. Perhaps this is a first hint towards such a development.

Today's EU is not stable. Without a decisive step forward, it will be unsustainable. In perspective, citizens must be sovereign and equal before the law in European democracy, the European Parliament must make decisions and there must be separation of powers. Doing this would amount to the 'Great Reformation' of

Europe! In order to accomplish this radical new beginning for Europe, we simply have to remember what Jean Monnet always said: 'L'Europe, nous ne coalisons pas des états, mais nous unisons des hommes' ('Europe does not mean to integrate states, but to unite people').

New horizons for a political union

By Jo Leinen

The EU can be characterized as a large common market and a monetary union, with related policies around these core projects. Identification with this EU is high in the industrial and commercial sectors but quite low among citizens and in civil society in the twenty-seven member states.

Political union requires a much higher level of acceptance – it needs ownership from citizens, both directly and indirectly. Citizens must be central to decision making, and policies should focus on citizens' interests. The Conference on the Future of Europe is a perfect opportunity to respond to these objectives.

The idea of a united Europe was always more than simply an economic and financial project. The vision is much more profound than that: a union based on fundamental values, where people can live, work and meet each other without discrimination based on their ethnicity or religious background.

A European Republic would be the best way to express the aspirations and expectations of millions of people, taking into account the decades of European integration since the early 1950s.

Democracy would be at the heart of this European Republic. The sovereign are the citizens of the EU. Political power derives from different levels of people's participation.

FUTURE DEVELOPMENT

The EU should be further developed into a full-fledged parliamentary democracy. As the citizens' chamber, the European Parliament must be granted all the necessary competences for exercising its role of representing the EU's citizens. That is:

- the right to legislate, co-decision as the rule (i.e. the legislative decision-making process by both the European Parliament and the Council of the European Union on equal footing);
- the right of initiative (i.e. the right for the European Parliament to submit legislative proposals);
- the right of inquiry;
- budgetary rights, with co-decision for income (own resources), as for spending; and
- the right to elect and control the EU executive (through election of the Commission's president as well as the College of Commissioners).

REFORM OF THE EU EXECUTIVE

The EU executive is opaque and lacks transparency. It must be reformed.

The EU should have one (double-headed) president through fusing the president of the European Commission and the president of the European Council. The Council of Ministers should be transformed into a Chamber of States (i.e. a second chamber). And the rotating presidency system should be abolished.

DEMOCRATIC INFRASTRUCTURE

To achieve this political union (the European Republic), we will need a democratic infrastructure.

European political parties must be empowered to exercise their roles and functions in the parliamentary democracy. They need to be an integral part of European elections through organizing European lists with a *Spitzenkandidat* at the top who runs for Commission president.

National, regional and local parliamentarians must be given a platform to participate in programming the EU agenda, and the mechanisms required for doing so.

More possibilities for citizens and civil society to participate in and influence EU policymaking should be created. As well as the Structured Dialogue with the Commission and the European Citizens' Initiative, we need more ideas for better communication and participation in EU affairs. The digital revolution brings with it new possibilities for novel multilingual and transnational channels for consultation and deliberation, and for making recommendations.

Social partners, cities, youth councils and other civic coalitions should become more involved, activating the potential they have for contributing to EU development.

The media is of crucial importance to a transnational democracy. Misinformation, fake news and hate speech are all dangerous to the successful functioning of democratic institutions. A European Media Compact and Action Plan is necessary.

The question of 'how' the political union functions as a democracy is important. 'What' the EU should achieve and 'what' the purpose of this particular European union will be are equally existential questions.

SOVEREIGNTY AND STRATEGIC AUTONOMY

In a world that is full of challenges, crises, conflicts and power games, the EU must protect the values and interests of our continent. As a political union, the EU must strive for sovereignty and strategic autonomy.

Monetary sovereignty, with the euro, should be accomplished. Sovereignty over data, especially big data, must be organized and achieved. Tax sovereignty – working against tax fraud, tax avoidance and tax oases – is crucial. The EU must strive for strategic autonomy over basic needs: food, energy, health. And sovereignty over security issues, internal ones as well as external ones, is imperative.

THE EUROPEAN REPUBLIC

The European Republic is more than a common market and a shared currency. It has a social, sustainable and innovative profile. It has a social, sustainable and innovative profile. The EU should be:

- ... the model for a sustainable society (i.e. one that is carbon neutral, and has a circular economy and rich biodiversity), fulfilling the 2030 agenda of the UN.

- ... a health union. It needs to have all the tools it requires to protect its citizens against diseases and pandemics, with a European Health Card that allows for non-discriminatory treatment anywhere in the twenty-seven member states.
- ... a Social Union, with social rights, no discrimination and fair transition mechanisms, and it must fight against poverty and exclusion.
- ... a partner for fair trade, demanding that social and ecological standards are met when it exchanges goods and services with other countries.
- ... a community of values, defending democracy and human rights against authoritarian regimes and behaviours both inside the bloc and outside it.
- ... a key player when it comes to promoting multilateralism, resolving conflicts and peace-keeping, and it should organize the security of its own people too.

The deliberations that make up the Conference on the Future of Europe must lead to the next big step forwards for the EU, based on citizenship, democratic decision making and the ability to deliver public goods for its people.

The European Republic will be a good place to live, and it will be a good partner to others around the world.

Conclusion
A European legend

By Maria João Rodrigues

We Europeans have invented the best and the worst of humanity.

- Philosophy and science, but also sophisticated war plans.
- Freedom of thought and freedom of speech, but also totalitarian doctrines.
- Freedom of initiative and larger market opportunities, but also large-scale exploitation.
- Universal education, but also exquisite aristocratic privileges.
- Welfare systems, but also entrenched child poverty.
- Democracy, but also totalitarian regimes.
- Human rights, but also the Holocaust.
- Women's emancipation, but also sophisticated discrimination.
- The connecting of the world across continents, but also the organization of enduring colonial regimes.

In the past century we triggered two world wars. After we saw the abyss that these wars created, we decided to turn the page forever by committing to building something unique in world history: a continent governed by a multilevel architecture, starting at the local level and ending at a supranational one, with a strong commitment to the global multilateral system.

After exploring industrial and military cooperation, as is seen in the United States, we concluded that we should start with market cooperation in order to build European unity. For this to work, we coupled a common market with instruments for social cohesion and supranational decision making: a European Commission with the right of initiative, accountable to a Council and a European Parliament.

In the face of a globalized world, our road to updating democratic sovereignty continued. Building on the single market, we created both a single currency and a political union with legal entity and citizenship: the European Union. By the turn of the twentieth century we had defined a long-term development strategy to compete in the global economy – not by sacrificing our social standards but by investing in knowledge, culture, education, research and innovation.

This investment was then brutally curtailed by a financial crisis that transitioned into a eurozone crisis, unveiling the inherent flaws of the existing EU architecture. A lost generation in many European countries is the terrible price that has been paid.

The triptych of values that were invented for us by the French Revolution has to be translated not just at the national level but also at the European one. If the EU wants to survive, equality can only exist in a free world if it is underpinned by a stronger spirit of solidarity. Equality when it comes to the rights of European citizens can only exist if the free and open European market is underpinned by stronger instruments of European solidarity to invest in the future of everyone – and if this investment is financed with fairness by everyone as well.

The systemic bottleneck in the EU's construction only started to be overcome when the tragedy of the Covid-19 pandemic hit us. But by then, the EU had lost more than a decade. It had become obsolete when it came to shaping and taking advantage of the digital revolution.

We Europeans, the inventors of the World Wide Web, lost ground when the devices that empower people to benefit from it – smartphones, laptops, smart objects and apps – were largely invented elsewhere, mainly in the United States. This allowed big American platforms to emerge, selling people's data to invest in the technologies of the future. Europe is now losing even more ground in this new phase of the Internet of Things. Big data is being used to revolutionize supply chains, jobs and the international division of labour, and to transform wealth in all sectors through the use of algorithms that are not defined by Europeans or according to European values.

Nevertheless, we Europeans still carry three important torches: those of ecology, welfare and democracy. But we need to reinvent them for the future by shaping the current digital revolution. However, we can only succeed if we are able to coordinate and develop action on a European scale. The strategic raw material for doing so is big data, and the minimum level for being big is continental, although the level of international cooperation would be even better.

The springboard for Europe to shape the digital revolution is universal access to new social rights over health, education, environmental quality and democratic decision making, bringing EU citizenship to a new level.

We need to be critical about our flaws and ambitious about how we can overcome them, but we should remain hopeful and confident. The life chances of future generations need to be our compass. Our European experience can also inspire the kinds of solutions we need to build with our partners at a global level. Driving the digital revolution to promote sustainable development goals and gender equality is one of them.

The governance of the future of Europe and the governance of the future of the world will be closely intertwined.

Acknowledgements

I would like to express my gratitude to the members of the FEPS Expert Group on the Future of Europe* and to the entire FEPS team, as well as to the representatives of the EU institutions and the invited experts who have accompanied us on this journey: Alicia Homs, Allan Larsson, Alvaro Oleart, Andras Inotai, Ania Skrzypek, Anke Hassel, Björn Hacker, Britta Thomsen, Daniela Schwarzer, David Rinaldi, Diego Lopez Garrido, Domenec Ruiz Devesa, Enrique Baron Crespo, Fabien Dell, Francesco Cerasani, Francesco Corti, Francesco Lanzone, Francisco Aldecoa, Gabriele Bischoff, Gerda Falkner, Gerhard Stahl, Gesine Schwan, Giorgio Clarotti, Giovanni Grevi, Guillaume Klossa, Halliki Kreinin, Henning Meyer, Irene Wennemo, Jacqueline O'Reilly, Jan Zielonka, Jan-Erik Støstad, Jean-François Lebrun, Jean-Paul Buffat, Jo Leinen, Johanna Lutz, László Andor, Liva Vikmane, Lora Lyubenova, Lukas Hochscheidt, Macro Schwarz, Manuel Muniz, Marek Belka, Margarida Marques, Mario Telò, Maurizio Ferrera, Mercedes Bresso, Michael Landesmann, Nicoletta Pirozzi, Olivier Costa, Paolo Guerrieri, Peter Bofinger, Philippa Sigl-Glockner, Pier Carlo Padoan, Pier Virgilio Dastoli, Ronja Kempin, Saïd El Khadraoui, Sergio Fabbrini, Stefan Collignon, Stine Quorning, Tanja Boerzel, Ulrike Guerot, Uwe Optenhoegel, Vassilis Ntousas, Vivien Schmidt and Vytenis Andriukaitis. The good balance between women and men and between different generations has undoubtedly provided great chemistry.

My thanks go to Nicky Robinson, who contributed to the translation of two of the chapters and took on some early proofreading of submissions. My thanks also go the London Publishing Partnership team, particularly Sam Clark and Richard Baggaley, who edited this book and provided excellent work. Finally, I am particularly grateful to François Balate, a young European leader who is now the Head of Office of the FEPS President. In that capacity, he worked with me to organize and manage the FEPS project on the Future of Europe. This book is the first public outcome of this project.

Maria João Rodrigues
President of the Foundation for European Progressive Studies

---

* The views expressed in this book do not necessarilly reflect those of the members of the Expert Group.

Glossary

AI	Artificial Intelligence
ASGS	Annual Sustainable Growth Strategies (instruments of the EU)
BATX	Baidu, Alibaba, Tencent and Xiaomi
BSE	Bovine Spongiform Encephalopathy (mad cow disease)
CABM	Carbon Adjustment Border Mechanism
CAI	Comprehensive Agreement on Investment (proposal for a trade agreement between China and the EU)
CARD	Coordinated Annual Review on Defence Mechanism of the EU
CEE	Central and Eastern Europe
CoFoE	Conference on the Future of Europe
COP	Conference of Parties (usually referring to UN Climate Conference)
CSCE	Commission on Security and Cooperation in Europe (US government agency)
CSDP	Common Security and Defence Policy of the EU
CSO	Civil Society Organization
DG	Directorate General
ECB	European Central Bank
ECDC	European Centre for Disease Prevention and Control
ECEC	Early Childhood Education and Care
ECOFIN	Economic and Financial Affairs Council (meeting of the ministers of EU member states in charge of economic and financial affairs)
EEU	Eurasian Economic Union
EGF	European Globalisation Adjustment Fund
EHU	European Health Union
EMA	European Medicines Agency
EMU	Economic and Monetary Union
EP	European Parliament
EPSR	European Pillar of Social Rights
ESF	European Social Fund
ESM	European Stability Mechanism
ETS	Emissions Trading System
EU	European Union
EUBS	European Unemployment Benefit Scheme
EZ	Eurozone Countries using the EURO as their main currency
FEAD	Fund for European Aid to the most Deprived Fund of the EU
FEPS	Foundation for European Progressive Studies
FTT	Financial Transaction Tax
G20	Group of the world's 20 major economies (19 countries plus the EU)
G7	Group of 7 (Canada, France, Germany, Italy, Japan, UK, US, EU)
GAFAM	Google, Amazon, Facebook, Apple, Microsoft

GDP	Gross Domestic Product
GDPR	General Data Protection Regulation of the EU
GNI	Gross National Income
ICT	Information and Communications Technology
IMF	International Monetary Fund
IoT	Internet of Things
IT	Information Technology
MEP	Member of the European Parliament
MFF	Multiannual Financial Framework (the EU's long-term budget)
MMT	Modern Monetary Theory
MPCC	Military Planning and Conduct Capacity
NATO	North-Atlantic Treaty Organization
NGEU	Next Generation EU (the recovery plan of the EU in response to the Covid-19 pandemic)
NGO	Non-Governmental Organization
NRRP	National Resilience and Recovery Plans
OECD	Organisation for Economic Co-operation and Development
PEPP	Pandemic Emergency Purchasing Programme (instrument of the EU)
PES	Party of European Socialists
PESCO	Permament Structured Cooperation (mechanism of the EU)
PHS	Personal and Household Services
RCEP	Regional Comprehensive Economic Partnership (free trade agreement between the Asia-Pacific nations of Australia, Brunei, Cambodia, China, Indonesia, Japan, Laos, Malaysia, Myanmar, New Zealand, the Philippines, Singapore, South Korea, Thailand and Vietnam)
REACH	Registration, Evaluation, Authorisation and Restriction of Chemicals (regulation of the EU)
RRP	Resilience and Recovery Plans
S&D	Progressive Alliance of Socialists and Democrats in the European Parliament
SDG	Sustainable Development Goals
SIWS	Social Investment in the Welfare State
STEM	Science, Technology, Engineering and Mathematics
SURE	Support to mitigate Unemployment Risks in an Emergency (instrument of the EU)
TEU	Treaty on European Union
TFEU	Treaty on the Functioning of the European Union
TTIP	Transatlantic Trade and Investment Partnership Trade (now rejected agreement between the US and the EU)
UN	United Nations
VAT	Value-Added Tax
WHO	World Health Organization
WTO	World Trade Organization
YEI	Youth Employment Initiative (instrument of the EU)

About the editor and authors

ABOUT THE EDITOR

Maria João Rodrigues, former Portuguese Minister of Employment under PM Antonio Guterres, is a European politician with a long track record in different European institutions: EU Presidencies, the Council, the European Council, the European Commission and, more recently, the European Parliament, where she was vice-president of the S&D Group, the second most important European Parliament group, in charge of general coordination and collaboration with other EU institutions.

She has played a relevant role in several important European initiatives: the Lisbon Treaty, the Lisbon Strategy and the Europe 2020 strategy (the EU's agenda for growth and jobs), eurozone reform, collaboration with the EU's strategic partners, development of the roadmap for the EU's future and, more recently, the European Pillar of Social Rights. She is now involved in developing plans to respond to the Covid-19 crisis.

She is currently the president of the Foundation for European Progressive Studies, a European political foundation located in Brussels, financed from the EU budget with the aim of supporting EU policymaking and debate. It has UN observer status and has a network of partners across Europe and the world.

Academically, she has been a professor of European economic policy at the European Studies Institute–Université Libre de Bruxelles and in the Lisbon University Institute. She was also the chair of the European Commission's advisory board for socioeconomic sciences. She is the author of more than 100 publications.

ABOUT THE AUTHORS

László Andor is the secretary general of FEPS. He was the EU Commissioner for Employment, Social Affairs and Inclusion between 2010 and 2014 and a member of the EBRD Board of Directors in London before that. He has lectured at Hertie School (Berlin), ULB (Brussels), Sciences Po (Paris) and Corvinus University (Budapest). He was awarded the Legion of Honour in 2014.

Vytenis Povilas Andriukaitis served as European Commissioner for Health and Food Safety between 2014 and 2019. He was a practising surgeon for more than twenty years. He is the co-author of the Constitution of the Republic of Lithuania and was elected six times as an MP of the Republic of Lithuania. He led the Lithuanian delegation to the Convention on the Future of Europe. He was the minister for health of the Republic of Lithuania from 2012 to 2014.

François Balate is the Head of Office of the President at FEPS. He was previously the Policy & Advocacy Director of the European Youth Forum. He graduated from the College of Europe in Bruges and from the Université Libre de Bruxelles.

Peter Bofinger is a professor of international and monetary economics at the University of Würzburg. From 2004 to 2019 he was a member of the German Council of Economic Experts, which is an independent advisory body to the German federal government. He had previously been the vice-president of the University of

Würzburg and an economist at the Deutsche Bundesbank. He is a research fellow at the Center for Economic Policy Research in London and a member of the Institute for New Economic Thinking's 'Commission on Global Economic Transformation'. He conducts research on monetary theory and policy with a focus on the digitalization of money and the implications of alternative models for the financial sphere (real models versus monetary models) for the analysis of interest rates and international capital flows.

Tanja A. Börzel is a professor of political science and holds the Chair for European Integration at the Otto-Suhr-Institute for Political Science, Freie Universität Berlin. She is the director of the 'Contestations of the Liberal Script' Cluster of Excellence, alongside Michael Zürn.

Mercedes Bresso is an Italian economist who has been a professor of economics and environmental economics at the Polytechnic and the University of Torino. She was president of the province of Torino from 1995 to 2004 and of the Piemonte region from 2005 to 2010. She was president of the Committee of the Regions between 2010 and 2012 and of the UEF (Union of European Federalists). As an MEP in 2004–5 and 2014–19, she worked with Elmar Brok as rapporteur of 'Improving the functioning of the European Union, building on the potential of the Lisbon Treaty'. She is the author of many articles and books, mainly on environmental economics: 'Pensiero economico e ambiente' (Loescher), 'Per una economia ecologica' (NIS), 'Travail, espace, pouvoir' (with Claude Raffestin; *L'Age d'homme*), 'Per un'Europa forte e sovrana' (S&D group) and 'I duecentocinquantamila stadi di Eratostene al tempo del virus' (with Claude Raffestin; *Mimesis*). She has also published two books on Fanta ecology and numerous thrillers.

Stefan Collignon is ordinary professor of political economy at the Sant'Anna School of Advanced Studies in Pisa, and a visiting professor at the European Institute and at the London School of Economics, where he taught from 2001 to 2005. Between 2005 and 2007 he was a visiting professor at Harvard University. Based on his experience as Deputy Director General at the German Finance Ministry, Stefan's academic research has focussed on developing a republican paradigm for European integration to improve the governance of Europe. Stefan is also president of the Association France-Birmanie, which has supported human rights in Myanmar.

Olivier Costa is research professor in political science at the CNRS (Centre national de la recherche scientifique), within the CEVIPOF research centre of Sciences Po (Paris). He is also the Director of the Department of European Political and Governance Studies of the College of Europe (Bruges). He is executive editor of the *Journal of European Integration*.

Emma Dowling is a sociologist and political economist at the University of Vienna, where she is Assistant Professor for the Sociology of Social Change. Previously she has held teaching and research positions at institutions in Germany and the United Kingdom. She has published widely on topics that include feminist political economy, global justice, financialization and society, as well as the role of emotions at work. She is the author of *The Care Crisis: What Caused It and How Can We End It?* (London/New York: Verso, 2021).

ABOUT THE CONTRIBUTORS

Saïd El Khadraoui is a special adviser to the Foundation of European Progressive Studies on the European Green Deal. He is a former MEP and he was previously a sustainability adviser at the European Political Strategy Centre, the in-house think tank of the European Commission. He is currently also a fellow at the KULeuven Public Governance Institute.

Gerda Falkner directs the Centre for European Integration Research in the department of political science at the University of Vienna. Her publications focus on various EU policies and their implementation. Most recently, she set up a team researching the EU's role in the digital revolution and how to protect democracy.

Georg Fischer is a senior research associate at the Vienna Institute for International Economic Studies. His present focus is on social convergence in Europe. From 1996 to 2017 he was with the European Commission, where his last position was as Director for Social Affairs in DG EMPL. Before that he worked for the OECD and served in the cabinet of the minister of finance and in the Ministry of Labour in Austria. He has been a fellow at the WZB in Berlin, at the ECF in Tel Aviv, in the Yale University Macmillan Center and at the Upjohn Institute for Employment Research in Michigan.

Diego Lopez Garrido is an economist and has a chair in constitutional law. Elected as an MP for six terms, he was a member of the Convention for Drafting the European Constitution, representing the Spanish Parliament from 2002 to 2003. He is a specialist in human rights and the author of many books on politics and European community law. His other former institutional positions include being vice-president of the NATO Parliamentary Assembly (2015), the State Secretary for European Affairs (2008–2011), and the coordinator of the Spanish presidency of the Council of the European Union (2010).

Hedwig Giusto is FEPS's senior policy advisor and the editor-in-chief of *The Progressive Post*, FEPS's magazine. She holds a PhD in the history of international relations from the University of Florence and an MSc in the history of international relations from the London School of Economics.

Giovanni Grevi teaches European foreign policy and international relations at the College of Europe in Bruges, at Sciences Po in Paris (PSIA) and at the Brussels School of Governance. He is also a senior associate fellow with the European Policy Centre (EPC), where he previously headed the Europe in the World programme, and at ISPI. Before joining the EPC in 2016, he was the director of the Foundation for International Relations and External Dialogue (FRIDE). Previously, Giovanni served as a senior research fellow at the EU Institute for Security Studies (EUISS) from 2005 to 2010 and worked at the EPC as Policy Analyst and Associate Director of Studies from 1999 to 2005. He has developed innovative projects and published extensively on EU foreign and security policy, strategic affairs, global governance, US foreign policy, foresight and EU politics and institutions. He holds an MSc in European studies from the London School of Economics and Political Science and a PhD in international relations from the Université Libre de Bruxelles.

Ulrike Guérot is the head of the Department for European Policy and the Study of Democracy at Danube University Krems, Austria and the founder of the European Democracy Lab in Berlin, a think tank that generates innovative ideas for Europe. Besides working and teaching at universities in Europe and the United States, she has worked at and directed several European research institutes and think tanks. She has received numerous honorable awards for her work, such as the Paul Watzlawick Ehrenring and the Salzburger Landespreis für Zukunftsforschung. Her many books have been best sellers in Germany and have been widely translated and published throughout Europe.

Paolo Guerrieri is currently a visiting professor at the PSIA, Sciences Po Paris and in the Business School of USD in California. He was formerly a professor of economics at the University of Rome 'Sapienza'. He served as a senator of the Italian Republic from 2013 to 2018. He has served as consultant to European and international institutions and has been a visiting professor at the University of California, Berkeley, at ULB in Belgium and at many other institutions. He is the author or editor of some sixteen books, monographs and anthologies, and more than 150 articles and book chapters on the European economy, international political economy, international trade and technological change.

Lukas Hochscheidt is a research assistant at the German Trade Union Confederation (the DGB). He holds a BA in political and social sciences and is currently studying for an MA in European affairs at Sciences Po in Paris. His research interests include the political economy of the welfare state and EU social policy.

Robin Huguenot-Noël is a researcher at the European University Institute (EUI). His dissertation focuses on employment growth and welfare state developments in the context of EMU integration. He has published several reports on the EU budget, structural reforms and social policy in the EU for the European institutions.

Guillaume Klossa was formerly a special adviser in the field of AI and digital for the European Commission. He was also a sherpa of the reflection group on the future of Europe (European Council) and a former director of the European Broadcasting Union. A European thinker and practitioner, he has taught at the College of Europe, ENA and Sciences Po Paris. He writes for international newspapers and is the founder and emeritus president of EuropaNova and copresident of Civico Europa. He also has leading positions in the business world.

Halliki Kreinin is a teaching and research associate and a PhD candidate at the Ecological Economics Institute/Socioeconomics of Work Institute at WU Vienna. She cocoordinated the 'Strategies for Social-Ecological Transformation' 2020 Vienna Degrowth Conference, in collaboration with the Austrian Chamber of Labour and the Austrian Trade Union Federation. Her research interests include environmental labour studies, sustainable work and social–ecological transformation.

Michael A. Landesmann was formerly the Scientific Director of the Vienna Institute for International Economic Studies (wiiw) between 1996 and 2016, and he is a professor of economics at the Johannes Kepler University in Austria. He has a DPhil from Oxford University and taught in Cambridge University's Department of Applied Economics and at Jesus College, Cambridge. His research focuses on international economic integration, industrial structural change, labour markets and migration.

Jean-François Lebrun joined the European Commission in 1987 and has dealt mainly with issues related to employment and social policy. Since his retirement he has worked as an expert on personal and household services (PHS) for several international, European and national

organizations. Between 2014 and 2017 he was seconded to the General Directorate of the Treasury in Paris, where he carried out an evaluation mission in the field of personal services.

At the European Commission he was the adviser in charge of PHS. Before that he was the head of the unit called 'New Skills for New Jobs, Adaptation to Change, Corporate Social Responsibility and the European Globalization Fund'. Many years ago he was assistant professor and researcher at the Free University Brussels. He is a graduate in economics and has a masters in econometrics.

Jo Leinen is a former Minister for the Environment in Saarland (Germany). He is also a former MEP and was the chair of the AFCO and ENVI committees. He is the honorary president of the European Movement International. He graduated in law and economics from the University of Saarbrücken, the University of Bonn, the College of Europe in Bruges and the Institute of World Affairs in Connecticut, USA.

Lora Lyubenova is a PhD student at Sofia University 'St. Kliment Ohridski'. Her research topic there is 'Political actors and interest groups, which influenced and shaped the European Pillar of Social Rights'. She is member of FEPS's Young Academics Network.

Justin Nogarede leads FEPS's digital and industrial policy portfolio. He previously worked as policy officer in the Secretariat-General of the European Commission. He started in the Directorate for Better Regulation and then proceeded to take on the digital policy portfolio in the president's and vice-president's Briefing Unit. After that, he became a policy coordinator, working on digital and single market policy files. In recent years Justin has, among other things, been involved in drafting the European Commission's mid-term review of its Digital Single Market Strategy, and in developing policy on standards and standard-essential patents, audio-visual media, internet governance, the collaborative economy, product liability and the internal market for goods.

Vassilis Ntousas is the Senior International Relations Policy Advisor at the Foundation for European Progressive Studies in Brussels and an Academy Associate at Chatham House in London. His research interests lie in European foreign policy and the EU's global engagement.

Alvaro Oleart is a postdoctoral researcher at Maastricht University-Studio Europa Maastricht, a scientific collaborator at the Université Libre de Bruxelles and a member of the Jean Monnet Network 'OpenEUDebate'. He is the author of the book *Framing TTIP in the European Public Spheres: Towards an Empowering Dissensus for EU Integration* (2021).

Carlota Perez is currently an honorary professor at IIPP, at UCL and at SPRU, University of Sussex, UK. She is an adjunct professor at TalTech, Estonia and an academic in residence at Anthemis UK. She is the author of *Technological Revolutions and Financial Capital: The Dynamics of Bubbles and Golden Ages* and acts worldwide as a consultant and lecturer.

David Rinaldi is the Director of Studies & Policy at FEPS, where he is in charge of economic and social policy and of coordinating the policy impact of the foundation. He teaches European Economic Governance at the ULB Institute for European Studies and is the co-founder of ProgressiveActs. Before joining FEPS, David worked at CEPS, the Jacques Delors Institute, the College of Europe and the Council of Europe.

ABOUT THE CONTRIBUTORS

Barbara Roggeveen is a PhD researcher in Russian international relations at Oxford University. Her research focuses on Eurasian integration, EU–Russia relations and Euro-Atlantic security. She has held research positions at the Atlantic Council, the University of Amsterdam and the OSCE Academy in Bishkek.

Vivien A. Schmidt is Jean Monnet Professor of European Integration in the Pardee School at Boston University and an honorary professor at LUISS University. Her research focuses on European political economy and democracy. She was recently named a Chevalier in the French Legion of Honor and received the European Union Studies Association's Lifetime Achievement Award.

Ania Skrzypek PhD is FEPS's Director for Research and Training. She obtained her degree cum laude in 2009 at Warsaw University for a dissertation on 'Cooperation of the socialists and social democratic parties in uniting Europe: from Liaison Bureau to PES 1957–2007' (published as a book in 2010). Before joining FEPS in 2009, she worked as a young researcher in the faculty of journalism and political science at Warsaw University, and she has also twice served as the elected Secretary General of Young European Socialists (ECOSY).

Mario Telò is a professor at ULB-Bruxelles, LUISS-Rome, and a visiting professor at Macau IEEM, CFAU-China and FGV-Rio. He is the Emeritus President of the IEE and a member of the Royal Academy of Sciences. He has served as a consultant to the EU Commission, the European Council and the European Parliament. He leads the 'Globalization Europe Multilateralism' research programme and edits the associated Routledge book series. Among his books are

Europe: A Civilian Power? (2005), *La place de l'UE dans le monde du 21ième siècle* (2018) and *Towards a New Multilateralism* (2021).

Britta Thomsen was a Danish MEP from 2004 to 2014. She has an MA in history, studied at the University of Lisbon and worked with European labour markets. She wrote the book *The Necessary Immigration* about immigration in Europe. Thomsen is an adjunct professor in the Copenhagen Business School and a board member of ACER.